D062007

Essential SQLAlchemy

Other resources from O'Reilly

Related titles
Learning Python   SQL in a Nutshell
Programming Python   The Art of SQL
Python in a Nutshell

oreilly.com
oreilly.com is more than a complete catalog of O'Reilly books. You'll also find links to news, events, articles, weblogs, sample chapters, and code examples.

oreillynet.com is the essential portal for developers interested in open and emerging technologies, including new platforms, programming languages, and operating systems.

Conferences
O'Reilly brings diverse innovators together to nurture the ideas that spark revolutionary industries. We specialize in documenting the latest tools and systems, translating the innovator's knowledge into useful skills for those in the trenches. Visit *conferences.oreilly.com* for our upcoming events.

Safari Bookshelf (*safari.oreilly.com*) is the premier online reference library for programmers and IT professionals. Conduct searches across more than 1,000 books. Subscribers can zero in on answers to time-critical questions in a matter of seconds. Read the books on your Bookshelf from cover to cover or simply flip to the page you need. Try it today for free.

Essential SQLAlchemy

Rick Copeland

O'REILLY®

Beijing · Cambridge · Farnham · Köln · Sebastopol · Taipei · Tokyo

Essential SQLAlchemy
by Rick Copeland

Copyright © 2008 Richard D. Copeland, Jr. All rights reserved.
Printed in the United States of America.

Published by O'Reilly Media, Inc., 1005 Gravenstein Highway North, Sebastopol, CA 95472.

O'Reilly books may be purchased for educational, business, or sales promotional use. Online editions are also available for most titles (*http://safari.oreilly.com*). For more information, contact our corporate/institutional sales department: (800) 998-9938 or *corporate@oreilly.com*.

Editor: Mary E. Treseler	**Indexer:** Joe Wizda
Production Editor: Sumita Mukherji	**Cover Designer:** Karen Montgomery
Copyeditor: Genevieve d'Entremont	**Interior Designer:** David Futato
Proofreader: Sumita Mukherji	**Illustrator:** Jessamyn Read

Printing History:

June 2008:   First Edition.

Nutshell Handbook, the Nutshell Handbook logo, and the O'Reilly logo are registered trademarks of O'Reilly Media, Inc. *Essential SQLAlchemy*, the image of largescale flying fish, and related trade dress are trademarks of O'Reilly Media, Inc.

Many of the designations uses by manufacturers and sellers to distinguish their products are claimed as trademarks. Where those designations appear in this book, and O'Reilly Media, Inc. was aware of a trademark claim, the designations have been printed in caps or initial caps

While every precaution has been taken in the preparation of this book, the publisher and author assume no responsibility for errors or omissions, or for damages resulting from the use of the information contained herein.

ISBN: 978-0-596-51614-7

[M]

1211553300

Table of Contents

Preface

If you're an application programmer, you've probably run into a relational database at some point in your professional career. Whether you're writing enterprise client-server applications or building the next killer Web 2.0 application, you need someplace to put the persistent data for your application. Relational databases, accessed via SQL, are some of the most common places to put that data.

SQL is a powerful language for querying and manipulating data in a database, but sometimes it's tough to integrate it with the rest of your application. You may have used some language that tries to merge SQL syntax into your application's programming language, such as Oracle's Pro*C/C++ precompiler, or you may have used string manipulation to generate queries to run over an ODBC interface. If you're a Python programmer, you may have used a DB-API module. But there is a better way.

This book is about a very powerful and flexible Python library named SQLAlchemy that bridges the gap between relational databases and traditional object-oriented programming. While SQLAlchemy allows you to "drop down" into raw SQL to execute your queries, it encourages higher-level thinking through a "pythonic" approach to database queries and updates. It supplies the tools that let you map your application's classes and objects onto database tables once and then to "forget about it," or to return to your model again and again to fine-tune performance.

SQLAlchemy is powerful and flexible, but it can also be a little daunting. SQLAlchemy tutorials expose only a fraction of what's available in this excellent library, and though the online documentation is extensive, it is often better as a reference than as a way to learn the library initially. This book is meant as a learning tool and a handy reference for when you're in "implementation mode" and need an answer *fast*.

This book covers the 0.4 release series of conservatively versioned SQLAlchemy.

Audience

First of all, this book is intended for those who want to learn more about how to use relational databases with their Python programs, or have heard about SQLAlchemy and want more information on it. Having said that, to get the most out of this book, the reader should have intermediate-to-advanced Python skills and at least moderate exposure to SQL databases. SQLAlchemy provides support for many advanced SQL constructs, so the experienced DBA will also find plenty of information here.

The beginning Python or database programmer would probably be best served by reading a Python book such as *Learning Python* by Mark Lutz (O'Reilly) and/or a SQL book such as *Learning SQL* by Alan Beaulieu (O'Reilly), either prior to this book or as a reference to read in parallel with this book.

Assumptions This Book Makes

This book assumes basic knowledge about Python syntax and semantics, particularly versions 2.4 and later. In particular, the reader should be familiar with object-oriented programming in Python, as a large component of SQLAlchemy is devoted entirely to supporting this programming style. The reader should also know basic SQL syntax and relational theory, as this book assumes familiarity with the SQL concepts of defining schemas, tables, SELECTs, INSERTs, UPDATEs, and DELETEs.

Contents of This Book

Chapter 1, *Introduction to SQLAlchemy*
> This chapter takes you on a whirlwind tour through the main components of SQLAlchemy. It demonstrates connecting to the database, building up SQL statements, and mapping simple objects to the database. It also describes SQLAlchemy's philosophy of letting tables be tables and letting classes be classes.

Chapter 2, *Getting Started*
> This chapter walks you through installing SQLAlchemy using *easy_install*. It shows you how to create a simple database using SQLite, and walks though some simple queries against a sample database to to illustrate the use of the Engine and the SQL expression language.

Chapter 3, *Engines and MetaData*
> This chapter describes the various engines (methods of connecting to database servers) available for use with SQLAlchemy, including the connection parameters they support. It then describes the MetaData object, which is where SQLAlchemy stores information about your database's schema, and how to manipulate MetaData objects.

Chapter 4, *SQLAlchemy Type Engines*
> This chapter describes the way that SQLAlchemy uses its built-in types. It also shows you how to create custom types to be used in your schema. You will learn the requirements for creating custom types as well as the cases where it is useful to use custom rather than built-in types.

Chapter 5, *Running Queries and Updates*
> This chapter tells you how to perform INSERTs, UPDATEs, and DELETEs. It covers result set objects, retrieving partial results, and using SQL functions to aggregate and sort data in the database server.

Chapter 6, *Building an Object Mapper*
> This chapter describes the object-relational mapper (ORM) used in SQLAlchemy. It describes the differences between the object mapper pattern (used in SQLAlchemy) and the active record pattern used in other ORMs. It then describes how to set up a mapper, and how the mapper maps your tables by default. You will also learn how to override the default mapping and how to specify various relationships between tables.

Chapter 7, *Querying and Updating at the ORM Level*
> This chapter shows you how to create objects, save them to a session, and flush them to the database. You will learn about how Session and Query objects are defined, their methods, and how to use them to insert, update, retrieve, and delete data from the database at the ORM level. You will learn how to use result set mapping to populate objects from a non-ORM query and when it should be used.

Chapter 8, *Inheritance Mapping*
> This chapter describes how to use SQLAlchemy to model object-oriented inheritance. The various ways of modeling inheritance in the relational model are described, as well as the support SQLAlchemy provides for each.

Chapter 9, *Elixir: A Declarative Extension to SQLAlchemy*
> This chapter describes the Elixir extension to SQLAlchemy, which provides a declarative, active record pattern for use with SQLAlchemy. You will learn how to use Elixir extensions such as acts_as_versioned to create auxiliary tables automatically, and when Elixir is appropriate instead of "bare" SQLAlchemy.

Chapter 10, *SqlSoup: An Automatic Mapper for SQLAlchemy*
> This chapter introduces the SQLSoup extension, which provides an automatic metadata and object model based on database reflection. You will learn how to use SQLSoup to query the database with a minimum of setup, and learn the pros and cons of such an approach.

Chapter 11, *Other SQLAlchemy Extensions*
> This chapter covers other, less comprehensive extensions to SQLAlchemy. It describes the extensions that are currently used in the 0.4 release series of SQLAlchemy, as well as briefly describing deprecated extensions and the functionality in SQLAlchemy that supplants them.

Conventions Used in This Book

The following typographical conventions are used in this book:

Italic

> Indicates new terms, URLs, email addresses, filenames, file extensions, pathnames, directories, and Unix utilities.

`Constant width`

> Indicates commands, options, switches, variables, attributes, keys, functions, types, classes, namespaces, methods, modules, properties, parameters, values, objects, events, event handlers, the contents of files, or the output from commands.

`Constant width italic`

> Shows text that should be replaced with user-supplied values.

ALL CAPS

> Shows SQL keywords and queries.

 This icon signifies a tip, suggestion, or general note.

 This icon indicates a warning or caution.

Using Code Examples

This book is here to help you get your job done. In general, you may use the code in this book in your programs and documentation. You do not need to contact us for permission unless you're reproducing a significant portion of the code. For example, writing a program that uses several chunks of code from this book does not require permission. Selling or distributing a CD-ROM of examples from O'Reilly books does require permission. Answering a question by citing this book and quoting example code does not require permission. Incorporating a significant amount of example code from this book into your product's documentation does require permission.

We appreciate, but do not require, attribution. An attribution usually includes the title, author, publisher, and ISBN. For example: "*Essential SQLAlchemy* by Rick Copeland. Copyright 2008 Richard D. Copeland, Jr., 978-0-596-51614-7."

If you feel your use of code examples falls outside fair use or the permission given here, feel free to contact us at *permissions@oreilly.com*.

How to Contact Us

Please address comments and questions concerning this book to the publisher:

O'Reilly Media, Inc.
1005 Gravenstein Highway North
Sebastopol, CA 95472
800-998-9938 (in the United States or Canada)
707-829-0515 (international or local)
707-829-0104 (fax)

We have a web page for this book, where we list errata, examples, and any additional information. You can access this page at:

http://www.oreilly.com/catalog/9780596516147

To comment or ask technical questions about this book, send email to:

bookquestions@oreilly.com

For more information about our books, conferences, Resource Centers, and the O'Reilly Network, see our web site at:

http://www.oreilly.com

Acknowledgments

Many thanks go to Tatiana Apandi, Barry Hart, Grig Gheorghiu, and Catherine Devlin for their critical pre-publication feedback, without whom this book would have undoubtedly had many technical snafus.

My appreciation goes out to Noah Gift, whose recommendation led to this book being written in the first place. I still remember how his phone call started: "You know SQLAlchemy, right?..."

Thanks to my employer, Predictix, for allowing me the time and energy to finish the book, and to my coworkers for being unwitting guinea pigs for many of the ideas and techniques in this book.

Finally, my heartfelt gratitude goes to my beloved wife Nancy, whose support in the presence of a husband glued to the computer was truly the fuel that allowed this book to be written at all.

## CHAPTER 1

Introduction to SQLAlchemy

What Is SQLAlchemy

SQLAlchemy is a Python Library created by Mike Bayer to provide a high-level, Pythonic (idiomatically Python) interface to relational databases such as Oracle, DB2, MySQL, PostgreSQL, and SQLite. SQLAlchemy attempts to be unobtrusive to your Python code, allowing you to map plain old Python objects (POPOs) to database tables without substantially changing your existing Python code. SQLAlchemy includes a database server-independent SQL expression language and an object-relational mapper (ORM) that lets you use SQL to persist your application objects automatically. This chapter will introduce you to SQLAlchemy, illustrating some of its more powerful features. Later chapters will provide more depth for the topics covered here.

If you have used lower-level database interfaces with Python, such as the DB-API, you may be used to writing code such as the following to save your objects to the database:

```
sql="INSERT INTO user(user_name, password) VALUES (%s, %s)"
cursor = conn.cursor()
cursor.execute(sql, ('rick', 'parrot'))
```

Although this code gets the job done, it is verbose, error-prone, and tedious to write. Using string manipulation to build up a query as done here can lead to various logical errors and vulnerabilities such as opening your application up to SQL injection attacks. Generating the string to be executed by your database server verbatim also ties your code to the particular DB-API driver you are currently using, making migration to a different database server difficult. For instance, if we wished to migrate the previous example to the Oracle DB-API driver, we would need to write:

```
sql="INSERT INTO user(user_name, password) VALUES (:1, :2)"
cursor = conn.cursor()
cursor.execute(sql, 'rick', 'parrot')
```

SQL Injection Attacks

SQL injection is a type of programming error where carefully crafted user input can cause your application to execute arbitrary SQL code. For instance, suppose that the DB-API code in the earlier listing had been written as follows:

```
sql="INSERT INTO user(user_name, password) VALUES ('%s', '%s')"
cursor = conn.cursor()
cursor.execute(sql % (user_name, password))
```

In most cases, this code will work. For instance, with the user_name and password variables just shown, the SQL that would be executed is INSERT INTO user(user_name, password) VALUES ('rick', 'parrot'). A user could, however, supply a maliciously crafted password: parrot'); DELETE FROM user; --. In this case, the SQL executed is INSERT INTO user(user_name, password) VALUES ('rick', 'parrot'); DELETE FROM user; --', which would probably delete all users from your database. The use of bind parameters (as in the first example in the text) is an effective defense against SQL injection, but as long as you are manipulating strings directly, there is always the possibility of introducing a SQL injection vulnerability into your code.

In the SQLAlchemy SQL expression language, you could write the following instead:

```
statement = user_table.insert(user_name='rick', password='parrot')
statement.execute()
```

To migrate this code to Oracle, you would write, well, exactly the same thing.

SQLAlchemy also allows you to write SQL queries using a Pythonic expression-builder. For instance, to retrieve all the users created in 2007, you would write:

```
statement = user_table.select(and_(
    user_table.c.created >= date(2007,1,1),
    user_table.c.created <  date(2008,1,1))
result = statement.execute()
```

In order to use the SQL expression language, you need to provide SQLAlchemy with information about your database schema. For instance, if you are using the user table mentioned previously, your schema definition might be the following:

```
metadata=MetaData('sqlite://') # use an in-memory SQLite database
user_table = Table(
    'tf_user', metadata,
    Column('id', Integer, primary_key=True),
    Column('user_name', Unicode(16), unique=True, nullable=False),
Column('email_address', Unicode(255), unique=True, nullable=False),
    Column('password', Unicode(40), nullable=False),
    Column('first_name', Unicode(255), default=''),
    Column('last_name', Unicode(255), default=''),
    Column('created', DateTime, default=datetime.now))
```

If you would rather use an existing database schema definition, you still need to tell SQLAlchemy which tables you have, but SQLAlchemy can reflect the tables using the database server's introspection capabilities. In this case, the schema definition reduces to the following:

```
users_table = Table('users', metadata, autoload=True)
```

Although the SQLAlchemy SQL expression language is quite powerful, it can still be tedious to manually specify the queries and updates necessary to work with your tables. To help with this problem, SQLAlchemy provides an ORM to automatically populate your Python objects from the database and to update the database based on changes to your Python objects. Using the ORM is as simple as writing your classes, defining your tables, and mapping your tables to your classes. In the case of the user table, you could perform a simple mapping via the following code:

```
class User(object): pass
mapper(User, user_table)
```

Notice that there is nothing particularly special about the User class defined here. It is used to create "plain old Python objects," or POPOs. All the magic of SQLAlchemy is performed by the mapper. Although the class definition just shown is empty, you may define your own methods and attributes on a mapped class. The mapper will create attributes corresponding to the column names in the mapped table as well as some private attributes used by SQLAlchemy internally. Once your table is mapped, you can use a Session object to populate your objects based on data in the user table and flush any changes you make to mapped objects to the database:

```
>>> Session = sessionmaker()
>>> session = Session()
>>>
>>> # Insert a user into the database
... u = User()
>>> u.user_name='rick'
>>> u.email_address='rick@foo.com'
>>> u.password='parrot'
>>> session.save(u)
>>>
>>> # Flush all changes to the session out to the database
... session.flush()
>>>
>>> query = session.query(User)
>>> # List all users
... list(query)
[<__main__.User object at 0x2abb96dae3d0>]
>>>
>>> # Get a particular user by primary key
... query.get(1)
<__main__.User object at 0x2abb96dae3d0>
>>>
>>> # Get a particular user by some other column
... query.get_by(user_name='rick')
<__main__.User object at 0x2abb96dae3d0>
>>>
>>> u = query.get_by(user_name='rick')
>>> u.password = 'foo'
```

```
>>> session.flush()
>>> query.get(1).password
'foo'
```

As you can see, SQLAlchemy makes persisting your objects simple and concise. You can also customize and extend the set of properties created by SQLAlchemy, allowing your objects to model, for instance, a many-to-many relationship with simple Python lists.

The Object/Relational "Impedance Mismatch"

Although a SQL database is a powerful and flexible modeling tool, it is not always a good match for the object-oriented programming style. SQL is good for some things, and object-oriented programming is good for others. This is sometimes referred to as the object/relational "impedance mismatch," and it is a problem that SQLAlchemy tries to address in the ORM. To illustrate the object/relational impedance mismatch, let's first look at how we might model a system in SQL, and then how we might model it in an object-oriented way.

SQL databases provide a powerful means for modeling data and allowing for arbitrary queries of that data. The model underlying SQL is the *relational model*. In the relational model, modeled items (*entities*) can have various attributes, and are related to other entities via *relationships*. These relationships can be one-to-one, one-to-many, many-to-many, or complex, multientity relationships. The SQL expression of the entity is the table, and relationships are expressed as foreign key constraints, possibly with the use of an auxiliary "join" table. For example, suppose we have a user permission system that has users who may belong to one or more groups. Groups may have one or more permissions. Our SQL to model such a system might be something like the following:

```
CREATE TABLE tf_user (
        id INTEGER NOT NULL,
        user_name VARCHAR(16) NOT NULL,
        email_address VARCHAR(255) NOT NULL,
        password VARCHAR(40) NOT NULL,
        first_name VARCHAR(255),
        last_name VARCHAR(255),
        created TIMESTAMP,
        PRIMARY KEY (id),
         UNIQUE (user_name),
         UNIQUE (email_address));
CREATE TABLE tf_group (
        id INTEGER NOT NULL,
        group_name VARCHAR(16) NOT NULL,
        PRIMARY KEY (id),
         UNIQUE (group_name));
CREATE TABLE tf_permission (
        id INTEGER NOT NULL,
        permission_name VARCHAR(16) NOT NULL,
        PRIMARY KEY (id),
         UNIQUE (permission_name));
```

```
-- Relate the user and group tables
CREATE TABLE user_group (
        user_id INTEGER,
        group_id INTEGER,
    PRIMARY KEY(user_id, group_id),
        FOREIGN KEY(user_id) REFERENCES tf_user (id),
        FOREIGN KEY(group_id) REFERENCES tf_group (id));
-- Relate the group and permission tables
CREATE TABLE group_permission (
        group_id INTEGER,
        permission_id INTEGER,
    PRIMARY KEY(group_id, permission_id),
        FOREIGN KEY(group_id) REFERENCES tf_group (id),
        FOREIGN KEY(permission_id) REFERENCES tf_permission (id));
```

Notice the two auxiliary tables used to provide many-to-many joins between users and groups, and between groups and users. Once we have this schema in place, a common scenario is to check whether a particular user has a particular permission. In SQL, we might write:

```
SELECT COUNT(*) FROM tf_user, tf_group, tf_permission WHERE
        tf_user.user_name='rick' AND tf_user.id=user_group.user_id
        AND user_group.group_id = group_permission.group_id
        AND group_permission.permission_id = tf_permission.id
        AND permission_name='admin';
```

In a single statement, we join the three entities—user, group, and permission—together to determine whether the user "rick" has the "admin" permission.

In the object-oriented world, we would probably model the system quite differently. We would still have users, groups, and permissions, but they would probably have an ownership relationship between them:

```
class User(object):
    groups=[]

class Group(object):
    users=[]
    permissions=[]

class Permission(object):
    groups=[]
```

Suppose we wanted to print out a summary of all of a given user's groups and permissions, something an object-oriented style would do quite well. We might write something like the following:

```
print 'Summary for %s' % user.user_name
for g in user.groups:
    print '  Member of group %s' % g.group_name
    for p in g.permissions:
        print '    ... which has permission %s' % p.permission_name
```

On the other hand, if we wanted to determine whether a user has a particular permission, we would need to do something like the following:

```
def user_has_permission(user, permission_name):
    for g in user.groups:
        for p in g.permissions:
            if p.permission_name == 'admin':
                return True
    return False
```

In this case, we needed to write a nested loop, examining every group the user is a member of to see if that group had a particular permission. SQLAlchemy lets you use object-oriented programming where appropriate (such as checking for a user's permission to do something) and relational programming where appropriate (such as printing a summary of groups and permissions). In SQLAlchemy, we could print the summary information exactly as shown, and we could detect membership in a group with a much simpler query. First, we need to create mappings between our tables and our objects, telling SQLAlchemy a little bit about the many-to-many joins:

```
mapper(User, user_table, properties=dict(
    groups=relation(Group, secondary=user_group, backref='users')))
mapper(Group, group_table, properties=dict(
    permissions=relation(Permission, secondary=group_permission,
                         backref='groups')))
mapper(Permission, permission_table)
```

Now, our model plus the magic of the SQLAlchemy ORM allows us to detect whether the given user is an administrator:

```
q = session.query(Permission)
rick_is_admin = q.count_by(permission_name='admin',
... user_name='rick')
```

SQLAlchemy was able to look at our mappers, determine how to join the tables, and use the relational model to generate a single call to the database. The SQL generated by SQLAlchemy is actually quite similar to what we would have written ourselves:

```
SELECT count(tf_permission.id)
FROM tf_permission, tf_user, group_permission, tf_group, user_group
WHERE (tf_user.user_name = ?
    AND ((tf_permission.id = group_permission.permission_id
    AND tf_group.id = group_permission.group_id)
    AND (tf_group.id = user_group.group_id
    AND tf_user.id = user_group.user_id)))
    AND (tf_permission.permission_name = ?)
```

SQLAlchemy's real power comes from its ability to bridge the object/relational divide; it allows you to use whichever model is appropriate to your task at hand. Aggregation is another example of using SQLAlchemy's relational model rather than the object-oriented model. Suppose we wanted a count of how many users had each permission type. In the traditional object-oriented world, we would probably loop over each permission, then over each group, and finally count the users in the group (without forgetting to remove duplicates!). This leads to something like this:

```
for p in permissions:
    users = set()
```

```
    for g in p.groups:
        for u in g.users:
            users.add(u)
print 'Permission %s has %d users' % (p.permission_name, len(users))
```

In SQLAlchemy, we can drop into the SQL expression language to create the following query:

```
q=select([Permission.c.permission_name,
         func.count(user_group.c.user_id)],
       and_(Permission.c.id==group_permission.c.permission_id,
          Group.c.id==group_permission.c.group_id,
          Group.c.id==user_group.c.group_id),
       group_by=[Permission.c.permission_name],
       distinct=True)
rs=q.execute()
for permission_name, num_users in q.execute():
print 'Permission %s has %d users' % (permission_name, num_users)
```

Although the query is a little longer in this case, we are doing all of the work *in the database*, allowing us to reduce the data transferred and potentially increase performance substantially due to reduced round-trips to the database. The important thing to note is that SQLAlchemy makes "simple things simple, and complex things possible."

SQLAlchemy Philosophy

SQLAlchemy was created with the goal of letting your objects be objects, and your tables be tables. The SQLAlchemy home page puts it this way:

SQLAlchemy Philosophy

SQL databases behave less and less like object collections the more size and performance start to matter; object collections behave less and less like tables and rows the more abstraction starts to matter. SQLAlchemy aims to accommodate both of these principles.

—From *http://www.sqlalchemy.org*

Using the object mapper pattern (where plain Python objects are mapped to SQL tables via a mapper object, rather than requiring persistent objects to be derived from some Persistable class) achieves much of this separation of concerns. There has also been a concerted effort in SQLAlchemy development to expose the full power of SQL, should you wish to use it.

In SQLAlchemy, your objects are POPOs until you tell SQLAlchemy about them. This means that it is entirely possible to "bolt on" persistence to an existing object model by mapping the classes to tables. For instance, consider an application that uses users, groups, and permissions, as shown. You might prototype your application with the following class definitions:

```
class User(object):

    def __init__(self, user_name=None, password=None, groups=None):
```

```
            if groups is None: groups = []
            self.user_name = user_name
            self.password = password
            self._groups = groups

    def join_group(self, group):
        self._groups.append(group)

    def leave_group(self, group):
        self._groups.remove(group)

class Group(object):

    def __init__(self, group_name=None, users=None, permissions=None):
            if users is None: users = []
            if permissions is None: permissions = []
            self.group_name = group_name
            self._users = users
            self._permissions = permissions

    def add_user(self, user):
        self._users.append(user)

    def del_user(self, user):
        self._users.remove(user)

    def add_permission(self, permission):
        self._permissions.append(permission)

    def del_permission(self, permission):
        self._permissions.remove(permission)

class Permission(object):

    def __init__(self, permission_name=None, groups=None):
        self.permission_name = permission_name
        self._groups = groups

    def join_group(self, group):
        self._groups.append(group)

    def leave_group(self, group):
        self._groups.remove(group)
```

Once your application moves beyond the prototype stage, you might expect to have to write code to manually load objects from the database or perhaps some other kind of persistent object store. On the other hand, if you are using SQLAlchemy, you would just define your tables:

```
user_table = Table(
    'tf_user', metadata,
    Column('id', Integer, primary_key=True),
    Column('user_name', Unicode(16), unique=True, nullable=False),
    Column('password', Unicode(40), nullable=False))
```

```
group_table = Table(
    'tf_group', metadata,
    Column('id', Integer, primary_key=True),
    Column('group_name', Unicode(16), unique=True, nullable=False))

permission_table = Table(
    'tf_permission', metadata,
    Column('id', Integer, primary_key=True),
    Column('permission_name', Unicode(16), unique=True,
        nullable=False))

user_group = Table(
    'user_group', metadata,
    Column('user_id', None, ForeignKey('tf_user.id'),
        primary_key=True),
    Column('group_id', None, ForeignKey('tf_group.id'),
        primary_key=True))

group_permission = Table(
    'group_permission', metadata,
    Column('group_id', None, ForeignKey('tf_group.id'),
        primary_key=True),
    Column('permission_id', None, ForeignKey('tf_permission.id'),
        primary_key=True))
```

and your mappers:

```
mapper(User, user_table, properties=dict(
_groups=relation(Group, secondary=user_group, backref='_users')))
mapper(Group, group_table, properties=dict(
    _permissions=relation(Permission, secondary=group_permission,
                        backref='_groups')))
mapper(Permission, permission_table)
```

and you're done. No modification of your objects is required—they are still simply new-style (derived from the **object** class) Python classes, and they still have whatever methods you have defined, as well as a few attributes added by SQLAlchemy (described in the sidebar "Instrumentation on Mapped Classes"). Your old methods **join_group**, **leave_group**, etc. *still work*, even without modifying the class code. This means that you can modify mapped "collection" properties (properties modeling 1:N or M:N relationships) with regular list operations, and SQLAlchemy will track your changes and flush them to the database automatically.

Instrumentation on Mapped Classes

Mapped classes are actually fairly unmolested by the default SQLAlchemy mapper. In particular, the mapped class is given the following new attributes:

c

> This attribute contains a collection of the columns in the table being mapped. This is useful when constructing SQL queries based on the mapped class, such as referring to **User.c.user_name**.

_state
SQLAlchemy uses this property to track whether a mapped object is "clean" (freshly fetched from the databaes), "dirty" (modified since fetching from the database), or "new" (as-yet unsaved to the database). This property generally should not be modified by the application programmer.

mapped properties
One attribute will be added to the mapped class for each property specified in the mapper, as well as any "auto-mapped" properties, such as columns. In the previous example, the mapper adds user_name, password, id, and _groups to the User class.

So, if you are planning on using SQLAlchemy, you should stay away from naming any class attributes c or _state, and you should be aware that SQLAlchemy will instrument your class based on the properties defined by the mapper.

SQLAlchemy also allows you the full expressiveness of SQL, including compound (multicolumn) primary keys and foreign keys, indexes, access to stored procedures, the ability to "reflect" your tables from the database into your application, and even the ability to specify cascading updates and deletes on your foreign key relationships and value constraints on your data.

SQLAlchemy Architecture

SQLAlchemy consists of several components, including the aforementioned database-independent SQL expression language object-relational mapper. In order to enable these components, SQLAlchemy also provides an Engine class, which manages connection pools and SQL dialects, a MetaData class, which manages your table information, and a flexible type system for mapping SQL types to Python types.

Engine

The beginning of any SQLAlchemy application is the Engine. The engine manages the SQLAlchemy connection pool and the database-independent SQL dialect layer. In our previous examples, the engine was created implicitly when the MetaData was created:

```
metadata=MetaData('sqlite://')
engine = metadata.bind
```

It is also possible to create an engine manually, using the SQLAlchemy function create_engine():

```
engine=create_engine('sqlite://')
```

This engine can later be bound to a MetaData object just by setting the bind attribute on the MetaData:

```
metadata.bind = engine
```

The engine can also be used in SQL statements such as table creation if the `MetaData` is *unbound* (not connected to a particular engine):

```
user_table.create(bind=engine)
```

The engine can be used to execute queries directly on the database via dynamic SQL:

```
for row in engine.execute("select user_name from tf_user"):
    print 'user name: %s' % row['user_name']
```

Most of the time, you will be using the higher-level facilities of the SQL expression language and ORM components of SQLAlchemy, but it's nice to know that you can always easily drop down all the way to raw SQL if you need to.

Connection pooling

Thus far, we have glossed over the use of database connections. In fact, all of our examples up to this point have used SQLAlchemy's powerful connection pooling subsystem. In order to execute queries against a database, a connection is required, and the establishment of a new connection is typically an expensive operation, involving a network connection, authentication of the user, and any database session setup required. To amortize the costs, the typical solution is to maintain a pool of database connections that are used over and over again in the application.

The `Engine` object in SQLAlchemy is responsible for managing a pool of low-level DB-API connections. In fact, the engine and the low-level connection objects obey a `Connectable` protocol, allowing you to execute dynamic SQL queries either directly against a connection, or against the engine (in which case the engine will automatically allocate a connection for the query).

In another instance of making simple things simple and complex things possible, SQLAlchemy does The Right Thing most of the time with connections, and allows you to override its strategy when required. SQLAlchemy's default strategy is to acquire a connection for each SQL statement, and when that connection is no longer used (when its result set is closed or garbage-collected) to return it to the pool. If you would like to manually manage your collections, you can also do that via the `connect()` method on the engine object:

```
engine = create_engine('sqlite://')
connection = engine.connect()
result = connection.execute("select user_name from tf_user")
for row in result:
    print 'user name: %s' % row['user_name']
result.close()
```

SQLAlchemy has another strategy for connection pooling that has some performance benefits in many cases: the "thread-local" strategy. In the thread-local strategy, a connection that is currently in use by a thread will be reused for other statements within that thread. This can reduce database server load, which is especially important when you could have several applications accessing the database simultaneously. If you want to use the thread-local strategy, simply create the Engine object and set the strategy to threadlocal:

```
engine = create_engine('sqlite://', strategy='threadlocal')
```

SQL dialect management

Although SQL is a standardized language, many database vendors either do not fully implement it or simply create extensions to the standard. The dialect object attempts to manage the idiosyncrasies of each supported SQL dialect as well as manage the low-level DB-API modules implementing the connection.

The dialect is mostly used as a transparent layer for your application programming. The main exception to this rule is when you want to access a data type that is supported only for particular database servers. For instance, MySQL has BigInteger and Enum types. To use these types, you must import them directly from the appropriate module in the sqlalchemy.databases package:

```
from sqlalchemy.databases.mysql import MSEnum, MSBigInteger

user_table = Table('tf_user', meta,
    Column('id', MSBigInteger),
Column('honorific', MSEnum('Mr', 'Mrs', 'Ms', 'Miss', 'Dr',
... 'Prof')))
```

MetaData Management

The MetaData object in SQLAlchemy is used to collect and organize information about your table layout (i.e., your database *schema*). We alluded to MetaData management before in describing how to create tables. A MetaData object must be created before any tables are defined, and each table must be associated with a MetaData object. MetaData objects can be created "bound" or "unbound," based on whether they are associated with an engine. The following is an example of the different ways you can create MetaData objects:

```
# create an unbound MetaData
unbound_meta = MetaData()

# create an Engine and bind the MetaData to it
db1 = create_engine('sqlite://')
unbound_meta.bind = db1

# Create an engine and then a bound MetaData
db2 = MetaData('sqlite:///test1.db')
bound_meta1 = MetaData(db2)

# Create a bound MetaData with an implicitly created engine
bound_meta2 = MetaData('sqlite:///test2.db')
```

Although tables can be defined against unbound `MetaData`, it is often more convenient to eventually bind the metadata to an engine, as this allows the `MetaData` and the `Table` objects defined for it to access the database directly:

```
# Create a bound MetaData
meta = MetaData('sqlite://')

# Define a couple of tables
user_table = Table(
    'tf_user', meta,
    Column('id', Integer, primary_key=True),
    Column('user_name', Unicode(16), unique=True, nullable=False),
    Column('password', Unicode(40), nullable=False))

group_table = Table(
    'tf_group', meta,
    Column('id', Integer, primary_key=True),
    Column('group_name', Unicode(16), unique=True, nullable=False))

# Create all the tables in the (empty) database
meta.create_all()

# Select all the groups from the tf_group table
result_set = group_table.select().execute()
```

As mentioned previously, you can also *reflect* your schema by setting the `autoload` parameter to `True` in your `Table` creation. Reflection, however, requires a database connection to function properly. (SQLAlchemy must query the database to determine the structure of the tables.) Binding the `MetaData` to an engine is a convenient way to provide this connection. Note, however, that you are never *required* to bind the `MetaData` object; any operation that you can perform with a bound `MetaData` or a table defined on it can also be performed by passing the engine or connection to the individual method. This might be useful if you wish to use the same `MetaData` object for multiple distinct database engines:

```
meta = MetaData()
engine1 = create_engine('sqlite:///test1.db')
engine2 = create_engine('sqlite:///test2.db')

# Use the engine parameter to load tables from the first engine
user_table = Table(
    'tf_user', meta, autoload=True, autoload_with=engine1)
group_table = Table(
    'tf_group', meta, autoload=True, autoload_with=engine1)
permission_table = Table(
    'tf_permission', meta, autoload=True, autoload_with=engine1)
user_group_table = Table(
    'user_group', meta, autoload=True, autoload_with=engine1)
group_permission_table = Table(
    'group_permission', meta, autoload=True, autoload_with=engine1)

# Create the tables in the second engine
meta.create_all(engine2)
```

```
# Select some data
result_set = engine1.execute(user_table.select())
```

Types System

In many cases, SQLAlchemy can map SQL types to Python types in a straightforward way. To do this, SQLAlchemy provides a set of TypeEngine-derived classes that convert SQL data to Python data in the `sqlalchemy.types` module. TypeEngine subclasses are used to define the MetaData for tables.

Sometimes, in keeping with the SQLAlchemy philosophy of letting your objects be objects, you may find that the provided TypeEngine classes do not express all of the data types you wish to store in your database. In this case, you can write a custom TypeEngine that converts data being saved to the database to a database-native type, and converts data being loaded from the database to a Python native type. Suppose, for instance, that we wished to have a column that stored images from the Python Imaging Library (PIL). In this case, we might use the following TypeEngine definition:

```
class ImageType(sqlalchemy.types.Binary):

    def convert_bind_param(self, value, engine):
        sfp = StringIO()
        value.save(sfp, 'JPEG')
        return sfp.getvalue()

    def convert_result_value(self, value, engine):
        sfp = StringIO(value)
        image = PIL.Image.open(sfp)
        return image
```

Once we have defined ImageType, we can use that type in our table definitions, and the corresponding PIL image will be automatically created when we select from the database or serialized when we insert or update the database.

SQL Expression Language

SQLAlchemy's SQL expression language provides an API to execute queries and updates against your tables, all from Python, and all in a database-independent way (managed by the SQLAlchemy-provided Dialect). For instance, the following expression:

```
select([user_table.c.user_name, user_table.c.password],
    where=user_table.c.user_name=='rick')
```

would yield the following SQL code:

```
SELECT tf_user.user_name, tf_user.password
FROM tf_user
WHERE tf_user.user_name = ?
```

Notice how the SQL generated uses a question mark for the user name value. This is known as a "bind parameter." When the query is run, SQLAlchemy will send the query string (with bind parameters) and the actual variables (in this case, the string `"rick"`) to the database engine. Using the SQLAlchemy SQL-generation layer has several advantages over hand-generating SQL strings:

Security

Application data (including user-generated data) is safely escaped via bind parameters, making SQL injection-style attacks extremely difficult.

Performance

The likelihood of reusing a particular query string (from the database server's perspective) is increased. For instance, if we wanted to select another user from the table, the SQL generated would be identical, and a different bind parameter would be sent. This allows the database server in some cases to reuse its execution plan from the first query for the second, increasing performance.

Portability

Although SQL is a standardized language, different database servers implement different parts of the standard, and to different degrees of faithfulness. SQLAlchemy provides you a way to write database-independent SQL in Python without tying you to a particular database server. With a little bit of planning, the same SQLAlchemy-based application can run on SQLite, Oracle, DB2, PostgreSQL, or any other SQLAlchemy-supported database without code changes.

Most of the time, you will be using the SQL expression language by creating expressions involving the attributes of the *table*.c object. This is a special attribute that is added to `Tables` you have defined in the metadata, as well as any objects you have mapped to tables or other selectables. The ".c" objects represent database columns, and they can be combined via a rich set of operators:

```
# Select all users with a username starting with 'r' who were
#    created before June 1, 2007
q = user_table.select(
    user_table.c.user_name.like('r%')
    & user_table.c.created < datetime(2007,6,1))

# Alternate syntax to do the same thing
q = user_table.select(and_(
    user_table.c.user_name.like('r%'),
    user_table.c.created < datetime(2007,6,1)))
```

You can also use mapped classes in the same way:

```
q = session.query(User)
q = q.filter(User.c.user_name.like('r%')
             & User.c.created > datetime(2007,6,1))
```

Of course, you aren't required to use the SQL expression language; you can always insert custom SQL instead:

```
q = user_table.select("""tf_user.user_name LIKE 'r%'""")
```

You can also use SQL functions in your queries by using the SQLAlchemy-supplied
func object:

```
q=select([Permission.c.permission_name,
          func.count(user_group.c.user_id)],
       and_(Permission.c.id==group_permission.c.permission_id,
          Group.c.id==group_permission.c.group_id,
          Group.c.id==user_group.c.group_id),
       group_by=[Permission.c.permission_name],
       distinct=True)
```

Object Relational Mapper (ORM)

Although you can do a lot with the Engine, Metadata, TypeEngine, and SQL expression
language, the true power of SQLAlchemy is found in its ORM. SQLAlchemy's ORM
provides a convenient, unobtrusive way to add database persistence to your Python
objects without requiring you to design your objects around the database, or the
database around the objects. To accomplish this, SQLAlchemy uses the data mapper
pattern. In this pattern, you can define your tables (or other selectables, such as joins)
in one module, your classes in another, and the mappers between them in yet another
module.

SQLAlchemy provides a great deal of flexibility in mapping tables, as well as a sensible
set of default mappings. Suppose that we defined the following tables, classes, and
mappers:

```
user_table = Table(
    'tf_user', metadata,
    Column('id', Integer, primary_key=True),
    Column('user_name', Unicode(16), unique=True, nullable=False),
Column('email_address', Unicode(255), unique=True, nullable=False),
    Column('password', Unicode(40), nullable=False),
    Column('first_name', Unicode(255), default=''),
    Column('last_name', Unicode(255), default=''),
    Column('created', DateTime, default=datetime.now))

group_table = Table(
    'tf_group', metadata,
    Column('id', Integer, primary_key=True),
    Column('group_name', Unicode(16), unique=True, nullable=False))

user_group = Table(
    'user_group',  metadata,
Column('user_id', None, ForeignKey('tf_user.id'), primary_key=True),
Column('group_id', None, ForeignKey('tf_group.id'),
... primary_key=True))

class User(object): pass

class Group(object): pass
```

```
mapper(User, user_table)
mapper(Group, group_table)
```

Here, the mapper would create properties on the User class for the columns of the table: id, user_name, email_address, password, first_name, last_name, and created. On the Group class, the id and group_name properties would be defined. The mapper, however, has a great deal more flexibility. If we wished to store only a hash of the user's password in the database, rather than the actual plaintext password, we might modify the User class and mapper to the following:

```
import sha
class User(object):

    def _get_password(self):
        return self._password
    def _set_password(self, value):
        self._password = sha.new(value).hexdigest()
    password=property(_get_password, _set_password)

    def password_matches(self, password):
        return sha.new(password).hexdigest() == self._password

mapper(User, user_table, properties=dict(
    _password=user_table.c.password))
```

By providing an application-level override for the password property, we can ensure that only hashed passwords are ever stored to the database. By telling the mapper to map user_table.c.password to the protected property _password, we prevent SQLAlchemy from providing the default mapping for the password column.

Perhaps the most powerful feature of the ORM is the ability to use regular Python data structures to model relationships between tables. In the preceding user/group example, we can modify the user mapper a bit more to provide the User class with a groups property, and the Group class with a users property:

```
mapper(User, user_table, properties=dict(
    _password=user_table.c.password,
    groups=relation(Group, secondary=user_group, backref='users')))
```

Now we can access all the groups that a user is a member of by simply accessing the groups property. We can also add a user to a group by either appending the user to the group's users property, *or* appending the group to the user's groups property:

```
# user1's "groups" property will automatically be updated
group1.users.append(user1)

# group2's "users" property will automatically be updated
user2.groups.append(group2)
```

The ORM uses a Session object to keep track of objects loaded from the database and the changes made to them. Sessions are used to persist objects created by the application, and they provide a query interface to retrieve objects from the database. Rather than executing the database code to synchronize your objects with your tables every time an object is modified, the Session simply tracks all changes until its flush() method is called, at which point all the changes are sent to the database in a single unit of work.

A Session class is created using the sessionmaker() function, and a Session object is created by instantiating the class returned from sessionmaker(). Although you can instantiate the Session object directly, the sessionmaker function is a convenient way to fix the parameters that will be passed to the Session's constructor, rather than repeating them wherever a Session is instantiated.

To insert objects into the database, we simply need to save them to the session:

```
Session=sessionmaker()
session=Session()
u = User()
u.user_name='rick'
u.password='foo'
u.email_address='rick@pyatl.org'
session.save(u) # tell SQLAlchemy to track the object
session.flush() # actually perform the insert
```

To retrieve objects from the database, we need to first obtain a query object from the session and then use its methods to specify which objects we retrieve:

```
q = session.query(User)

user = q.get(1) # retrieve by primary key

# retrieve one object by property
user = q.get_by(user_name='rick')

# retrieve multiple objects
users = list(q.filter_by(first_name=None))

# retrieve multiple objects using the SQL expression language
users = list(q.filter(User.c.first_name==None))
```

Note that the filter_by() method takes keyword arguments whose names match the mapped properties. This is often a useful shortcut because you avoid having to type out "User.c." over and over, but is less flexible than the filter method, which can take arbitrary SQL expressions as its criteria for selection. One powerful feature of SQLAlchemy is its ability, in the filter_by() method, to automatically search your joined tables for a matching column:

```
# Retrieve all users in a group named 'admin'
users = list(q.filter_by(group_name='admin'))
```

SQLAlchemy will automatically search for tables with foreign key relationships that contain the queried object to find columns to satisfy the keyword arguments. This can be very powerful, but can also sometimes find the wrong column, particularly if you are querying based on a common column name, such as name, for instance. In this case, you can manually specify the joins that SQLAlchemy will perform in the query via the join() method.

```
q = session.query(User)
q = q.join('groups') # use the mapped property name for joins
q = q.filter(Group.c.group_name=='admin')
users = list(q)
```

You can even specify a "join chain" by using a list of properties for the argument to join():

```
q = session.query(User)
# groups is a property of a User, permissions is a property of a
... Group
q = q.join(['groups', 'permissions'])
q = q.filter(Permission.c.permission_name=='admin')
users = list(q)
```

The power of SQLAlchemy to construct complex queries becomes clear when we compare the previous code to the SQL generated:

```
SELECT tf_user.first_name AS tf_user_first_name,
    tf_user.last_name AS tf_user_last_name,
    tf_user.created AS tf_user_created,
    tf_user.user_name AS tf_user_user_name,
    tf_user.password AS tf_user_password,
    tf_user.email_address AS tf_user_email_address,
    tf_user.id AS tf_user_id
FROM tf_user
    JOIN user_group ON tf_user.id = user_group.user_id
    JOIN tf_group ON tf_group.id = user_group.group_id
JOIN group_permission ON tf_group.id = group_permission.group_id
JOIN tf_permission ON tf_permission.id =
... group_permission.permission_id
WHERE tf_permission.permission_name = ? ORDER BY tf_user.oid
```

## CHAPTER 2

Getting Started

This chapter guides you through installing version 0.4 of SQLAlchemy (the version documented by this book) via EasyInstall. It will also give you a quick tutorial on the basic features of SQLAlchemy to "get your hands dirty" as soon as possible.

Installing SQLAlchemy

In order to use SQLAlchemy, you need to install the SQLAlchemy package as well as a Python database driver for your database. This section will guide you through installing both.

Installing the SQLAlchemy Package

Installing the SQLAlchemy is a straightforward process involving the widely used *SetupTools* package.

Installing setup tools

SQLAlchemy is distributed as an EGG file via the Python package index (PyPI), also known as the CheeseShop. If you have installed EGGs before using *easy_install*, you can skip to the next section. Otherwise, you will need to install *SetupTools*, a package that enhances the Python standard library-provided *distutils* package.

> *SetupTools* includes a tool called *easy_install*, which can be used to install various Python modules from the CheeseShop. *easy_install* is particularly good at resolving dependencies between Python packages and installing a package's dependencies along with the package itself. If you intend to take advantage of the rich library of free software available in the CheeseShop, or if you intend to take advantage of the benefits of distributing your own code through *SetupTools*, it is a good idea to become familiar with all its features. You can find more documentation on *SetupTools* at *http://peak.telecommunity.com/DevCenter/EasyInstall*.

To install *SetupTools*, first download the bootstrap script *ez_setup.py* from *http://peak.telecommunity.com/dist/ez_setup.py*. You will then need to run the script to download the rest of *SetupTools*.

 In Windows, you must make certain that you have administrator privileges before running *easy_install* or *ez_setup.py*, as both of these scripts modify your Python site-packages directory.

In Windows, it's also a good idea to make sure that Python and your Python scripts directories are on your path. In the default Python installation, these directories are *c:\python25* and *c:\python25\scripts*.

In Unix-like systems, including Linux, BSD, and OS X, you can install *SetupTools* as follows:

```
$ sudo python ez_setup.py
```

In Windows, you will need to open a command prompt and run the bootstrap script as follows:

```
c:\>python ez_setup.py
```

Once you have installed *SetupTools* using *ez_setup*, you are ready to install SQLAlchemy.

Installing SQLAlchemy with easy_install

To install SQLAlchemy using *easy_install* on a Unix-like system, simply type the following:

```
$ sudo easy_install -UZ SQLAlchemy
```

On Windows, the corresponding command is as follows (as long as your scripts directory, generally *c:\python25\scripts*, is on your path):

```
c:\>easy_install -UZ SQLAlchemy
```

This will download and install SQLAlchemy to your Python site-packages directory. If you wish to install a particular version of SQLAlchemy, add a version specifier to the *easy_install* command line. In Unix, this would be:

```
$ sudo easy_install -UZ SQLAlchemy==0.4.1
```

In Windows, the command is similar:

```
c:\>easy_install -UZ SQLAlchemy==0.4.1
```

Python EGGs are typically distributed and installed as ZIP files. Although this is convenient for distribution, it is often nice to see the actual source code. *easy_install* includes an option to specify that the EGG should be unzipped. The -UZ options as shown specify that SQLAlchemy should be Updated if already installed and should not be Zipped. If you are installing SQLAlchemy for the first time, you can leave off the -U, and if you don't care to look at the source code, you can leave off the -Z.

Testing the install

To verify that your installation of SQLAlchemy has been successful, simply open up an interactive Python interpreter and try importing the module and verifying its version:

```
>>> import sqlalchemy
>>> sqlalchemy.__version__
'0.4.1'
```

This book covers the 0.4 release of SQLAlchemy, so confirm that the version installed on your system is at least 0.4.0.

SQLAlchemy also has an extensive unit test suite that can be downloaded separately (not via *easy_install*) from *http://sqlalchemy.org* if you wish to test the installation more extensively.

Installing Some Database Drivers

The next step is installing the appropriate DB-API database drivers for the database you wish to use. If you are using a version of Python greater than or equal to 2.5, you already have the SQLite driver installed, as it is included in the standard Python library. If you are using Python 2.3 or 2.4, you will need to install the SQLite driver separately.

Installing the SQLite driver on Python versions before 2.5

For many of the examples in this book, we use the SQLite database driver, mainly because it requires no separate database server installation, and you can use it to generate throwaway in-memory databases. Even if your production database is not SQLite, it can be advantageous to install the driver for prototyping code and running the examples in this book. The SQLite database driver became part of the Python standard library in version 2.5, so if you are running more recent versions of Python, you can skip this section.

Installing SQLite is different depending on whether you are using Windows or another operating system. If you are using Windows, you can download the *pysqlite* binary module from *http://pysqlite.org/* and install it. If you are using another operating system, you will also need to install the SQLite library from *http://sqlite.org/*.

Other supported drivers

If you wish to connect to other databases, you must install the appropriate DB-API driver module. The complete list of supported databases and drivers follows:

PostgreSQL
> *psycopg2* at *http://www.initd.org/pub/software/psycopg/*

SQLite
> *pysqlite* at *http://initd.org/pub/software/pysqlite/* or *sqlite3* (included with Python versions 2.5 and greater)

MySQL
> *MySQLdb* at *http://sourceforge.net/projects/mysql-python*

Oracle
> *cx_Oracle* at *http://www.cxtools.net/*

SQL Server
> Support for Microsoft SQL server is provided by multiple drivers as follows:
> - *pyodbc* at *http://pyodbc.sourceforge.net/* (recommended driver)
> - *adodbapi* at *http://adodbapi.sourceforge.net/*
> - *pymssql* at *http://pymssql.sourceforge.net/*

Firebird
> *kinterbasdb* at *http://kinterbasdb.sourceforge.net/*

Informix
> *informixdb* at *http://informixdb.sourceforge.net/*

SQLAlchemy Tutorial

Once you have installed SQLAlchemy and the SQLite driver (either *pysqlite* or *sqlite3*), you can start really exploring SQLAlchemy. This tutorial shows off some of the basic features of SQLAlchemy that you can use to become immediately productive. This tutorial is based on a stripped-down version of a user authentication module that might be used in a web application.

Connecting to the Database and Creating Some Tables

Before doing anything, we need to import the modules we will use. In this case, for simplicity's sake, we will simply import everything from the *sqlalchemy* package. We will also import the `datetime` class from the *datetime* package for use in defining default values for our tables.

```
from sqlalchemy import *
from datetime import datetime
```

To connect to the database, we will create a `MetaData` object, which is used by SQLAlchemy to keep track of the tables we define:

```
metadata = MetaData('sqlite:///tutorial.sqlite')
```

The `MetaData` object we create is *bound* to a particular database `Engine`, in this case a SQLite engine connected to the database in the file *tutorial.sqlite*. If *tutorial.sqlite* does not already exist, it will be created automatically by SQLite.

Once we have created our `MetaData`, we can define our tables. The first table defined is the user table:

```
user_table = Table(
    'tf_user', metadata,
    Column('id', Integer, primary_key=True),
    Column('user_name', Unicode(16),
            unique=True, nullable=False),
    Column('password', Unicode(40), nullable=False),
    Column('display_name', Unicode(255), default=''),
    Column('created', DateTime, default=datetime.now))
```

Notice how the `Table` constructor is given the SQL name of the table (`'tf_user'`), a reference to the metadata object, and a list of columns. The columns are similarly defined with their SQL names, data types, and various optional constraints. In this case, since we defined an `'id'` column as a primary key, SQLAlchemy will automatically create the column with an auto-increment default value. Also note that we can specify uniqueness and nullability constraints on columns, provide literal defaults, or provide Python callables (e.g., `datetime.now`) as defaults.

Next, we define our group and permission tables:

```
group_table = Table(
    'tf_group', metadata,
    Column('id', Integer, primary_key=True),
    Column('group_name', Unicode(16),
            unique=True, nullable=False))

permission_table = Table(
    'tf_permission', metadata,
    Column('id', Integer, primary_key=True),
    Column('permission_name', Unicode(16),
            unique=True, nullable=False))
```

Each table is simply defined with an auto-increment primary key and a unique name.

Finally, we define the join tables that provide a many-to-many relationship between users and groups and groups and permissions:

```
user_group_table = Table(
    'tf_user_group', metadata,
    Column('user_id', None, ForeignKey('tf_user.id'),
            primary_key=True),
    Column('group_id', None, ForeignKey('tf_group.id'),
            primary_key=True))
```

```
group_permission_table = Table(
    'tf_group_permission', metadata,
    Column('permission_id', None, ForeignKey('tf_permission.id'),
           primary_key=True),
    Column('group_id', None, ForeignKey('tf_group.id'),
           primary_key=True))
```

Note in particular the use of compound primary keys (each table is keyed by two columns) and the use of foreign key constraints. We also specified the data type of the foreign key columns as None. When a foreign key column is specified with this datatype, SQLAlchemy will examine the column on the related table (e.g., 'tf_user.id') to determine the data type for the foreign key column.

Once the tables have been defined, we can create them in the database using the following code:

```
metadata.create_all()
```

If you were not creating the database, but rather connecting to an existing database, you could, of course, leave out the call to metadata.create_all(). SQLAlchemy will in any case create tables using the IF NOT EXISTS syntax, so a metadata.create_all() is a safe operation.

Performing Queries and Updates

Once we have defined the tables in our schema, we can insert some data. To create a new user, we use SQLAlchemy to construct an INSERT statement using the following syntax:

```
stmt = user_table.insert()
```

Once the insert statement has been created, it can be executed multiple times with different values:

```
stmt.execute(user_name='rick', password='secret',
             display_name='Rick Copeland')
stmt.execute(user_name='rick1', password='secret',
             display_name='Rick Copeland Clone')
```

If we wish to see the actual SQL generated, we can instruct SQLAlchemy to log the queries using the metadata.bind.echo property:

```
>>> metadata.bind.echo = True
>>> stmt.execute(user_name='rick2', password='secret',
...              display_name='Rick Copeland Clone 2')
2007-09-06 10:19:52,317 INFO sqlalchemy.engine.base.Engine.0x..50
... INSERT INTO tf_user (user_name, password, display_name, created)
...
... VALUES (?, ?, ?, ?)
2007-09-06 10:19:52,318 INFO sqlalchemy.engine.base.Engine.0x..50
... ['rick2', 'secret', 'Rick Copeland Clone 2', '2007-09-06
... 10:19:52.317540']
2007-09-06 10:19:52,319 INFO sqlalchemy.engine.base.Engine.0x..50
... COMMIT
```

```
<sqlalchemy.engine.base.ResultProxy object at 0x2b7ee8ffb610>
>>> metadata.bind.echo = False
```

Note again that SQLAlchemy uses bind parameters for the values to be inserted, and that SQLAlchemy automatically generates the created column value based on the result of calling datetime.now() when the insert was executed.

To select data back out of the table, we can use the table's select() method as follows:

```
>>> stmt = user_table.select()
>>> result = stmt.execute()
>>> for row in result:
...     print row
...
(1, u'rick', u'secret1', u'Rick Copeland',
... datetime.datetime(2007, 9, 7, 10, 6, 4, 415754))
(2, u'rick1', u'secret', u'Rick Copeland Clone',
... datetime.datetime(2007, 9, 7, 10, 6, 4, 476505))
(3, u'rick2', u'secret', u'Rick Copeland Clone 2',
... datetime.datetime(2007, 9, 7, 10, 6, 4, 543650))
```

We can also retrieve values from each row of the result using dict-like indexing or simple attribute lookup as follows:

```
>>> result = stmt.execute()
>>> row =result.fetchone()
>>> row['user_name']
u'rick'
>>> row.password
u'secret1'
>>> row.created
datetime.datetime(2007, 9, 7, 10, 6, 4, 415754)
>>> row.items()
[(u'id', 1), (u'user_name', u'rick'), (u'password', u'secret1'),
... (u'display_name', u'Rick Copeland'),
... (u'created', datetime.datetime(2007, 9, 7, 10, 6, 4, 415754))]
```

To restrict the rows that are returned from the select() method, we can supply a where clause. SQLAlchemy provides a powerful SQL expression language to assist in the construction of where clauses, as shown in the following example:

```
>>> stmt = user_table.select(user_table.c.user_name=='rick')
>>> print stmt.execute().fetchall()
[(1, u'rick', u'secret1', u'Rick Copeland',
... datetime.datetime(2007, 9, 7, 10, 6, 4, 415754))]
```

The SQL expression language is covered in more detail in Chapter 5.

We can also use the SQL expression language to generate updates and deletes by passing clauses to the update() and delete() methods on Table objects:

```
>>> # Create an update constrained by user name
... stmt = user_table.update(user_table.c.user_name=='rick')
>>> # Execute the update, setting the password column to secret123
... stmt.execute(password='secret123')
<sqlalchemy.engine.base.ResultProxy object at 0xa20c50>
```

```
>>>
>>> # Create a delete statement that deletes all users
... #    except for 'rick'
... stmt = user_table.delete(user_table.c.user_name != 'rick')
>>> stmt.execute()
<sqlalchemy.engine.base.ResultProxy object at 0x2b12bf430210>
>>> # Select the users back from the database
... user_table.select().execute().fetchall()
[(1, u'rick', u'secret123', u'Rick Copeland',
... datetime.datetime(2007, 9, 7, 18, 35, 35, 529412))]
>>> # Add the users back
... stmt = user_table.insert()
>>> stmt.execute(user_name='rick1', password='secret',
...              display_name='Rick Copeland Clone')
<sqlalchemy.engine.base.ResultProxy object at 0xa20c90>
>>> stmt.execute(user_name='rick2', password='secret',
...              display_name='Rick Copeland Clone 2')
<sqlalchemy.engine.base.ResultProxy object at 0xa20cd0>
>>>
```

SQLAlchemy also provides for more generalized queries via the `insert()`, `select()`, `update()`, and `delete()` *functions* (rather than the *methods* on `Table` objects) to allow you to specify more complex SQL queries. Again, this is covered in more detail in Chapter 5.

Mapping Objects to Tables

In addition to the SQL-level features covered thus far, SQLAlchemy also provides a powerful object-relational mapper (ORM) that allows you to map tables (and other "selectable" objects, such as SELECT statements) to objects, making those objects automatically "SQL-persistable." In order to use the ORM, we need to import the appropriate names:

```
from sqlalchemy.orm import *
```

The simplest case of mapping is to just declare empty classes for our application objects and declare an empty mapper:

```
class User(object): pass
class Group(object): pass
class Permission(object): pass

mapper(User, user_table)
mapper(Group, group_table)
mapper(Permission, permission_table)
```

Now that we have declared the mapping between our classes and tables, we can start doing queries. First off, though, we need to understand the unit of work (UOW) pattern. In UOW as implemented by SQLAlchemy, there is an object known as a `Session` that tracks changes to mapped objects and can `flush()` them out *en masse* to the database in a single "unit of work." This can lead to substantial performance improvement when compared to executing multiple separate updates. In SQLAlchemy, the Session class is created using the `sessionmaker()` function, and the Session object is created by instantiating the class returned from `sessionmaker()`. The intent is that `sessionmaker()` should be called once (at the module level), with its return value used to create individual sessions:

```
Session = sessionmaker()
session = Session()
```

Once we have the session object, we use it to obtain access to a Query object for our class:

```
query = session.query(User)
```

The simplest way to use the Query object is as an iterator for all the objects in the database. Since we have already inserted a row in the user_table, we can retrieve that row as a User object:

```
>>> list(query)
[<__main__.User object at 0xb688d0>,
... <__main__.User object at 0xb68910>,
... <__main__.User object at 0xb68c10>]
>>> for user in query:
...      print user.user_name
...
rick
rick1
rick2
```

We can also retrieve an object from the database by using its primary key with the `get()` method on the Query object:

```
>>> query.get(1)
<__main__.User object at 0xb688d0>
```

If we want to filter the results retrieved by the Query object, we can use the `filter()` and `filter_by()` methods:

```
>>> for user in query.filter_by(display_name='Rick Copeland'):
...      print user.id, user.user_name, user.password
...
1 rick secret123
>>> for user in query.filter(User.c.user_name.like('rick%')):
...      print user.id, user.user_name, user.password
...
1 rick secret123
2 rick1 secret
3 rick2 secret
```

Note the use of the .c attribute of the User object. It was added by the mapper as a convenience to access the names of mapped columns. If we wanted to, we could freely substitute `user_table.c.user_name` for `User.c.user_name`, and vice versa.

To insert objects into the database, we simply create an object in Python and then use the **save()** method to notify the session about the object:

```
>>> newuser = User()
>>> newuser.user_name = 'mike'
```

```
>>> newuser.password = 'password'
>>> session.save(newuser)
```

Due to the UOW pattern, the new user has not yet been saved to the database. If we try to count the users using the **user_table**, we still get 3:

```
>>> len(list(user_table.select().execute()))
3
```

If, however, we try to use the **Query** object, the ORM recognizes the need to perform a **flush()** on the **Session**, inserts the new user, and we get a count of 4:

```
>>> metadata.bind.echo = True
>>> query.count()
2007-09-09 21:33:09,482 INFO sqlalchemy.engine.base.Engine.0x..50
... INSERT INTO tf_user (user_name, password, display_name, created)
...
... VALUES (?, ?, ?, ?)
2007-09-09 21:33:09,482 INFO sqlalchemy.engine.base.Engine.0x..50
... ['mike', 'password', '', '2007-09-09 21:33:09.481854']
2007-09-09 21:33:09,485 INFO sqlalchemy.engine.base.Engine.0x..50
... SELECT count(tf_user.id)
FROM tf_user
2007-09-09 21:33:09,486 INFO sqlalchemy.engine.base.Engine.0x..50 []
4
```

You can disable the auto-flushing behavior of SQLAlchemy by specifying **autoflush=False** in the call to **sessionmaker()**.

To update objects in the database, we simply make changes to the object in Python and allow the SQLAlchemy **Session** to track our changes and eventually flush everything out to the database:

```
>>> newuser.password = 'password1'
>>> newuser.display_name = 'Michael'
>>>
>>> rick = query.get(1)
>>> rick.display_name = 'Richard'
>>>
>>> session.flush()
2007-09-09 21:40:21,854 INFO sqlalchemy.engine.base.Engine.0x..50
... UPDATE tf_user SET display_name=? WHERE tf_user.id = ?
2007-09-09 21:40:21,854 INFO sqlalchemy.engine.base.Engine.0x..50
... ['Richard', 1]
2007-09-09 21:40:21,856 INFO sqlalchemy.engine.base.Engine.0x..50
... UPDATE tf_user SET password=?, display_name=? WHERE tf_user.id =
... ?
2007-09-09 21:40:21,857 INFO sqlalchemy.engine.base.Engine.0x..50
['password1', 'Michael', 4]
```

To delete an object, simply call the **session**'s **delete()** method with the object to be deleted. To flush the **session** and commit the transaction, we call **session.commit()**:

```
>>> session.delete(newuser)
>>>
>>> session.commit()
```

```
2007-09-09 21:42:56,327 INFO sqlalchemy.engine.base.Engine.0x..50
... DELETE FROM tf_user WHERE tf_user.id = ?
2007-09-09 21:42:56,328 INFO sqlalchemy.engine.base.Engine.0x..50
... [4]
2007-09-09 21:42:56,328 INFO sqlalchemy.engine.base.Engine.0x..50
... COMMIT
```

The SQLAlchemy ORM also includes support for managing relationships between classes, as well as flexible overrides of its column-mapping conventions. The ORM is covered in more detail in Chapters 6, 7, and 8.

## CHAPTER 3

Engines and MetaData

This chapter introduces SQLAlchemy's `Engine` and `MetaData` classes. The `Engine` class provides database connectivity, including a connection pool with various strategies for acquiring connections from the pool. The `MetaData` class maintains information about your database schema, including any tables and indexes defined. In this chapter, you will learn how to define a new database schema using `MetaData` as well as how to connect a `MetaData` instance to an existing schema.

Engines and Connectables

The SQLAlchemy-provided `Engine` class is responsible for managing the connection to the database. It does this by incorporating a database connection pool and a database-specific `Dialect` layer to translate the SQL expression language (Chapter 5) into database-specific SQL.

To get started using an `Engine`, you use the `create_engine()` function:

```
# Create a connection to a SQLite in-memory database
engine = create_engine('sqlite://')

# Create a connection to a SQLite on-disk database "data.sqlite"
engine = create_engine('sqlite:///data.sqlite')

# Create a connection to a PostGreSQL database
engine = create_engine('postgres://rick:foo@localhost:5432/pg_db')

# Create a connection to a MySQL database
engine = create_engine('mysql://localhost/mysql_db')

# Create a connection to an Oracle database (via TNS)
engine = create_engine('oracle://rick:foo@oracle_tns')

# Create a connection to an Oracle database (without a TNS name)
engine =
... create_engine('oracle://rick:foo@localhost:1521/oracle_sid')
```

The first argument to `create_engine()` is the RFC-1738 style URL specifying the database. The general form of the url is: *driver://username:password@host:port/database*.

Of course, the various database drivers interpret these URLs in slightly different ways, as illustrated here. It is also possible to pass additional arguments to the low-level DB-API driver created by SQLAlchemy via either a URL query string:

```
url='postgres://rick:foo@localhost/pg_db?arg1=foo&arg2=bar'
engine = create_engine(url)
```

or via the connect_args parameter to create_engine():

```
engine = create_engine('postgres://rick:foo@localhost/pg_db',
    connect_args=dict(arg1='foo', arg2='bar'))
```

If you wish complete control over the connection creation process, you can even pass a function (or other callable object) that returns a DB-API connection to create_engine() in the creator argument:

```
import psycopg
def connect_pg():
    return psycopg.connect(user='rick', host='localhost')
engine = create_engine('postgres://', creator=connect_pg)
```

The full set of keyword arguments accepted by create_engine() are specified in here:

connect_args
>A dictionary of options to be passed to the DB-API's connect() method. The default is {}.

convert_unicode
>Indicates whether the engine should convert all unicode values into raw byte strings before going into the database, and convert raw byte strings to unicode coming out of result sets. This can be useful, for instance, when dealing with a database server or schema that does not provide unicode support natively. The default is False.

creator
>A callable that returns a DB-API connection. The default is None.

echo
>A flag that tells SQLAlchemy to echo all statements and bind parameter values to its logger. The default is None.

echo_pool
>A flag that tells SQLAlchemy to log all connection pool checkins and checkouts. The default is False.

encoding
>Specifies the encoding to use in all translations between raw byte strings and Python unicode objects. The default is False.

module
>Specifies which module to use when a database implementation can use more than one (such as PostgreSQL and Oracle). The default is None.

pool

Use an existing connection pool rather than creating a new one. The default is None.

poolclass

If the engine is creating its own connection pool, the class (a subclass of sqlalchemy.pool.Pool) to use when constructing the pool object. If no pool class is specified, sqlalchemy.pool.QueuePool will be used for all database drivers except for SQLite, which uses the sqlalchemy.pool.SingletonThreadPool. The default is None.

max_overflow

The number of connections to allow the connection pool to overflow to (only applicable with the QueuePool). The default is 10.

pool_size

The number of connections to keep alive in the connection pool (only applicable to the QueuePool and SingletonThreadPool pool classes). The default is 5.

pool_recycle

Close and reopen connections after this number of seconds of inactivity, or, if −1 (the default), disable connection recycling. This is useful if the database server times out connections after a period of inactivity, as MySQL does.

pool_timeout

The number of seconds to wait when getting a connection from the pool before giving up, (applicable only to QueuePool connection pools). The default is 30.

strategy

Selects an alternate implementation of the engine; the only current strategies are 'plain' and 'threadlocal'. 'threadlocal' reuses connections for multiple statements within a thread; 'plain' (the default) uses a new connection for each statement.

threaded

Used only by cx_Oracle, makes the engine threadsafe. If this is not required, performance might be improved by setting this parameter to False.

use_ansi

Used only by Oracle to correct for a quirk of Oracle versions 8 and earlier when handling LEFT OUTER JOINs.

use_oids

Used only by PostgreSQL to enable the column name "oid" (object ID).

Configuring SQLAlchemy Logging

SQLAlchemy uses the Python standard library logging module to log various actions. The echo and echo_pool arguments to create_engine() and the echo_uow flag used on Session objects all affect the regular loggers.

One useful debugging strategy is to add a logfile for a particular class of operations that SQLAlchemy is performing. For instance, to capture all of the engine-related operations, we could set up the logger as follows:

```
import logging
handler = logging.FileHandler('sqlalchemy.engine.log')
handler.level = logging.DEBUG
logging.getLogger('sqlalchemy.engine').addHandler(handler)
```

The loggers used with SQLAlchemy are listed next. Note that several of these loggers deal with material covered in later chapters (in particular, the `sqlalchemy.orm.*` loggers):

- `sqlalchemy.engine`—control SQL echoing. `logging.INFO` logs SQL query output, `logging.DEBUG` logs result sets as well.
- `sqlalchemy.pool`—control connection pool logging. `logging.INFO` logs checkins and checkouts.
- `sqlalchemy.orm`—control logging of ORM functions. `logging.INFO` logs configurations and unit of work dumps.
  - `sqlalchemy.orm.attributes`—logs instrumented attribute operations.
  - `sqlalchemy.orm.mapper`—logs mapper configurations and operations.
  - `sqlalchemy.orm.unitofwork`—logs unit of work operations, including dependency graphs.
  - `sqlalchemy.orm.strategies`—logs relation loader operations (lazy and eager loads).
  - `sqlalchemy.orm.sync`—logs synchronization of attributes from one object to another during a flush.

Database Connections and ResultProxys

Although the Engine is the normal method of performing database operations, SQLAlchemy does make the lower-level `Connection` object available through the `connect()` method on the engine, as shown in the following example:

```
conn = engine.connect()
result = conn.execute('select user_name, email_address from
... tf_user')
for row in result:
    print 'User name: %s Email address: %s' % (
        row['user_name'], row['email_address'])
conn.close()
```

The `Connection` object is actually an instance of the `sqlalchemy.engine.Connection` class, which serves as a proxy for the particular DB-API connection object. The `result` object is an instance of the `sqlalchemy.engine.ResultProxy` class, which has many features in common with a database cursor.

Both Engines and Connections are implementations of the Connectable interface, which has two important methods: connect(), which in the case of a Connection simply returns itself, and execute(), which executes some SQL and generates a ResultProxy. Most SQLAlchemy functions that therefore take an Engine as a parameter (usually named bind) can also take a Connection, and vice versa.

The ResultProxy object has several useful methods and attributes for returning information about the query:

__iter__()
> Allows iteration over a result proxy, generating RowProxy objects

fetchone()
> Fetches the next RowProxy object from the ResultProxy

fetchall()
> Fetches all RowProxy objects at once

scalar()
> Fetches the next row from the cursor and treat it as a scalar (i.e., not a RowProxy)

keys
> List of the column names in the result set

rowcount
> The total number of rows in the result set

close()
> Closes the ResultProxy, possibly returning the underlying Connection to the pool

The RowProxy object generated by the ResultProxy provides several useful methods that allow you to retrieve data, such as a tuple, dictionary, or object:

__getattr__()
> Provides access to data via object.*column name*

__getitem__()
> Provides access to data via object[*column name*] or object[*column position*]

keys()
> Provides a list of all the column names in the row

values()
> Provides a list of all the values in the row

items()
> Provides a list of (*column name*, *value*) tuples for the row

Connection Pooling

SQLAlchemy provides the connection pool as an easy and efficient way to manage connections through the database. Normally, you don't need to worry about the connection pool because it is automatically managed by the Engine class. The connection pool can, however, be used on its own to manage regular DB-API connections. If you wish to manage such a pool, you could do the following:

```
from sqlalchemy import pool
import psycopg2
psycopg = pool.manage(psycopg2)

connection = psycopg.connect(database='mydb',
    username='rick', password='foo')
```

The pool.manage() call sets up a connection pool (the exact object is an instance of sqlalchemy.pool.DBProxy). The connect() method then works just as the Engine's connect() method, returning a proxy for the DB-API connection from the managed connection pool. When the connection proxy is garbage collected, the underlying DB-API connection is returned to the connection pool.

By default, the connect() method returns the same connection object if it is called multiple times in a given thread (the same "threadlocal" strategy used by the Engine). To specify that the pool should generate a new connection each time that connect() is called, pass use_threadlocal=False to the pool.manage() function.

If you wish to use a particular connection pool class instead of the DBProxy as shown previously, SQLAlchemy provides the ability to directly instantiate the pool:

```
from sqlalchemy import pool
import psycopg2
import sqlite

def getconn_pg():
    c = psycopg2.connect(database='mydb', username='rick',
        password='foo')
    return c

def getconn_sl():
    c = sqlite.connect(filename='devdata.sqlite')
    return c

pool_pg = pool.QueuePool(getconn_pg, use_threadlocal=True)

# SQLite requires use of the SingletonThreadPool
        pool_sl = pool.SingletonThreadPool(getconn_sl)
```

Some of the various pool types that are available in the sqlalchemy.pool module are:

AssertionPool

Allows only one connection to be checked out at a time and raises an AssertionError when this constraint is violated.

NullPool

Does no pooling; instead, actually opens and closes the underlying DB-API connection on each checkout/checkin of a connection.

QueuePool
> Maintains a fixed-size connection pool. This is the default connection pool class used for nonsqlite connections.

SingletonThreadPool
> Maintains a single connection per thread. It is used with sqlite because this database driver does not handle using a single connection in multiple threads well.

StaticPool
> Maintains a single connection that is returned for all connection requests.

MetaData

SQLAlchemy provides the MetaData class, which collects objects that describe tables, indexes, and other schema-level objects. Before using any of the higher-level features of SQLAlchemy, such as the SQL query language and the ORM, the schema of the database must be described using metadata. In some cases, you can *reflect* the structure of schema items into the MetaData from the database. In this case, you need only specify the name of the entity, and its structure will be loaded from the database directly.

Getting Started with MetaData

To create a new MetaData object, you simply call its constructor, possibly with information about how to connect to the database. If the constructor is called with no arguments, it is considered to be *unbound*; if it is called with either an Engine or a SQL connection URI, it is considered *bound*. Shortcuts are available to bound MetaData and to objects within a bound MetaData to facilitate the execution of statements against the bound engine. Most of the time you will probably use a bound MetaData object. However, it is sometimes useful to use an unbound MetaData if you need to connect to multiple database servers, where each server contains the same database schema.

The various ways to construct MetaData objects are illustrated in the following examples:

```
# create an unbound MetaData
unbound_meta = MetaData()

# create an Engine and bind the MetaData to it
db1 = create_engine('sqlite://')
unbound_meta.bind = db

# Create an engine and then a bound MetaData
db2 = MetaData('sqlite:///test1.db')
bound_meta1 = MetaData(db2)

# Create a bound MetaData with an implicitly created engine
bound_meta2 = MetaData('sqlite:///test2.db')
```

Note that you are never required to bind the MetaData object; all operations that rely on a database connection can also be executed by passing the Engine explicitly as the keyword parameter bind. This is referred to as *explicit execution*. If a MetaData instance is bound, then the bind parameter can be omitted from method calls that rely on the database connection. This is referred to as *implicit execution*. The "bound-ness" of a MetaData object is shared by all Tables, Indexes, and Sequences in the MetaData, so a Table attached to a bound MetaData, for instance, would be able to create itself via:

```
table.create()
```

whereas a Table in an unbound MetaData would need to supply a bind parameter:

```
table.create(bind=some_engine_or_connection)
```

Defining Tables

The most common use of the MetaData object is in defining the tables in your schema. To define tables in the MetaData, you use the Table and Column classes as shown in the following example:

```
from sqlalchemy import *
from datetime import datetime

metadata=MetaData()
user_table = Table(
    'tf_user', metadata,
    Column('id', Integer, primary_key=True),
    Column('user_name', Unicode(16), unique=True, nullable=False),
Column('email_address', Unicode(255), unique=True, nullable=False),
    Column('password', Unicode(40), nullable=False),
    Column('first_name', Unicode(255), default=''),
    Column('last_name', Unicode(255), default=''),
    Column('created', DateTime, default=datetime.now))
```

Unlike some other database mapping libraries, SQLAlchemy fully supports the use of composite and noninteger primary and foreign keys:

```
brand_table = Table(
    'brand', metadata,
    Column('id', Integer, primary_key=True),
    Column('name', Unicode(255), unique=True, nullable=False))

product_table = Table(
    'product', metadata,
Column('brand_id', Integer, ForeignKey('brand.id'),
... primary_key=True),
    Column('sku', Unicode(80), primary_key=True))

style_table = Table(
    'style', metadata,
    Column('brand_id', Integer, primary_key=True),
    Column('sku', Unicode(80), primary_key=True),
    Column('code', Unicode(80), primary_key=True),
    ForeignKeyConstraint(['brand_id', 'sku'],
```

```
                ['product.brand_id',
                 'product.sku']))
```

To actually create a table, you can call the **create()** method on it. Here, we will create the style table on an in-memory SQLite database and view the generated SQL:

```
>>> style_table.create(bind=create_engine('sqlite://', echo=True))
2007-08-25 08:05:44,396 INFO sqlalchemy.engine.base.Engine.0x..50
CREATE TABLE style (
        brand_id INTEGER NOT NULL,
        sku VARCHAR(80) NOT NULL,
        code VARCHAR(80) NOT NULL,
        PRIMARY KEY (brand_id, sku, code),
FOREIGN KEY(brand_id, sku) REFERENCES product (brand_id, sku)
)


2007-08-25 08:05:44,396 INFO sqlalchemy.engine.base.Engine.0x..50
... None
2007-08-25 08:05:44,397 INFO sqlalchemy.engine.base.Engine.0x..50
... COMMIT
```

We see that the composite primary key and foreign key constraints are correctly generated. Although the foreign key constraints are ignored by SQLite, it is still useful to generate them, as SQLAlchemy can use this information to perform joins automatically based on the foreign key relationships between tables.

The Table constructor Table.__init__(self, name, metadata,*args, **kwargs), takes the following arguments:

name
> The table name as known by the database (may be combined with the schema parameter).

metadata
> The MetaData object to which to attach this table.

*args
> The series of Column and Constraint objects to define for this table.

schema
> The schema name for this table, if required by the database. In **kwargs, the default is None.

autoload
> Indicates whether to reflect the columns from the database. In **kwargs, the default is False.

autoload_with
> The Connectable used to autoload the columns. In **kwargs, the default is None.

include_columns

The list of column names (strings) to be reflected if autoload=True. If None, all columns are reflected. If not None, any columns omitted from the list will not be represented on the reflected Table object. In **kwargs, the default is None.

mustexist

Indicates that the table must already be defined elsewhere in the Python application (as part of this MetaData). An exception is raised if this is not true. In **kwargs, the default is False.

useexisting

Directs SQLAlchemy to use the previous Table definition for this table name if it exists elsewhere in the application. (SQLAlchemy disregards the rest of the constructor arguments if this is True.) in **kwargs, the default is False.

owner

Specifies the owning user of the table. This is useful for some databases (such as Oracle) to help with table reflection. In **kwargs, the default is None.

quote

Forces the table name to be escaped and quoted before being sent to the database (useful for table names that conflict with SQL keywords, for example). In **kwargs, the default is False.

quote_schema

Forces the schema name to be escaped and quoted before being sent to the database. In **kwargs, the default is False.

The Table constructor also supports database-specific keyword arguments. For instance, the MySQL driver supports the mysql_engine argument to specify the backend database driver (i.e., 'InnoDB' or 'MyISAM', for instance).

Table reflection

Tables can also be defined using reflection from an existing database. This requires a database connection, and so either a bound MetaData must be used, or a Connectable must be supplied via the autoload_with parameter:

```
db = create_engine('sqlite:///devdata.sqlite')
brand_table = Table('brand', metadata, autoload=True,
... autoload_with=db)
```

You can also override the reflected columns if necessary. This can be particularly useful when specifying custom column data types, or when the database's introspection facilities fail to identify certain constraints.

```
brand_table = Table('brand', metadata,
    Column('name', Unicode(255)), # override the reflected type
    autoload=True)
```

If you want to reflect the entire database schema, you may do so by specifying reflect=True in the metadata constructor. Of course, in this case, the MetaData must be created as a bound `MetaData`. When reflecting an entire schema in this way, the individual tables can be accessed via the `MetaData`'s `tables` attribute:

```
db = create_engine('sqlite:///devdata.sqlite')
metadata = MetaData(bind=db, reflect=True)
brand_table = metadata.tables['brand']
```

You can also use the `reflect()` method of the `MetaData` to load the schema. `MetaData.reflect(bind=None, schema=None, only=None)` takes the following arguments:

bind
: A `Connectable` used to access the database; required only when the `MetaData` is unbound. The default is `None`.

schema
: Specifies an alternate schema from which to reflect tables. The default is `None`.

only
: Directs the `MetaData` to load only a subset of the available tables. This can be specified either as a sequence of the names to be loaded or as a boolean callable that will be called for each available table with the parameters *only(metadata, table name)*. If the callable returns `True`, the table will be reflected. The default is `None`.

The `MetaData` constructor itself has the definition `MetaData.__init__(bind=None, reflect=None)`.

Column Definitions

The `Column` constructor `Column.__init__(self, name, type_, *args, **kwargs)` takes the following arguments:

name
: The name of the column as it is known by the database.

type_
: The `TypeEngine` for this column. This can also be `None` if the column is a `ForeignKey`, in which case the type will be the same as the referenced column.

*args
: `Constraint`, `ForeignKey`, `ColumnDefault`, and `Sequence` objects that apply to the column.

key
: An alias for this column. If specified, the column will be identified everywhere in Python by this name rather than by its SQL-native name. In `**kwargs`, the default is `None`.

primary_key
: If `True`, marks the column as part of the primary key. (Alternatively, the `Table` can have a `PrimaryKeyConstraint` defined.) In `**kwargs`, the default is `False`.

nullable

> If set to False, this does not allow None as a value for the column. In **kwargs, the default is True, unless the column is a primary key.

default

> A Python callable or a SQL expression language construct specifying a default value for this column. Note that this is an *active* (Python-generated) default when a callable is specified; the SQL has the generated value inserted as a literal. In **kwargs, the default is None.

index

> Indicates that the column is indexed (with an autogenerated index name). Alternatively, use an Index object in the table declaration instead. In **kwargs, the default is False.

unique

> Indicates that the column has a unique constraint. Alternatively, use a UniqueConstraint object in the table declation instead. In **kwargs, the default is False.

onupdate

> Specifies an active default value (generated by SQLAlchemy rather than the database server) to be used when updating (but not inserting) a row in the table. In **kwargs, the default is None.

autoincrement

> Indicates that integer-based primary keys should have autoincrementing behavior. This is applicable only if the column has no default value and is a type or subtype of Integer. In **kwargs, the default is True.

quote

> This forces the column name to be escaped and quoted before being sent to the database (useful for column names that conflict with SQL keywords, for example). In **kwargs, the default is False.

Constraints

SQLAlchemy also supports a variety of constraints, both at the column level and at the table level. All constraints are derived from the Constraint class, and take an optional name parameter.

 If the name is not specified, SQLAlchemy auto-generates a suitable name if necessary.

Primary keys

The usual way to declare primary key columns is to specify `primary_key=True` in the `Column` constructor:

```
product_table = Table(
    'product', metadata,
Column('brand_id', Integer, ForeignKey('brand.id'),
... primary_key=True),
    Column('sku', Unicode(80), primary_key=True))
```

You can also specify primary keys using the `PrimaryKeyConstraint` object:

```
product_table = Table(
    'product', metadata,
    Column('brand_id', Integer, ForeignKey('brand.id')),
    Column('sku', Unicode(80)),
    PrimaryKeyConstraint('brand_id', 'sku', name='prikey'))
```

To see the SQL generated to create such a table, we can create it on the in-memory SQLite database:

```
>>> product_table.create(bind=create_engine('sqlite://', echo=True))
2007-08-25 14:26:56,706 INFO sqlalchemy.engine.base.Engine.0x..d0
CREATE TABLE product (
        brand_id INTEGER,
        sku VARCHAR(80),
        CONSTRAINT prikey PRIMARY KEY (brand_id, sku),
         FOREIGN KEY(brand_id) REFERENCES brand (id)
)


2007-08-25 14:26:56,706 INFO sqlalchemy.engine.base.Engine.0x..d0
... None
2007-08-25 14:26:56,707 INFO sqlalchemy.engine.base.Engine.0x..d0
... COMMIT
```

Foreign keys

Foreign keys are references from a row in one table to a row in another table. The usual way to specify simple (noncomplex) foreign keys is by passing a `ForeignKey` object to the `Column` constructor. The `ForeignKey` constructor `ForeignKey.__init__(self, column, constraint=None, use_alter=False, name=None, onupdate=None, ondelete=None)` takes the following parameters:

column

Either a `Column` object or a database-recognized string, such as *tablename.columnname* or *schemaname.tablename.columnname*, that specifies the referenced column.

constraint

The owning `ForeignKeyConstraint`, if any. If left unspecified, a new `ForeignKeyConstraint` will be created and added to the parent table. The default is None.

use_alter

> Use an ALTER TABLE command to create the constraint (passed along to the owning `ForeignKeyConstraint`). Otherwise, the constraint will be created in the CREATE TABLE statement. The default is `False`.

name

> The name of the constraint (passed along to the owning `ForeignKeyConstraint`). The default is `None`.

onupdate

> Generates an ON UPDATE clause in the SQL for the constraint (e.g., `onupdate='CASCADE'` would generate "ON UPDATE CASCADE" to cascade changes in the referenced columns to the foreign key). Commonly supported values for ON UPDATE are RESTRICT (raise an error), CASCADE (shown previously), SET NULL (set the column to NULL), and SET DEFAULT (set the column to its passive default). The default for this parameter is `None`. Not supported for all database drivers/backends.

ondelete

> Generates an ON DELETE clause in the SQL for the constraint (e.g., `ondelete='CASCADE'` would generate "ON DELETE CASCADE" to cascade deletions of the referenced row to the row with the foreign key). The default is `None`. Not supported for all database drivers/backends.

If you need to reference a compound primary key, SQLAlchemy provides the `ForeignKeyConstraint` class for increased flexibility. To use the `ForeignKeyConstraint`, simply pass a list of columns in the local table (the compound foreign key) and a list of columns in the referenced table (the compound primary key):

```
style_table = Table(
    'style', metadata,
    Column('brand_id', Integer, primary_key=True),
    Column('sku', Unicode(80), primary_key=True),
    Column('code', Unicode(80), primary_key=True),
    ForeignKeyConstraint(
        ['brand_id', 'sku'],
        ['product.brand_id', 'product.sku']))
```

The `ForeignKeyConstraint` constructor `ForeignKeyConstraint.__init__(self, columns, refcolumns, name=None, onupdate=None, ondelete=None, use_alter=False)` takes the same parameters as the `ForeignKey` constructor except for `columns` and `refcolumns`:

columns

> Either a list of `Column` objects or a list of database-recognized strings (such as *tablename.columnname* or *schemaname.tablename.columnname*) that specifies the referenced column in the local table (the compound foreign key)

refcolumns

Either a list of Column objects or a list of database-recognized strings (such as *tablename.columnname* or *schemaname.tablename.columnname*) that specifies the referenced column in the remote table (the compound primary key)

UNIQUE constraints

UniqueConstraint is a more flexible version of specifying unique=True in the Column definition, as it allows multiple columns to participate in a uniqueness constraint:

```
product_table = Table(
    'product', metadata,
    Column('id', Integer, primary_key=True),
    Column('brand_id', Integer, ForeignKey('brand.id')),
    Column('sku', Unicode(80)),
    UniqueConstraint('brand_id', 'sku'))
```

The SQL generated is just as we would expect:

```
>>> product_table.create(bind=create_engine('sqlite://', echo=True))
2007-08-25 13:55:19,450 INFO sqlalchemy.engine.base.Engine.0x..50
CREATE TABLE product (
        id INTEGER NOT NULL,
        brand_id INTEGER,
        sku VARCHAR(80),
        PRIMARY KEY (id),
         FOREIGN KEY(brand_id) REFERENCES brand (id),
         UNIQUE (brand_id, sku)
)


2007-08-25 13:55:19,450 INFO sqlalchemy.engine.base.Engine.0x..50
... None
2007-08-25 13:55:19,451 INFO sqlalchemy.engine.base.Engine.0x..50
COMMIT
```

CHECK constraints

CheckConstraints can also be specified, either at the column level (in which case they should only refer to the column on which they are defined), or at the Table level (in which case they should refer only to any column in the table). CheckConstraints are specified with a text constraint that will be passed directly through to the underlying database implementation, so care should be taken if you want to maintain database independence in the presence of CheckConstraints. MySQL and SQLite, in particular, do not actively support such constraints.

For instance, if you wanted to validate that payments were always positive amounts, you might create a payment table similar to the following:

```
payment_table = Table(
    'payment', metadata,
    Column('amount', Numeric(10,2), CheckConstraint('amount > 0')))
```

To see the SQL generated, we can execute the table creation statements on SQLite (recognizing that SQLite will not enforce the CHECK constraint):

```
>>> payment_table.create(bind=create_engine('sqlite://', echo=True))
2007-08-25 14:13:13,132 INFO sqlalchemy.engine.base.Engine.0x..90
CREATE TABLE payment (
        amount NUMERIC(10, 2) CHECK (amount > 0)
)


2007-08-25 14:13:13,133 INFO sqlalchemy.engine.base.Engine.0x..90
... None
2007-08-25 14:13:13,133 INFO sqlalchemy.engine.base.Engine.0x..90
... COMMIT
```

You can also generate CHECK constraints involving multiple columns:

```
>>> discount_table = Table(
...     'discount', metadata,
...     Column('original', Numeric(10,2), CheckConstraint('original
... > 0')),
...     Column('discounted', Numeric(10,2),
... CheckConstraint('discounted > 0')),
...     CheckConstraint('discounted < original',
... name='check_constraint_1'))
>>>
>>> discount_table.create(bind=create_engine('sqlite://',
... echo=True))
2007-08-25 14:17:57,600 INFO sqlalchemy.engine.base.Engine.0x..d0
CREATE TABLE discount (
        original NUMERIC(10, 2) CHECK (original > 0),
        discounted NUMERIC(10, 2) CHECK (discounted > 0),
        CONSTRAINT check_constraint_1  CHECK (discounted < original)
)


2007-08-25 14:17:57,601 INFO sqlalchemy.engine.base.Engine.0x..d0
... None
2007-08-25 14:17:57,602 INFO sqlalchemy.engine.base.Engine.0x..d0
... COMMIT
```

Defaults

SQLAlchemy provides several methods of generating default values for columns when inserting and updating rows. These default values fall into one of two categories: *active defaults* or *passive defaults*.

Active defaults

Active defaults are values that are generated by SQLAlchemy and then sent to the database in a separate statement. Active defaults include constants, Python callables, SQL expressions (including function calls) to be executed before the insert or update, or a pre-executed sequence. In all of these cases, SQLAlchemy manages the generation of the default value and the statement that actually sends the default to the database.

Active defaults are divided into two classes: insert defaults and the update defaults, which are specified separately (allowing a different default on insert and update, if that is desired). To specify an insert default, use the `default` parameter when creating the Column object. `default` can be a constant, a Python callable, an SQL expression, or an SQL sequence. For instance, to record the time at which a user record was created, you might use the following:

```
from datetime import datetime
user_table = Table(
    'tf_user', MetaData(),
    Column('id', Integer, primary_key=True),
    Column('user_name', Unicode(16), unique=True, nullable=False),
    Column('password', Unicode(40), nullable=False),
    Column('first_name', Unicode(255), default=''),
    Column('last_name', Unicode(255), default=''),
    Column('created_apptime', DateTime, default=datetime.now),
    Column('created_dbtime', DateTime,
            default=func.current_timestamp(),
    Column('modified', DateTime, onupdate=datetime.now)))
```

Here, we have created several defaults with constants, as well as two "created" defaults. One is the standard library function `datetime.now()`, and the other is the SQL function CURRENT_TIMESTAMP. The `created_apptime` column, upon insertion, will contain the current time on the application's machine, whereas the `created_dbtime` column will contain the database server's current time. The SQL generated is illustrative:

```
>>> e=create_engine('sqlite://', echo=True)
>>> user_table.create(bind=e)
2007-08-25 14:52:17,595 INFO sqlalchemy.engine.base.Engine.0x..50
CREATE TABLE tf_user (
        id INTEGER NOT NULL,
        user_name VARCHAR(16) NOT NULL,
        password VARCHAR(40) NOT NULL,
        first_name VARCHAR(255),
        last_name VARCHAR(255),
        created_apptime TIMESTAMP,
        created_dbtime TIMESTAMP,
        modified TIMESTAMP,
        PRIMARY KEY (id),
         UNIQUE (user_name)
)❶


2007-08-25 14:52:17,596 INFO sqlalchemy.engine.base.Engine.0x..50
... None
2007-08-25 14:52:17,597 INFO sqlalchemy.engine.base.Engine.0x..50
... COMMIT
>>>
>>> e.execute(user_table.insert(), user_name='rick', password='foo')
2007-08-25 14:52:17,604 INFO sqlalchemy.engine.base.Engine.0x..50
... SELECT current_timestamp ❷
```

```
2007-08-25 14:52:17,605 INFO sqlalchemy.engine.base.Engine.0x..50 []
2007-08-25 14:52:17,606 INFO sqlalchemy.engine.base.Engine.0x..50
... INSERT INTO tf_user (user_name, password, first_name,
... last_name, created_apptime, created_dbtime) VALUES (?,
... ?, ?, ?, ?, ?)
2007-08-25 14:52:17,606 INFO sqlalchemy.engine.base.Engine.0x..50
... ['rick', 'foo', '', '', '2007-08-25 14:52:17.604140',
... u'2007-08-25 18:52:17'] ❸
2007-08-25 14:52:17,607 INFO sqlalchemy.engine.base.Engine.0x..50
... COMMIT
<sqlalchemy.engine.base.ResultProxy object at 0x2aff31673690>
>>> e.execute(user_table.update(user_table.c.user_name=='rick'),
... password='secret')
2007-08-25 15:01:48,804 INFO sqlalchemy.engine.base.Engine.0x..50
... UPDATE tf_user SET password=?, modified=?
... ❹  WHERE
... tf_user.user_name = ?
2007-08-25 15:01:48,805 INFO sqlalchemy.engine.base.Engine.0x..50
... ['secret', '2007-08-25 15:01:48.774391', 'rick']
2007-08-25 15:01:48,805 INFO sqlalchemy.engine.base.Engine.0x..50
... COMMIT
<sqlalchemy.engine.base.ResultProxy object at 0x2adaf2551e50>
>>>
```

❶ The SQL generated for the table creation had no reference to the default values. This is because these values were *active defaults*, as opposed to the *passive defaults* covered in the next section.

❷ The `current_timestamp` is selected from the database for use in the insert statement.

❸ Two different timestamps are sent to the database, one for `created_apptime`, and one for `created_dbtime`. In this case, the application machine's native Python time resolution is greater than the `current_timestamp` provided by SQLite.

❹ Though we did not specify an update to the `modified` column, SQLAlchemy provides an update value based on the `onupdate` parameter of the column definition.

Passive defaults

Passive defaults are default values provided by the database itself. If a column is marked with a `PassiveDefault` instance, then the column will have a database-level default value *and* SQLAlchemy will make the `Engine` aware of the passive default. The `Engine` will, in turn, mark the `ResultProxy` as having passive default values. The `ResultProxy` is actually inspected by the object-relational mapping system to determine whether to refetch the row after an insert to get the default column values.

We can enhance the previous example by providing a passive default for the `created_dbtime` column:

```
from sqlalchemy import *
from datetime import datetime

user_table = Table(
```

```
    'tf_user', MetaData(),
    Column('id', Integer, primary_key=True),
    Column('user_name', Unicode(16), unique=True, nullable=False),
    Column('password', Unicode(40), nullable=False),
    Column('first_name', Unicode(255), default=''),
    Column('last_name', Unicode(255), default=''),
    Column('created_apptime', DateTime, default=datetime.now),
    Column('created_dbtime', DateTime, PassiveDefault('sysdate')),
    Column('modified', DateTime, onupdate=datetime.now))
```

Again, it is illustrative to see the creation and manipulation SQL:

```
>>> e=create_engine('sqlite://', echo=True)
>>> user_table.create(bind=e)
2007-08-25 15:50:49,912 INFO sqlalchemy.engine.base.Engine.0x..50
CREATE TABLE tf_user (
        id INTEGER NOT NULL,
        user_name VARCHAR(16) NOT NULL,
        password VARCHAR(40) NOT NULL,
        first_name VARCHAR(255),
        last_name VARCHAR(255),
        created_apptime TIMESTAMP,
        created_dbtime TIMESTAMP DEFAULT current_timestamp,
        modified TIMESTAMP,
        PRIMARY KEY (id),
         UNIQUE (user_name)
)❶



2007-08-25 15:50:49,912 INFO sqlalchemy.engine.base.Engine.0x..50
... None
2007-08-25 15:50:49,913 INFO sqlalchemy.engine.base.Engine.0x..50
... COMMIT
>>>
>>> rs = e.execute(user_table.insert(), user_name='rick',
... password='foo')
2007-08-25 15:50:49,930 INFO sqlalchemy.engine.base.Engine.0x..50
... INSERT INTO tf_user (user_name, password, first_last_name,
... created_apptime) VALUES (?, ?, ?, ?, ?)
... ❷
2007-08-25 15:50:49,931 INFO sqlalchemy.engine.base.Engine.0x..50
... ['rick', 'foo', '', '', '2007-08-25 15:50:49.930339']
2007-08-25 15:50:49,932 INFO sqlalchemy.engine.base.Engine.0x..50
... COMMIT
>>> if rs.lastrow_has_defaults(): ❸
...     prikey = rs.last_inserted_ids()
...     row = e.execute(user_table.select(
...         user_table.c.id == prikey[0])).fetchone()
...     print 'Created at', row.created_dbtime
...
2007-08-25 15:50:50,966 INFO sqlalchemy.engine.base.Engine.0x..50
... SELECT tf_user.id, tf_user.user_name, tf_user.password,
... tf_user.first_name, tf_user.last_name, tf_user.created_apptime,
... tf_user.created_dbtime, tf_user.modified
FROM tf_user
WHERE tf_user.id = ?
```

```
2007-08-25 15:50:50,966 INFO sqlalchemy.engine.base.Engine.0x..50
... [1]
Created at 2007-08-25 19:50:49
```

❶ The SQL generated for the table creation *does* contain a reference to the default
created_dbtime, unlike the active default example.

❷ The created_dbtime is *not* provided to the database in the insert statement; it will be
provided by the database itself.

❸ The result set is flagged as having a passive default via the lastrow_has_defaults()
function, and so we recognize the need to fetch the row back from the database.

PostgreSQL does not support passive defaults for primary keys. This is
due to the fact that SQLAlchemy does not use the PostgreSQL OIDs to
determine the identity of rows inserted (OIDs are actually disabled by
default in PostgreSQL version 8.), and psycopg2's cursor.lastrowid()
function only returns OIDs. Thus, the only way to know the primary
key of a row that is being inserted is to provide it as an active default.

Defining Indexes

Once your database grows to a certain size, you will probably need to consider adding
indexes to your tables to speed up certain selects. The easiest way to index a column
is to simply specify index=True when defining the Column:

```
user_table = Table(
    'tf_user', MetaData(),
    Column('id', Integer, primary_key=True),
Column('user_name', Unicode(16), unique=True, nullable=False,
... index=True),
    Column('password', Unicode(40), nullable=False),
    Column('first_name', Unicode(255), default=''),
    Column('last_name', Unicode(255), default='', index=True))
```

In this case, the index will be created with an auto-generated name. If a column is
defined with both index=True and unique=True, then the UNIQUE constraint is created
on the index rather than on the column. The SQL generated for the previous table
definition is illustrative:

```
>>> e = create_engine('sqlite://', echo=True)
>>> user_table.create(bind=e)
2007-08-25 16:30:36,542 INFO sqlalchemy.engine.base.Engine.0x..90
CREATE TABLE tf_user (
        id INTEGER NOT NULL,
        user_name VARCHAR(16) NOT NULL,
        password VARCHAR(40) NOT NULL,
        first_name VARCHAR(255),
        last_name VARCHAR(255),
        PRIMARY KEY (id)
)
```

```
2007-08-25 16:30:36,542 INFO sqlalchemy.engine.base.Engine.0x..90
... None
2007-08-25 16:30:36,543 INFO sqlalchemy.engine.base.Engine.0x..90
... COMMIT
2007-08-25 16:30:36,544 INFO sqlalchemy.engine.base.Engine.0x..90
... CREATE UNIQUE INDEX ix_tf_user_user_name ON tf_user
... (user_name)
2007-08-25 16:30:36,544 INFO sqlalchemy.engine.base.Engine.0x..90
... None
2007-08-25 16:30:36,545 INFO sqlalchemy.engine.base.Engine.0x..90
... COMMIT
2007-08-25 16:30:36,546 INFO sqlalchemy.engine.base.Engine.0x..90
... CREATE INDEX ix_tf_user_last_name ON tf_user (last_name)
2007-08-25 16:30:36,546 INFO sqlalchemy.engine.base.Engine.0x..90
... None
2007-08-25 16:30:36,547 INFO sqlalchemy.engine.base.Engine.0x..90
... COMMIT
```

The Index object

Although the `index=True` syntax is convenient in column definition, SQLAlchemy also provides an independent `Index` object, which can be used to:

- Define indexes on multiple columns
- Define named indexes
- Create indexes independently of the table (useful when adding an index to an existing table)

To create an index using the `Index` object, simply instantiate the object using the column attributes of the *table*.c object:

```
i = Index('idx_name', user_table.c.first_name,
... user_table.c.last_name,
        unique=True)
```

If the index is defined before the table is created, then the index will be created along with the table. Otherwise, you can create the index independently via its own `create()` function:

```
>>> i = Index('idx_name', user_table.c.first_name,
... user_table.c.last_name,
...          unique=True)
>>> i.create(bind=e)
2007-08-25 16:30:36,566 INFO sqlalchemy.engine.base.Engine.0x..90
... CREATE UNIQUE INDEX idx_name ON tf_user (first_name, last_name)
2007-08-25 16:30:36,566 INFO sqlalchemy.engine.base.Engine.0x..90
... None
2007-08-25 16:30:36,567 INFO sqlalchemy.engine.base.Engine.0x..90
... COMMIT
Index("idx_name", Column('first_name', Unicode(length=255),
... default=ColumnDefault('')),
... Column('last_name',Unicode(length=255),
... default=ColumnDefault('')), unique=True)
```

Creating Explicit Sequences

In our examples up to this point, to generate a unique integer key for inserted rows, we have simply specified that the table's primary key was an integer value. In this case, SQLAlchemy does what is generally The Right Thing: it either generates a column with an auto-incrementing data type (AUTOINCREMENT, SERIAL, etc.) if one is available in the Dialect being used, or, if an auto-incrementing data type is not available (as in the case of PostgreSQL and Oracle), it implicitly generates a sequence and fetches values from that sequence.

SQLAlchemy also provides for the explicit use of a Sequence object to generate default values for columns (not just primary keys). To use such a sequence, simply add it to the parameter list of the Column object:

```
brand_table = Table(
    'brand', metadata,
Column('id', Integer, Sequence('brand_id_seq'), primary_key=True),
    Column('name', Unicode(255), unique=True, nullable=False))
```

The SQL generated to create this table is:

```
>>> e = create_engine('postgres://postgres:password@localhost/test',
... echo=True)
>>>
>>> brand_table.create(bind=e)
2007-08-25 18:25:40,624 INFO sqlalchemy.engine.base.Engine.0x..d0
... CREATE SEQUENCE brand_id_seq
2007-08-25 18:25:40,624 INFO sqlalchemy.engine.base.Engine.0x..d0
... None
2007-08-25 18:25:40,630 INFO sqlalchemy.engine.base.Engine.0x..d0
... COMMIT
2007-08-25 18:25:40,634 INFO sqlalchemy.engine.base.Engine.0x..d0
CREATE TABLE brand (
        id INTEGER,
        name VARCHAR(255) NOT NULL,
         UNIQUE (name)
)


2007-08-25 18:25:40,635 INFO sqlalchemy.engine.base.Engine.0x..d0
... None
2007-08-25 18:25:40,659 INFO sqlalchemy.engine.base.Engine.0x..d0
... COMMIT
```

The parameters accepted by the Sequence constructor Sequence.__init__(name, start=None, increment=None, optional=False, quote=False, for_update=False) are as follows:

name

> The name of the sequence to be created.

start
: The initial value of the sequence being created (default None). This may be ignored, depending on the Dialect.

increment
: The increment value of the sequence being created (default None). This may be ignored, depending on the Dialect.

optional
: If True, this specifies that the sequence should be used only if it is necessary (e.g., if no other method of generating autoincrementing columns is possible). The default is False.

quote
: This forces the sequence name to be escaped and quoted before being sent to the database (useful for names that conflict with SQL keywords, for example). The default is False.

for_update
: Uses the sequence when updating the row, not just when inserting. The default is False.

MetaData Operations

SQLAlchemy uses the MetaData object internally for several purposes, particularly inside the object relational mapper (ORM), which is covered in Chapter 6. MetaData can also be used in connection with Engine and other Connectable instances to create or drop tables, indexes, and sequences from the database.

Binding MetaData

As mentioned previously, MetaData can be *bound* to a database Engine. This is done in one of three ways:

- Specify the Engine URI in the MetaData constructor
- Specify an actual Engine or other Connectable object in the MetaData constructor
- Assign the bind attribute of an "unbound" MetaData to an Engine or other Connectable

The various ways of binding MetaData are illustrated in the following examples:

```
# Create a bound MetaData with an implicitly created engine
bound_meta2 = MetaData('sqlite:///test2.db')

# Create an engine and then a bound MetaData
db2 = MetaData('sqlite:///test1.db')
bound_meta1 = MetaData(db2)

# Create an unbound MetaData
unbound_meta = MetaData()
```

```
# Create an Engine and bind the MetaData to it
db1 = create_engine('sqlite://')
unbound_meta.bind = db1
```

Binding the `MetaData` object to an engine allows the `MetaData` and the objects attached to it (Tables, Indexes, Sequences, etc.) to perform database operations without explicitly specifying an Engine:

```
from sqlalchemy import *

metadata = MetaData('sqlite://')

user_table = Table(
    'tf_user', metadata,
    Column('id', Integer, primary_key=True),
Column('user_name', Unicode(16), unique=True, nullable=False,
... index=True),
    Column('password', Unicode(40), nullable=False),
    Column('first_name', Unicode(255), default=''),
    Column('last_name', Unicode(255), default='', index=True))

user_table.create()  # we can omit the bind parameter
```

Create/drop MetaData and schema objects

Bound and unbound `MetaData` objects can create and drop schema objects either by using the `create()` and `drop()` methods on the objects, or by using the `MetaData` methods `create_all()` and `drop_all()`. The schema objects' (`Table`, `Index`, and `Sequence`) `create()` and `drop()` and methods take the following keyword parameters:

bind
> The `Engine` on which to execute the schema item creation (default is `None`).

checkfirst
> Add an `IF NOT EXISTS` or `IF EXISTS` clause, whichever is appropriate to the SQL generated (not supported for Indexes). The default is `False`.

The `MetaData` object itself supports the following arguments to its `create_all()` and `drop_all` methods:

bind
> The `Engine` on which to execute the operation. The default is `None`.

tables
> The `Table` objects to create/drop. If not specified, create/drop all schema items known to the `MetaData`. The default is `None`.

checkfirst
> Add an `IF NOT EXISTS` or `IF EXISTS` clause (whichever is appropriate to the SQL generated). The default is `False`.

Adapt Tables from one MetaData to another

A table that has been created against one `MetaData` can be adapted to another `MetaData` via the `Table.tometadata` (`self, metadata, schema=None`) method. This can be useful when working with the same schema in more than one `Engine` because it allows you to have bound `MetaData` and `Tables` for both engines. You can also use the `MetaData.table_iterator()` method to reflect an entire schema into another engine, for example:

```
meta1 = MetaData('postgres://postgres:password@localhost/test',
... reflect=True)
meta2 = MetaData('sqlite://')
for table in meta1.table_iterator():
    table.tometadata(meta2)
meta2.create_all()
```

## CHAPTER 4

SQLAlchemy Type Engines

This chapter introduces the SQLAlchemy type system. It covers the built-in types provided by SQLAlchemy: database-independent types and database-specific types. It then tells you how to create your own custom types for use in mapping application data onto your database schema.

Type System Overview

When defining the `MetaData` used by your application, it is necessary to supply the SQL data type used by each column of each table (unless the tables are defined with `autoload=True`, in which case SQLAlchemy provides the data types for you). These SQL data types are actually instances of SQLAlchemy-provided classes known as `TypeEngines`. `TypeEngine` objects convert Python values to native database values and vice versa. For instance, `String(40)` is an instance of a `TypeEngine` that represents a `VARCHAR(40)`. `TypeEngines` also supply SQL text for use when creating tables using `metadata`.create_all() or `table`.create().

SQLAlchemy provides three different ways of constructing types for use in your application. First, it provides a set of generic `TypeEngines`, which are fairly portable across different database engines. Second, it provides database server-specific `TypeEngines`, which can be used to exploit particular types supported by certain databases. Third, SQLAlchemy allows you to define application-specific custom `TypeEngines` if you wish to further customize object conversion to/from the database.

Built-in Types

SQLAlchemy provides a fairly complete set of built-in `TypeEngines` for support of basic SQL column types. The SQLAlchemy-provided `TypeEngines` are broken into the generic types (those portable across multiple database engines) and the dialect-specific types, which work only on particular databases.

If you want to keep your application portable across database servers, it is a good idea to stick to the generic types and (possibly) application-specific custom types, as any code that relies on database dialect-specific TypeEngines will need to be modified if the database changes. In the SQLAlchemy tradition of not getting in your way, however, full support is provided for dialect-specific TypeEngines if you wish to exploit database server-specific types.

Generic Types

The generic TypeEngines provided by SQLAlchemy are found in the *sqlalchemy.types* package. These TypeEngines cover a fairly complete set of portable column types. The TypeEngines supported, their corresponding Python type, and their SQL representation, are listed in Table 4-1. Note that there are several TypeEngines defined in all caps (such as CLOB). These are derived from other TypeEngines and may or may not be further specialized to allow finer-grained specification of the underlying database type.

Table 4-1. Built-in generic TypeEngines

Class name	Python type	SQL type (for SQLite driver)	Arguments
String	string	TEXT or VARCHAR	length (default is unbounded)
Integer	int	INTEGER	none
SmallInteger	int	SMALLINT	none
Numeric	float, Decimal	NUMERIC	precision=10, length=2
Float(Numeric)	float	NUMERIC	precision=10
DateTime	datetime.datetime	TIMESTAMP	none
Date	datetime.date	DATE	none
Time	datetime.time	TIME	none
Binary	byte string	BLOB	length (default is unbounded)
Boolean	bool	BOOLEAN	none
Unicode	unicode	TEXT or VARCHAR	length (default is unbounded)
PickleType	any object that can be pickled	BLOB	none
FLOAT(Numeric)	float, Decimal	NUMERIC	precision=10, length=2
TEXT(String)	string	TEXT	length (default is unbounded)
DECIMAL(Numeric)	float, Decimal	NUMERIC	precision=10, length=2
INT, INTEGER(Integer)	int	INTEGER	none
TIMESTAMP(DateTime)	datetime.datetime	TIMESTAMP	none

Class name	Python type	SQL type (for SQLite driver)	Arguments
DATETIME(DateTime)	datetime.date time	TIMESTAMP	none
CLOB(String)	string	TEXT	length (default is unbounded)
VARCHAR(String)	string	VARCHAR or TEXT	length (default is unbounded)
CHAR(String)	string	CHAR or TEXT	length (default is unbounded)
NCHAR(Unicode)	string	VARCHAR, NCHAR, or TEXT	length (default is unbounded)
BLOB(Binary)	byte string	BLOB	length (default is unbounded)
BOOLEAN(Boolean)	bool	BOOLEAN	none

When using TypeEngines to specify columns in Tables, you can use an instance of the TypeEngine class or the class itself. If you use the class, the default parameters will be used when constructing the SQL type. For instance, the following Python code:

```
test_table3 = Table(
    'test3', metadata,
    Column('c0', Numeric),
    Column('c1', Numeric(4,6)),
    Column('c3', String),
    Column('c4', String(10)))
```

yields the following SQL creation (in SQLite):

```
CREATE TABLE test3 (
        c0 NUMERIC(10, 2),
        c1 NUMERIC(4, 6),
        c3 TEXT,
        c4 VARCHAR(10)
)
```

Dialect-Specific Types

To generate appropriate dialect-specific SQL CREATE TABLE statements from these generic types, SQLAlchemy compiles those generic TypeEngines into dialect-specific TypeEngines. In some cases, in addition to implementing the generic types, a dialect may provide dialect-specific types (such as IP address, etc.).

Some of the dialect-specific types don't actually provide any special support for converting between database values and Python values; these are generally used for completeness, particularly when reflecting tables. In this case, no conversion is done between the value supplied by the DB-API implementation and the application. This behavior is indicated in the following tables by listing "none" as the Python type for that TypeEngine. Tables 4-2 through 4-5 list some of the types provided by particular database engines that are not automatically used by SQLAlchemy.

Table 4-2. MS SQL server types

Class name	Python type	SQL type	Arguments
MSMoney	none	MONEY	none
MSSmallMoney	none	SMALLMONEY	none
AdoMSNVarchar	unicode	NVARCHAR	length
MSBigInteger	int	BIGINT	none
MSTinyInteger	int	TINYINT	none
MSVariant	none	SQL_VARIANT	none
MSUniqueIdentifier	none	UNIQUEIDENTIFIER	none

Table 4-3. MySQL types

Class name	Python type	SQL type	Arguments
MSEnum	string	ENUM	values
MSTinyInteger	int	TINYINT	length
MSBigInteger	int	BIGINT	length
MSDouble	float	DOUBLE	length=10,precision=2
MSTinyText	string	TINYTEXT	none
MSMediumText	string	MEDIUMTEXT	none
MSLongText	string	LONGTEXT	none
MSNVarChar	unicode	NATIONAL VARCHAR	length
MSTinyBlob	byte string	TINYBLOB	none
MSMediumBlob	byte string	MEDIUMBLOB	none
MSLongBlob	byte string	LONGBLOB	none
MSBinary	byte string	BINARY	length
MSVarBinary	byte string	VARBINARY	length
MSSet	set	SET	set values
MSYear	int	YEAR	length
MSBit	long	BIT	length

Table 4-4. Oracle types

Class name	Python type	SQL type	Arguments
OracleRaw	byte string	RAW	length

Table 4-5. PostgreSQL types

Class name	Python type	SQL type	Arguments
PGArray	any TypeEngine	*type engine*[]	TypeEngine
PGBigInteger	int, long	BIGINT	none
PGInet	none	INET	none
PGInterval	none	INTERVAL	none

Application-Specific Custom Types

Although SQLAlchemy provides a rich set of generic and database-specific types, it is sometimes helpful to be able to create application-specific custom types. For instance, you may wish to emulate enumerations in a database engine that does not support enumerations by restricting the values that can be stored in a column.

In SQLAlchemy, there are two ways to create an application-specific custom type. If you wish to implement a type that is similar to an existing TypeEngine, you would implement a TypeDecorator. If your implementation is more involved, you can directly subclass TypeEngine.

Implementing a TypeDecorator

To implement a TypeDecorator, you must provide the base TypeEngine you are "implementing" as well as two functions, convert_bind_param() and convert_result_value(). convert_bind_param(self, value, engine) is used to convert Python values to SQL values suitable for the DB-API driver, and convert_result_value(self, value, engine) is used to convert SQL values from the DB-API driver back into Python values. The implemented TypeEngine is specified in the impl attribute on the TypeDecorator.

For instance, if you wish to implement a type for validating that a particular Integer column contains only the values 0, 1, 2, and 3 (e.g., to implement an enumerated type in a database that does not support enumerated types), you would implement the following TypeDecorator:

```
from sqlalchemy import types

class MyCustomEnum(types.TypeDecorator):

    impl=types.Integer

    def __init__(self, enum_values, *l, **kw):
        types.TypeDecorator.__init__(self, *l, **kw)
        self._enum_values = enum_values

    def convert_bind_param(self, value, engine):
        result = self.impl.convert_bind_param(value, engine)
        if result not in self._enum_values:
            raise TypeError, (
```

```
        "Value %s must be one of %s" % (result, self._enum_values))
            return result

    def convert_result_value(self, value, engine):
        'Do nothing here'
        return self.impl.convert_result_value(value, engine)
```

It is not necessary to specify in a TypeDecorator the SQL type used to implement the column, as this will be obtained from the impl attribute. The TypeDecorator is used only when an existing TypeEngine provides the correct SQL type for the type you are implementing.

Performance-Conscious TypeDecorators

SQLAlchemy has a second, undocumented (at the time of this book's writing) interface for providing bind parameter and result value conversion. If you provide a bind_processor() or result_processor() method in your TypeDecorator, then these will be used instead of the convert_bind_param() and convert_result_value() methods. The new "processor" interface methods take a database dialect as a parameter and return a conversion function (a "processor") that takes a single value parameter and returns the (possibly converted) value. If no processing is necessary, you can simply return None rather than a new processor:

```
>>> from sqlalchemy import types
>>> import sqlalchemy.databases.sqlite as sqlite
>>>
>>> class MyCustomEnum(types.TypeDecorator):
...     impl = types.Integer
...     def __init__(self, enum_values, *l, **kw):
...         types.TypeDecorator.__init__(self, *l, **kw)
...         self._enum_values = enum_values
...     def bind_processor(self, dialect):
...         impl_processor = self.impl.bind_processor(dialect)
...         if impl_processor:
...             def processor(value):
...                 result = impl_processor(value)
...                 assert value in self._enum_values, \
...                     "Value %s must be one of %s" % (result,
... self._enum_values)
...                 return result
...         else:
...             def processor(value):
...                 assert value in self._enum_values, \
...                     "Value %s must be one of %s" % (value,
... self._enum_values)
...                 return value
...         return processor
...
>>> mce=MyCustomEnum([1,2,3])
>>> processor = mce.bind_processor(sqlite.dialect())
>>> print processor(1)
1
>>> print processor(5)
Traceback (most recent call last):
  File "<stdin>", line 1, in <module>
```

```
    File "<stdin>", line 17, in processor
AssertionError: Value 5 must be one of [1, 2, 3]
```

Creating a New TypeEngine

If creating a TypeDecorator is insufficient for your new type (such as when supporting a new SQL type), you can directly subclass the TypeEngine class. In this case, in addition to providing the convert_bind_param() and convert_result_value() methods, you must also provide the get_col_spec method for SQLAlchemy to use in its create_table() implementation.

To create a new TypeEngine to implement the SQL type "NEWTYPE", for instance, you might use the following class declaration:

```
class NewType(types.TypeEngine):

    def __init__(self, *args):
        self._args = args

    def get_col_spec(self):
        return 'NEWTYPE(%s)' % ','.join(self._args)

    def convert_bind_param(self, value, engine):
        return value

    def convert_result_value(self, value, engine):
        return value
```

## CHAPTER 5

Running Queries and Updates

SQLAlchemy provides a rich Pythonic interface for constructing SQL updates and queries, known as the SQL Expression Language. This language is based around the concept of an SQL *statement*, which represents some database-independent SQL syntax that may have one or more bind variables, and that can be executed on an SQL Engine or other Connectable. This chapter introduces the various kinds of data manipulation supported by SQLAlchemy (SQL INSERT, UPDATE, and DELETE) and performed on the query interface (SQL SELECT).

Inserts, Updates, and Deletes

Insert, Update, and Delete constructs are created in SQLAlchemy via the Table methods insert, update, and delete, or via the insert, update, and delete functions. The functionality of these data manipulation language (DML) constructs is equivalent, regardless of whether they are constructed via methods or functions; the distinction is a question of style more than substance.

Although each DML construct has its own particulars regarding construction, they all end up generating a Statement. We can inspect the SQL text corresponding to the statement by printing it out:

```
>>> metadata=MetaData()
>>>
>>> simple_table = Table(
...     'simple', metadata,
...     Column('id', Integer, primary_key=True),
...     Column('col1', Unicode(20)))
>>>
>>> stmt = simple_table.insert()
>>> print stmt
INSERT INTO simple (id, col1) VALUES (:id, :col1)
```

Note in the previous example that SQLAlchemy has created bind parameters for each of the columns in the table we created in the insert statement. We can examine the bind parameters in a statement by compiling the statement and looking at its params attribute:

```
>>> compiled_stmt = stmt.compile()
>>> print compiled_stmt.params
ClauseParameters:{'id': None, 'col1': None}
```

To execute the statement, we can directly execute it on an `Engine`, or we can bind the `MetaData` used to construct the statement and use the `MetaData`'s engine:

```
>>> engine = create_engine('sqlite://')
>>> simple_table.create(bind=engine)
>>> engine.execute(stmt, col1="Foo")
<sqlalchemy.engine.base.ResultProxy object at 0x2b3210b00f10>
>>> metadata.bind = engine
>>> stmt.execute(col1="Bar")
<sqlalchemy.engine.base.ResultProxy object at 0x2b3210b020d0>
```

Note that the bind parameter values are supplied to the `execute()` method as keyword parameters. These parameters can either be supplied either directly to the `execute()` method or in the statement construction phase:

```
>>> stmt = simple_table.insert(values=dict(col1="Initial value"))
>>> print stmt
INSERT INTO simple (col1) VALUES (?)
>>> compiled_stmt = stmt.compile()
>>> print compiled_stmt.params
ClauseParameters:{'col1': 'Initial value'}
```

If parameters are supplied in the statement construction and the `execute()` call, the parameters supplied with the `execute()` call override those supplied when creating the statement.

Insert Statements

The `Insert` construct is perhaps the simplest. In order to create an `Insert` statement, you can use the `Table.insert()` method or the `insert()` function. (The method is actually just a wrapper for the function.) The `insert` takes two arguments: the table into which a row is being inserted, and an optional dictionary of values to be inserted. Each key in the dictionary represents a column and may be either the metadata `Column` object or its string identifier. The values provided can be one of the following:

- A literal Python value to be inserted.
- An SQL expression to be inserted, such as `func.current_timestamp()`, which will create the SQL `INSERT INTO simple2 (col1, col2) VALUES (?, current_timestamp)`.
- A `Select` statement (covered later in this chapter). In this case, the value to be inserted is provided by a subquery.

If we wish to insert multiple rows into the table, we can create an insert statement and execute it multiple times with different bind parameters:

```
>>> stmt = simple_table.insert()
>>> stmt.execute(col1="First value")
<sqlalchemy.engine.base.ResultProxy object at 0xd0a490>
>>> stmt.execute(col1="Second value")
<sqlalchemy.engine.base.ResultProxy object at 0xd0a050>
>>> stmt.execute(col1="Third value")
<sqlalchemy.engine.base.ResultProxy object at 0xd0a3d0>
```

It is also possible to use the DB API's executemany() to insert multiple rows in one database call. To do this, simply provide an list (or other iterable) of binding dictionaries to the execute() method on the statement or engine:

```
>>> stmt.execute([dict(col1="Fourth Value"),
...               dict(col1="Fifth Value"),
...               dict(col1="Sixth Value")])
<sqlalchemy.engine.base.ResultProxy object at 0xd0a310>
```

Update Statements

Update statements are similar to inserts, except that they can specify a "where" clause that indicates which rows to update. Like insert statements, update statements can be created by either the update() function or the update() method on the table being updated. The only parameters to the update() function are the table being updated (omitted if using the update() method), the where clause, and the values to be set.

The where clause of the update() query can be a SQL clause object (covered later in this chapter) or a text string specifying the update condition. In order to update every row of a table, you can simply leave off the where clause. To update this simple table, we can execute the following statement:

```
>>> stmt = simple_table.update(
... whereclause=text("col1='First value'"),
... values=dict(col1='1st Value'))❶
>>> stmt.execute()
<sqlalchemy.engine.base.ResultProxy object at 0xc77910>
>>> stmt = simple_table.update(text("col1='Second value'"))
>>> stmt.execute(col1='2nd Value') ❷
...
<sqlalchemy.engine.base.ResultProxy object at 0xc77950>
>>> stmt = simple_table.update(text("col1='Third value'"))
>>> print stmt
UPDATE simple SET id=?, col1=? WHERE col1='Third value'
... ❸
>>> engine.echo = True
>>> stmt.execute(col1='3rd value')
2007-09-25 08:57:11,253 INFO sqlalchemy.engine.base.Engine.0x..d0
... UPDATE simple SET col1=? WHERE col1='Third value'
2007-09-25 08:57:11,254 INFO sqlalchemy.engine.base.Engine.0x..d0
... ['3rd value']
2007-09-25 08:57:11,255 INFO sqlalchemy.engine.base.Engine.0x..d0
... COMMIT
<sqlalchemy.engine.base.ResultProxy object at 0xc77990>
```

❶ Here, we create an UPDATE statement, complete with both values to update and a where clause.

❷ Here, the where clause is bound when the statement is created, but the actual values to be updated are passed to the `execute()` method.

❸ Note that prior to execution, the SQL has a bind parameter for the `id` column, but when the statement is executed, `id` is omitted because no value was provided for it.

Correlated update statements can also be generated using the SQL expression language. A correlated update is an update whose values are provided by a select statement. Suppose that we have a product catalog with the schema in the following listing, and the data in Tables 5-1 through 5-3:

```
product_table = Table(
    'product', metadata,
    Column('sku', String(20), primary_key=True),
    Column('msrp', Numeric))
store_table = Table(
    'store', metadata,
    Column('id', Integer, primary_key=True),
    Column('name', Unicode(255)))
product_price_table = Table(
    'product_price', metadata,
    Column('sku', None, ForeignKey('product.sku'), primary_key=True),
    Column('store_id', None, ForeignKey('store.id'), primary_key=True),
    Column('price', Numeric, default=0))
```

Table 5-1. Contents of product table

sku	msrp
"123"	12.34
"456"	22.12
"789"	41.44

Table 5-2. Contents of store table

id	name
1	"Main Store"
2	"Secondary Store"

Table 5-3. Contents of product_price table (initial)

sku	store_id	price
"123"	1	0
"456"	1	0
"789"	1	0
"123"	2	0

sku	store_id	price
"456"	2	0
"789"	2	0

If we wish to globally set the price for all products in all stores to their MSRP price, we could execute the following update:

```
>>> msrp = select(
...       [product_table.c.msrp],
...       product_table.c.sku==product_price_table.c.sku,
...       limit=1)
>>> stmt = product_price_table.update(
...       values=dict(price=msrp))
>>> stmt.execute()
2007-09-26 10:05:17,184 INFO sqlalchemy.engine.base.Engine.0x..d0
... UPDATE product_price SET price=(SELECT product.msrp
FROM product
WHERE product.sku = product_price.sku
 LIMIT 1 OFFSET 0)
2007-09-26 10:05:17,184 INFO sqlalchemy.engine.base.Engine.0x..d0
... []
2007-09-26 10:05:17,185 INFO sqlalchemy.engine.base.Engine.0x..d0
... COMMIT
<sqlalchemy.engine.base.ResultProxy object at 0xd0e510>
```

This would cause the updated `product_price_table` to contain the values in Table 5-4.

Table 5-4. Contents of product_price_table (after update)

sku	store_id	price
"123"	1	12.34
"456"	1	22.12
"789"	1	41.44
"123"	2	12.34
"456"	2	22.12
"789"	2	41.44

Delete Statements

The `Delete` construct is used to delete data from the database. To create a `Delete` construct, you can use either the `delete()` function or the `delete()` method on the table from which you are deleting data. Unlike `insert()` and `update()`, `delete()` takes no `values` parameter, only an optional where clause (omitting the where clause will delete all rows from the table). To delete all rows from the `product_price` table for sku `123`, in the previous section, for instance, we would execute the code as shown here:

```
>>> stmt = product_price_table.delete(
...       text("sku='123'"))
```

```
>>> stmt.execute()
2007-09-27 19:22:51,612 INFO sqlalchemy.engine.base.Engine.0x..d0
... DELETE FROM product_price WHERE sku='123'
2007-09-27 19:22:51,612 INFO sqlalchemy.engine.base.Engine.0x..d0
... []
2007-09-27 19:22:51,613 INFO sqlalchemy.engine.base.Engine.0x..d0
... COMMIT
<sqlalchemy.engine.base.ResultProxy object at 0xd92510>
```

Queries

The real power of the SQL expression language is in its query interface. This includes the actual queries (SQL "SELECT" statements) as well as the syntax for specifying "WHERE" clauses (which may be used in UPDATEs and DELETEs, as well).

The goal of the SQL expression language, like the goal of SQLAlchemy in general, is to provide functionality that doesn't "get in your way" when you need to be more specific about the SQL you need. In that vein, you can always use the Text construct (used previously in the UPDATE and DELETE examples) to specify the exact SQL text you would like to use. For most operations, however, the SQL expression language makes for a succinct, secure, and less error-prone way of expressing your queries.

Basic Query Construction

SQLAlchemy makes simple SQL queries easy to express, while also enabling the construction of quite complex queries in a straightforward manner. This section describes the basic building blocks of query construction in SQLAlchemy.

The select( ) function versus the select( ) method

Like the DML statements INSERT, UPDATE, and DELETE, SELECT statements can be generated using either a function or a Table method. Unlike the DML statements, however, there is a minor difference in functionality between the select() function and the Table.select() method. The select() function requires you to specify which columns you want in your result set. So, to select one column from the prod uct_table shown previously, you could use the select() function:

```
>>> stmt = select([product_table.c.sku])
>>> for row in stmt.execute():
...     print row
...
(u'123',)
(u'456',)
(u'789',)
```

To select *all* columns from the product_table, you would use the Table.select() method:

```
>>> stmt = product_table.select()
>>> for row in stmt.execute():
```

```
...        print row
...
(u'123', Decimal("12.34"))
(u'456', Decimal("22.12"))
(u'789', Decimal("41.44"))
```

To achieve the same result using the select() function, simply provide the table in lieu of columns:

```
>>> stmt = select([product_table])
>>> for row in stmt.execute():
...        print row
...
(u'123', Decimal("12.34"))
(u'456', Decimal("22.12"))
(u'789', Decimal("41.44"))
```

The actual parameters used by select() are listed next. They are discussed in more detail later in the chapter.

columns=None
> A list of ClauseElement structures to be returned from the query.

bind=None
> An engine on a connectable object on which to execute the statement. If this is omitted, an engine binding will be inferred from referenced columns and/or tables, if possible.

whereclause=None
> A ClauseElement expression used to for the WHERE clause.

from_obj=[]
> A list of Tables or other selectable objects that will be used to form the FROM clause. If this is not specified, the FROM clause is inferred from the tables referenced in other clauses.

order_by=None
> A list of ClauseElements used to construct the ORDER BY clause.

group_by=None
> A list of ClauseElements used to construct the GROUP BY clause.

having=None
> A ClauseElement used to construct the HAVING clause.

distinct=False
> Adds a DISTINCT qualifier to the column list in the SELECT statement.

for_update=False
> Adds a FOR UPDATE qualifier to the SELECT statement. Some databases support other values for this parameter, such as MySQL, which supports "read" (translating to LOCK IN SHARE MODE), or Oracle, which supports "nowait" (translating to FOR UPDATE NOWAIT).

limit=None

The numerical limit for the number of rows returned. Typically this uses the LIMIT clause, but SQLAlchemy provides some support for LIMIT even when the underlying database does not support it directly.

offset=None

The numerical offset for the starting row that is returned. Typically this uses the OFFSET clause, but SQLAlchemy provides some support for OFFSET even when the underlying database does not support it directly.

correlate=True

Indicates that this SELECT statement is to be "correlated" with its enclosing SELECT statement if it is used as a subquery. In particular, any selectables present in both this statement's `from_obj` list and the enclosing statement's `from_obj` list will be omitted from this statement's FROM clause.

use_labels=False

Generates unique labels for each column in the `columns` list, to ensure there are no name collisions.

prefixes=None

A list of `ClauseElement`s to be included directly after the SELECT keyword in the generated SQL. This is used for dialect-specific SQL extensions, to insert text between the SELECT keyword and the column list.

Result set objects

Thus far, we have glossed over the return value of the `execute()` method on SQL statements, showing only that it is possible to iterate over this value and receive tuple-like objects. In fact, SQLAlchemy provides an object, defined in the `ResultProxy` class, to allow cursor-like access to the results of a query. Some of the useful methods and attributes available on the `ResultProxy` object are summarized here:

fetchone()

Fetch one result from the cursor.

fetchmany (size=None)

Fetch several results from the cursor (if size is omitted, fetch all results).

fetchall()

Fetch all results from the cursor.

__iter__()

Return an iterator through the result set.

close()

Close the `ResultProxy`, as well as the underlying cursor. This method is called automatically when all result rows are exhausted.

```
scalar()
```
Fetch the first column of the first row, and close the result set (useful for queries such as "SELECT DATETIME('NOW')").

`rowcount` *(valid only for DML statements)*

Return the number of rows updated, deleted, or inserted by the statement.

The "rows" returned from a `ResultProxy` object, either via the `fetch*()` methods or iteration, is actually a `RowProxy` object. As we have seen previously, it supports a tuple-like interface. We can also retrieve columns from the `RowProxy` object through its `dict`-like interface or its `object`-like interface:

```
>>> result = select([product_table]).execute()
>>> row = result.fetchone()
>>> print row
(u'123', 12.34)
>>> print row[0]
123
>>> print row['sku']
123
>>> print row[product_table.c.sku]
123
>>> print row.sku
123
>>> print row.items()
[('sku', u'123'), ('msrp', 12.34)]
>>> print row.keys()
['sku', 'msrp']
>>> print row.values()
[u'123', 12.34]
>>> print row.has_key('msrp')
True
>>> print row.has_key('price')
False
```

Operators and functions in WHERE clauses

To actually *construct* a SELECT statement with a WHERE clause, we can use either the `Text` construct (as shown previously) or the SQL expression language. The easiest way to use the SQL expression language to generate a WHERE clause is to use SQLAlchemy-provided operator overloading on the `Column` class:

```
>>> x = product_table.c.sku=="123"
>>> print type(x)
<class 'sqlalchemy.sql._BinaryExpression'>
>>> print x
product.sku = ?
>>> stmt=product_table.select(product_table.c.sku=="123")
>>> print stmt
SELECT product.sku, product.msrp
FROM product
WHERE product.sku = ? ❶
...
```

```
>>> print stmt.execute().fetchall()
2007-09-30 16:34:44,800 INFO sqlalchemy.engine.base.Engine.0x..10
... SELECT product.sku, product.msrp
FROM product
WHERE product.sku = ?
2007-09-30 16:34:44,800 INFO sqlalchemy.engine.base.Engine.0x..10
... ['123']❷
[(u'123', 12.34)]
```

❶ Note that the "123" literal has been replaced by a "?" placeholder. This is an example of SQLAlchemy using a *bind parameter*. By using bind parameters, SQLAlchemy ensures that the entire SQL string passed to the database driver was constructed by SQLAlchemy, and that it is safe from SQL-injection attacks. (Of course, this can be subverted via the `Text` construct, which passes whatever the programmer specifies to the database driver.)

❷ Here, SQLAlchemy provides the value of the bind parameter to the database driver directly.

All SQLAlchemy-provided operators generate a `ClauseElement`-derived object as a result of the operation. `ClauseElement`s provide the overloaded operators (and other SQL-constructing features) of the SQL expression language. This allows complex SQL expressions to be built up from complex Python expressions. SQLAlchemy provides overloading for most of the standard Python operators. This includes all the standard comparison operators (==, !=, <, >, <=, >=). Note in particular the conversion of "== None" to "IS NULL".

```
>>> print product_price_table.c.price == 12.34
product_price.price = ?
>>> print product_price_table.c.price != 12.34
product_price.price != ?
>>> print product_price_table.c.price < 12.34
product_price.price < ?
>>> print product_price_table.c.price > 12.34
product_price.price > ?
>>> print product_price_table.c.price <= 12.34
product_price.price <= ?
>>> print product_price_table.c.price >= 12.34
product_price.price >= ?
>>> print product_price_table.c.price == None
product_price.price IS NULL
```

Support is also provided for the arithmetic operators (+, -, *, /, and %), with special support for database-independent string concatenation:

```
>>> print product_price_table.c.price + 14.44
product_price.price + ?
>>> expr = product_table.c.sku + "-sku"
>>> print expr
product.sku || ?
>>> from sqlalchemy.databases.mysql import MySQLDialect
>>> print expr.compile(dialect=MySQLDialect())
product.sku + %s
```

Arbitrary SQL operators (such as MySQL's NULL-safe equality operator, <=>) are also supported via the op() method on ClauseElements:

```
>>> print product_table.c.sku.op('my_new_operator')(
...         product_table.c.msrp)
product.sku my_new_operator product.msrp
```

SQLAlchemy also provides for use of the SQL boolean operators AND, OR, and NOT, as well as the LIKE operator for comparing strings. The bitwise logical operators &, |, and ~ are used to implement AND, OR, and NOT, while the like() method on ClauseElements is used to implement LIKE. Special care must be taken when using the AND, OR, and NOT overloads because of Python operator precendence rules. For instance, & binds more closely than <, so when you write A < B & C < D, what you are actually writing is A < (B&C) < D, which is probably not what you intended. You can also use the SQLAlchemy-provided functions and_, or_, and not_ to represent AND, OR, and NOT if you prefer:

```
>>> print (product_table.c.msrp > 10.00) & (product_table.c.msrp <
... 20.00)
product.msrp > ? AND product.msrp < ?
>>> print and_(product_table.c.msrp > 10.00,
...            product_table.c.msrp < 20.00)
product.msrp > ? AND product.msrp < ?
>>> print product_table.c.sku.like('12%')
product.sku LIKE ?
>>> print ~((product_table.c.msrp > 10.00) &
...         (product_table.c.msrp < 20.00))
NOT (product.msrp > ? AND product.msrp < ?)
>>> print not_(and_(product_table.c.msrp > 10.00,
...                 product_table.c.msrp < 20.00))
NOT (product.msrp > ? AND product.msrp < ?)
```

SQLAlchemy also provides for the use of arbitrary SQL functions via the func variable, which generates functions using attribute access. You can also use the special function func._ to add parentheses around a subexpression if necessary:

```
>>> print func.now()
now()
>>> print func.current_timestamp
current_timestamp
>>> print func.abs(product_table.c.msrp)
abs(product.msrp)
>>> print func._(text('a=b'))
(a=b)
```

SQLAlchemy provides several other useful methods on ClauseElements, summarized here:

between(cleft, cright)
> Produces a BETWEEN clause like *column* BETWEEN *cleft* AND *cright*.

distinct()
> Adds a DISTINCT modifier like DISTINCT *column*.

startswith(other)
:   Produces the clause *column* LIKE *'other*%'.

endswith(other)
:   Produces the clause *column* LIKE *'%other'*.

in_(*other)
:   Produces an IN clause like *column* IN (*other[0]*, *other[1]*, ...). *other* can also be a subquery.

like(other)
:   Produces a LIKE clause like *column* LIKE *other*.

op(operator)
:   Produces an arbitrary operator like *column operator*.

label(name)
:   Produces an AS construct for the column (a column alias) like *column* AS *name*.

Using custom bind parameters

Up to this point, SQLAlchemy has been automatically creating bind parameters whenever we used a literal expression in the SQL query language. It is also possible to generate a custom bind parameter. This might be useful, for instance, if you wanted to generate a statement without knowing *a priori* what values would be used to bind the statement. You can also use this to speed up your queries when you have many statements that are identical except for the bind parameter values. (The Python overhead for executing each query is lower in such cases, and some database servers will cache the execution plan, making the server-side processing faster as well.) Using the schema introduced earlier in this chapter, we might generate a statement that selects the price for a given product using the following code:

```
>>> stmt = select([product_table.c.msrp],
...                whereclause=product_table.c.sku==bindparam('sku'))
>>> print stmt
SELECT product.msrp
FROM product
WHERE product.sku = ?
>>> print stmt.compile().get_params()
ClauseParameters:{'sku': None}
>>> print stmt.execute(sku='123').fetchall()
[(12.34,)]
>>> print stmt.execute(sku='456').fetchall()
[(22.120000000000001,)]
>>> print stmt.execute(sku='789').scalar()
41.44
```

The actual bindparam() parameters are summarized here:

key

> Either a string representing the bind parameter name or a `Column` object (which will be used to generate a bind parameter name). This name is used in the `execute()` call to provide a value for the bind parameter.

value=None

> The default value for this bind parameter (If no value is supplied in the `execute()` call, this value will be used instead.) If no value is supplied here or in the `execute()` call, an exception is raised.

type=None

> A `TypeEngine` object representing the type of the bind parameter. The `TypeEngine` is used to format the value provided to the bind parameter using the `TypeEngine`'s `convert_bind_param()` method.

shortname=None

> An alias for the bind parameter (this name can be used in the `execute()` call instead of the `key` parameter). This can be useful if the `key` name is cumbersome, as when using a `Column` object.

unique=False

> Generate a unique name for the bind parameter based on the `key`. This can be useful for ensuring there are no unintended name collisions. This is typically used along with the `value` parameter.

Using literal text in queries

We have already briefly seen the use of the `text()` in constructing customized SQL strings. In fact, even when we want to use custom SQL strings, we rarely need to use the `text()` function; SQLAlchemy can infer the need for it automatically in most cases. For instance, if we wanted to select the price for SKU "123", we could simply write:

```
>>> stmt = select(['product.msrp'],
...                from_obj=['product'],
...                whereclause="product.sku=='123'")
>>> print stmt
SELECT product.msrp
FROM product
WHERE product.sku=='123'
>>> print metadata.bind.execute(stmt).fetchall()
[(12.34,)]
>>> stmt2 = select([text('product.msrp')],
...                from_obj=[text('product')],
...                whereclause=text("product.sku=='123'"))
>>> print str(stmt2) == str(stmt)
True
```

We can use bind parameters with `text()` by using the "named colon" format (*:name*) for the bind parameters. We can also bind the clause constructed to a particular engine using the `bind` parameter to the `text()` function.

```
>>> stmt = text("SELECT product.msrp FROM product WHERE
... product.sku==:sku",
...               bind=metadata.bind)
>>> print stmt
SELECT product.msrp FROM product WHERE product.sku==?
>>> print stmt.compile().get_params()
ClauseParameters:{'sku': None}
>>> print stmt.execute(sku='456').fetchall()
[(22.120000000000001,)]
```

The actual parameters of the text() function are summarized here:

text
> The string with the SQL text to be constructed. Bind parameters can be used with the *parameter* syntax.

bind=None
> The engine to which to bind the constructed ClauseElement. Useful when constructing a statement entirely out of text() objects.

bindparams=None
> A list of bindparam( ) objects to be used to define the types and/or values of the bind parameters used.

typemap=None
> A dictionary mapping column names used in a SELECT statement to TypeEngines. Used to convert result set values to Python objects.

Ordering and grouping results, returning distinct values

SQLAlchemy supports the use of the ORDER BY, GROUP BY, HAVING, and UNIQUE clauses of SQL queries via the order_by, group_by, having, and unique parameters of the select() function and method.

The Difference Between WHERE and HAVING

Both the WHERE clause in SQL and the HAVING clause restrict results to those results matching a given SQL expression. The difference is that HAVING is always accompanied by grouping (typically via the GROUP BY clause), and the HAVING clause filters the results *after* they are grouped, whereas the WHERE clause filters the rows *before* they are grouped. WHERE clauses therefore can't reference the results of aggregation functions such as SUM or COUNT, but the HAVING clause can.

If we wanted to see the products in our database listed by price, for instance, we could use the following query:

```
>>> stmt = product_table.select(order_by=[product_table.c.msrp])
>>> print stmt
SELECT product.sku, product.msrp
FROM product ORDER BY product.msrp
>>> print stmt.execute().fetchall()
```

```
[(u'123', 12.34), (u'456', 22.120000000000001), (u'789',
... 41.439999999999998)]
>>> stmt =
... product_table.select(order_by=[desc(product_table.c.msrp)])
>>> print stmt
SELECT product.sku, product.msrp
FROM product ORDER BY product.msrp DESC
>>> print stmt.execute().fetchall()
[(u'789', 41.439999999999998), (u'456', 22.120000000000001),
... (u'123', 12.34)]
```

We could use the grouping provided by group_by (possibly filtered by having) to retrieve how many stores carry each product:

```
>>> stmt = select([product_price_table.c.sku,
...                 func.count(product_price_table.c.store_id)],
...                 group_by=[product_price_table.c.sku])
>>> print stmt
SELECT product_price.sku, count(product_price.store_id)
FROM product_price GROUP BY product_price.sku
>>> print stmt.execute().fetchall()
[(u'456', 2), (u'789', 2)]
>>>
>>> stmt = select([product_price_table.c.sku,
...                 func.count(product_price_table.c.store_id)],
...                 group_by=[product_price_table.c.sku],
...                 having=func.count(product_price_table.c.store_id)
... > 2)
>>> print stmt
SELECT product_price.sku, count(product_price.store_id)
FROM product_price GROUP BY product_price.sku
HAVING count(product_price.store_id) > ?
>>> print stmt.execute().fetchall()
[]
```

We have already seen how we can use the distinct() method on ClauseElements to specify that a column should be distinct in a result set. SQLAlchemy also provides support for selecting only distinct rows in a result set via the distinct parameter to select().

```
>>> stmt = select([product_price_table.c.sku,
...                 product_price_table.c.price])
>>> print stmt
SELECT product_price.sku, product_price.price
FROM product_price
>>> print stmt.execute().fetchall()
[(u'456', 22.120000000000001), (u'789', 41.439999999999998),
... (u'456', 22.120000000000001), (u'789', 41.439999999999998)]
>>> stmt = select([product_price_table.c.sku,
...                 product_price_table.c.price],
...                 distinct=True)
>>> print stmt
SELECT DISTINCT product_price.sku, product_price.price
FROM product_price
```

```
>>> print stmt.execute().fetchall()
[(u'456', 22.120000000000001), (u'789', 41.439999999999998)]
```

Limiting results returned

One common operation when working with large data sets is the use of the OFFSET
and LIMIT clauses to return only a subset of data from a cursor. SQLAlchemy supports
OFFSET and LIMIT (even in databases without direct support) through the use of
offset and limit with the `select()` function and method:

```
>>> stmt = product_table.select()
>>> print stmt.execute().fetchall()
[(u'123', 12.34), (u'456', 22.120000000000001), (u'789',
... 41.439999999999998)]
>>> stmt = product_table.select(offset=1, limit=1)
>>> print stmt
SELECT product.sku, product.msrp
FROM product
 LIMIT 1 OFFSET 1
>>> print stmt.execute().fetchall()
[(u'456', 22.120000000000001)]
```

Limiting and offsetting is done *after* ordering and grouping, so you can use this construct to provide a "paged" view of sorted data. This can be very useful, for instance,
when displaying sortable data on a web form.

Using the "generative" query interface

Up until this point, we have been using the `select()` function and method as a query
constructor, generating a complete SQL statement as a result of the `select()` call.
SQLAlchemy also supports a "generative" interface for the `select()` function and
method that allows us to build up the query, one piece at a time. For instance, suppose
we have a product table with the following defintion:

```
product_table = Table(
    'product', metadata,
    Column('id', Integer, primary_key=True),
    Column('sku', String(20), unique=True),
    Column('manufacturer', Unicode(255)),
    Column('department', Unicode(255)),
    Column('category', Unicode(255)),
    Column('class', Unicode(255)),
    Column('subclass', Unicode(255)))
```

Now, suppose we have a user interface that displays all the "product" records in the
system, optionally filtered by various criteria (manufacturer, department, etc.). We
might write the following function to return the filtered user list:

```
def get_prods(manufacturer=None,
            department=None,
            category=None,
            class_=None,
            subclass=None,
```

```
                offset=None,
                limit=None):
    where_parts = []
    if manufacturer is not None:
        where_parts.append(product_table.c.manufacturer
                            == manufacturer)
    if department is not None:
        where_parts.append(product_table.c.department
                            == department)
    if category is not None:
        where_parts.append(product_table.c.category
                            == category)
    if class_ is not None:
        where_parts.append(product_table.c.class_
                            == class_)
    if subclass is not None:
        where_parts.append(product_table.c.subclass
                            == subclass)
    whereclause=and_(*where_parts)
    query = product_table.select(whereclause,
                                 offset=offset, limit=limit)
    return query
```

We can use arbitrary filters, and the appropriate SQL WHERE clause will automatically be constructed for us automatically:

```
>>> q = get_prods()
>>> print q
SELECT product.id, product.sku, product.manufacturer,
... product.department, product.category, product.class,
... product.subclass
FROM product
>>> q = get_prods(manufacturer="Neon")
>>> print q
SELECT product.id, product.sku, product.manufacturer,
... product.department, product.category, product.class,
... product.subclass
FROM product
WHERE product.manufacturer = ?
>>> q = get_prods(manufacturer="Neon", department="Auto")
>>> print q
SELECT product.id, product.sku, product.manufacturer,
... product.department, product.category, product.class,
... product.subclass
FROM product
WHERE product.manufacturer = ? AND product.department = ?
```

The generative interface allows us to rewrite the previous function as the following:

```
def get_prods(manufacturer=None,
              department=None,
              category=None,
              class_=None,
              subclass=None,
              offset=None,
              limit=None):
```

```
query = product_table.select()
if manufacturer is not None:
    query = query.where(product_table.c.manufacturer
                        == manufacturer)
if department is not None:
    query = query.where(product_table.c.department
                        == department)
if category is not None:
    query = query.where(product_table.c.category
                        == category)
if class_ is not None:
    query = query.where(product_table.c.class_
                        == class_)
if subclass is not None:
    query = query.where(product_table.c.subclass
                        == subclass)
query = query.offset(offset)
query = query.limit(limit)
return query
```

Although the two functions have the same functionality, the second one (using the generative interface) is more flexible. Suppose we wanted to refactor the original function into multiple parts, with each part potentially adding a different filtering criterion. In that case, we would need to pass a where_parts list through all the intermediate functions. In the generative approach, all the information about the query is "wrapped up" in the query itself, allowing us to build up a query piecemeal in several different functions, without passing anything around but the query itself.

The generative interface actually consists of a set of methods on the statement constructed by the select() function or method. Those methods are summarized next. Note that none of these functions actually modify the query object in place; rather, they return a new query object with the new condition applied:

where(whereclause)

> Add a constraint to the WHERE clause. All constraints added this way will be AND-ed together to create the whole WHERE clause.

order_by(*clauses)

> Generate an ORDER BY clause (or append the given clauses to an existing ORDER BY clause).

group_by(*clauses)

> Generate a GROUP BY clause (or append the given clauses to an existing GROUP BY clause).

having(having)

> Generate a HAVING clause (or add to an existing HAVING clause). Like where(), the final statement's HAVING clause will be all of the clauses added via this function, AND-ed together.

select_from(fromclause)

> Generate a FROM clause or append to the existing one.

---

limit(limit)

Equivalent to the limit parameter in the select() function or method.

offset(offset)

Equivalent to the offset parameter in the select() function or method.

column(column)

Add a column to the list of columns being selected.

distinct()

Equivalent to passing distinct=True to the select() function or method.

count(whereclause=None, **params)

Generate a statement that will count the rows that would be returned from the query, optionally with a whereclause and additional params to be passed to the generated SELECT COUNT(...) statement.

apply_labels()

Equivalent to use_labels=True in the select() function/method.

prefix_with(clause)

Append a prefix to the generated SQL. (A prefix is inserted immediately after the SELECT keyword, as in the prefixes parameter to select().)

replace_selectable(old, alias)

Replace every occurrence of old with the alias alias. (Aliasing is covered in more detail in later in this chapter, "Using aliases"). This can be useful when it is necessary to modify a query to use an alias when that query was originally written to use a reference to the actual table, for instance.

union(other, **kwargs)

Return an UNION with this selectable and another (covered in more detail later under "Joins and Set Operations").

union_all(other, **kwargs)

Return an UNION ALL with this selectable and another (covered in more detail later under "Joins and Set Operations").

intersect(other, **kwargs)

Return an INTERSECT with this selectable and another (covered in more detail later under "Joins and Set Operations").

intersect_all(other, **kwargs)

Return an INTERSECT ALL with this selectable and another (covered in more detail under "Joins and Set Operations").

except_(other, **kwargs)

Return an EXCEPT with this selectable and another (covered in more detail under "Joins and Set Operations").

except_all(other, **kwargs)

Return an EXCEPT ALL with this selectable and another (covered in more detail under "Joins and Set Operations").

join(right, *args, **kwargs)
> Return a INNER JOIN between this selectable and another (covered in more detail under "Joins and Set Operations").

outerjoin(right, *args, **kwargs)
> Return a LEFT OUTER JOIN between this selectable and another (covered in more detail under "Joins and Set Operations").

as_scalar()
> Allows the query to be embedded in a column list of an enclosing query.

label(name)
> Label the result of this query with name for use in the column list of an enclosing query. Also implies as_scalar().

correlate(fromclause)
> Specify a table on which to correlate, or use None to disable SQLAlchemy's auto-correlation on embedded subqueries.

select(whereclauses, **params)
> Generate an enclosing SELECT statment that selects all columns of this select.

Joins and Set Operations

In addition to the interface for selecting, filtering, sorting, and grouping on SELECT statements from single tables, SQLAlchemy provides full support for operations that combine multiple tables or other selectables (JOINs), as well as set operations on selectables (UNION, INTERSECT, and EXCEPT).

Joining selectables

To join two selectables (in tables or other select statements) together, SQLAlchemy provides the join() (implementing INNER JOIN) and outerjoin() (implementing OUTER JOIN) functions, as well as join() and outerjoin() methods on all selectables. The only difference between the *join() methods and the *join() functions is that the methods implicitly use self as the lefthand side of the join.

If you are familiar with the JOIN constructs in SQL, then you are used to specifyingthe ON clause of the JOIN. For instance, to select all stores where the price of a product is different than its MSRP, you might write the following SQL:

```
SELECT store.name
FROM store
    JOIN product_price ON store.id=product_price.store_id
    JOIN product ON product_price.sku=product.sku
WHERE product.msrp != product_price.price;
```

Notice how we had to specify the join criteria for each of the joins in the statement. Wouldn't it be nice if the database could infer the ON clauses based on the foreign key constraints? Well, SQLAlchemy does this automatically:

```
>>> from_obj = store_table.join(product_price_table)
... .join(product_table)
>>> query = store_table.select()
>>> query = query.select_from(from_obj)
>>> query = query.where(product_table.c.msrp
... != product_price_table.c.price)
>>> print query
SELECT store.id, store.name
FROM store JOIN product_price ON store.id = product_price.store_id
... JOIN product ON product.sku = product_price.sku
WHERE product.msrp != product_price.price
```

In some cases, we are not using the JOINed table to filter results, but we would like to see the results from a JOINed table alongside results from the table we are using. In this case, we can either use the **select()** function or use the **column()** method of the query object:

```
>>> print query.column('product.sku')
SELECT store.id, store.name, product.sku
FROM store JOIN product_price ON store.id = product_price.store_id
... JOIN product ON product.sku = product_price.sku
WHERE product.msrp != product_price.price
>>> query2 = select([store_table, product_table.c.sku],
...                  from_obj=[from_obj],
...                  whereclause=(product_table.c.msrp
...                               !=product_price_table.c.price))
>>> print query2
SELECT store.id, store.name, product.sku
FROM store JOIN product_price ON store.id = product_price.store_id
... JOIN product ON product.sku = product_price.sku
WHERE product.msrp != product_price.price
```

But what if we want to return results that may not have matching rows in the JOINed table? For this, we use the **outerjoin** function/method:

```
>>> from_obj = store_table.outerjoin(product_price_table)
>>> from_obj = from_obj.outerjoin(product_table)
>>> query = store_table.select()
>>> query = query.select_from(from_obj)
>>> query = query.column('product.msrp')
>>> print query
SELECT store.id, store.name, product.msrp
FROM store LEFT OUTER JOIN product_price
... ON store.id = product_price.store_id
LEFT OUTER JOIN product
... ON product.sku = product_price.sku
```

In this case, if there is not a matching entry in the product_price table or the product table, then the query will insert **None** for the **msrp** column.

Although SQLAlchemy can automatically infer the correct join condition most of the time, support is also provided for custom ON clauses via the **onclause** argument to **join()** and **outerjoin()**, a **ClauseElement** specifying the join condition.

Set operations (UNION, INTERSECT, EXCEPT)

The SQL language and SQLAlchemy also support set operations on selectables. For instance, you may wish to retrieve the union of results from two queries (those rows satisfying either or both queries), the intersection (those rows satisfying both queries), or the difference (those rows satisfying the first query but not the second). For these functions, SQL provides the UNION, INTERSECT, and EXCEPT clauses, as well as the related UNION ALL, INTERSECT ALL, and EXCEPT ALL clauses (although the INTERSECT and EXCEPT clauses are not supported on all databases).

To support these constructs, SQLAlchemy provides the `union()`, `union_all()`, `intersect()`, `intersect_all()`, `except_()`, and `except_all()` functions and selectable methods. Like the `*join()` methods, the set-oriented methods are simply the corresponding functions with the first parameter bound to itself. Suppose we wanted to select all the products with prices greater than $10 but less than $20. One way we could do this is with the following simple query:

```
>>> query = product_table.select(and_(product_table.c.msrp > 10.00 ,
...                                    product_table.c.msrp < 20.00))
>>> print query
SELECT product.sku, product.msrp
FROM product
WHERE product.msrp > ? AND product.msrp < ?
>>> for r in query.execute():
...     print r
...
(u'123', Decimal("12.34"))
```

We could rewrite this query as an INTERSECT using the `intersect()` function:

```
>>> query0 = product_table.select(product_table.c.msrp > 10.00)
>>> query1 = product_table.select(product_table.c.msrp < 20.00)
>>> query = intersect(query0, query1)
>>> print query
SELECT product.sku, product.msrp
FROM product
WHERE product.msrp > ? INTERSECT SELECT product.sku, product.msrp
FROM product
WHERE product.msrp < ?
>>> for r in query.execute():
...     print r
(u'123', Decimal("12.34"))
```

Using aliases

When using joins, it is often necessary to refer to a table more than once. In SQL, this is accomplished by using *aliases* in the query. For instance, suppose we have the following (partial) schema that tracks the reporting structure within an organization:

```
employee_table = Table(
    'employee', metadata,
    Column('id', Integer, primary_key=True),
```

```
Column('manager', None, ForeignKey('employee.id')),
Column('name', String(255)))
```

Now, suppose we want to select all the employees managed by an employee named Fred. In SQL, we might write the following:

```
SELECT employee.name
FROM employee, employee AS manager
WHERE employee.manager_id = manager.id
    AND manager.name = 'Fred'
```

SQLAlchemy also allows the use of aliasing selectables in this type of situation via the `alias()` function or method:

```
>>> manager = employee_table.alias('mgr')
>>> stmt = select([employee_table.c.name],
...                and_(employee_table.c.manager_id==manager.c.id,
...                     manager.c.name=='Fred'))
>>> print stmt
SELECT employee.name
FROM employee, employee AS mgr
WHERE employee.manager_id = mgr.id AND mgr.name = ?
```

SQLAlchemy can also choose the alias name automatically, which is useful for guaranteeing that there are no name collisions:

```
>>> manager = employee_table.alias()
>>> stmt = select([employee_table.c.name],
...                and_(employee_table.c.manager_id==manager.c.id,
...                     manager.c.name=='Fred'))
>>> print stmt
SELECT employee.name
FROM employee, employee AS employee_1
WHERE employee.manager_id = employee_1.id AND employee_1.name = ?
```

Subqueries

SQLAlchemy provides rich support for subqueries (using a query inside another query). We have already seen one type of subquery in the use of the join and in set operation support. SQLAlchemy also allows subqueries to appear in the column list of a select statement, in the right hand side of the SQL IN operator (using the SQLAlchemy-provided `in_()` method on `ClauseElement`s), and as an argument to the `from_obj` parameter on the `select()` function.

Embedding subqueries in the column list

In order to embed a subquery in a column list, we need to use the `as_scalar()` method on the inner query to indicate that the query will return a single value. For instance, if we want to retrieve the number of stores that offer each product, we could use the following query:

```
>>> subquery = select(
...     [func.count(product_price_table.c.sku)],
```

```
...         product_price_table.c.sku==product_table.c.sku)
>>> print subquery
SELECT count(product_price.sku)
FROM product_price, product
WHERE product_price.sku = product.sku
>>> stmt = select([product_table.c.sku,
...                 product_table.c.msrp,
...                 subquery.as_scalar()])
>>> print stmt
SELECT product.sku, product.msrp, (SELECT count(product_price.sku)
FROM product_price
WHERE product_price.sku = product.sku)
FROM product
>>> for row in stmt.execute():
...     print row
...
(u'123', Decimal("12.34"), 0)
(u'456', Decimal("22.12"), 2)
(u'789', Decimal("41.44"), 2)
```

Correlated versus uncorrelated subqueries

You may have noticed in the previous example that when SQLAlchemy inserted the subquery into the main query, it left out the **product** table in the subquery's FROM list. This is because SQLAlchemy attempts to *correlate* subqueries with outer queries whenever they reference the same table. To disable this behavior, you can use the correlate() method on the subquery to manually specify a FROM clause to remove from the subquery, or, by passing **None**, to disable correlation in the subquery:

```
>>> stmt = select([product_table.c.sku,
...                 product_table.c.msrp,
...                 subquery.correlate(None).as_scalar()])
>>> print stmt
SELECT product.sku, product.msrp, (SELECT count(product_price.sku)
FROM product_price, product
WHERE product_price.sku = product.sku)
FROM product
>>> for row in stmt.execute():
...     print row
...
(u'123', Decimal("12.34"), 4)
(u'456', Decimal("22.12"), 4)
(u'789', Decimal("41.44"), 4)
```

Because the inner query is uncorrelated, rather than totaling the number of stores that carry the given product, the query repeatedly calculates the number of rows in the product_price table with *any* valid SKU.

Embedding subqueries in an IN clause

It is often useful in SQL to embed subqueries in an IN clause of another query. SQLAlchemy provides support for this as well, allowing you to specify a selectable as an argument for the ClauseElement's in_() method. For instance, if we wanted to retrieve all the employees whose names start with "Ted" and who do not have a manager, we could write the query as follows:

```
>>> subquery = select([employee_table.c.id],
...                    employee_table.c.manager_id==None)
>>> stmt = employee_table.select(
...        and_(employee_table.c.id.in_(subquery),
...             employee_table.c.name.like('Ted%')))
>>> print stmt
SELECT employee.id, employee.manager_id, employee.name
FROM employee
WHERE employee.id IN (SELECT employee.id
FROM employee
WHERE employee.manager_id IS NULL) AND employee.name LIKE ?
```

Embedding subqueries in the FROM clause

It is sometimes useful to generate a SQL query in multiple stages by using a subquery in the FROM clause of another query (and continuing this nesting if necessary). SQLAlchemy provides support for such subqueries by allowing you to specify any list of selectables (not just Table objects) to the from_obj parameter of the select(). If we follow this pattern, then the previous query could be rewritten as follows:

```
>>> subquery =
... employee_table.select(employee_table.c.manager_id==None)
>>> stmt = select([subquery.c.id, subquery.c.manager_id,
... subquery.c.name],
...                whereclause=subquery.c.name.like('Ted%'),
...                from_obj=[subquery])
>>> print stmt
SELECT id, manager_id, name
FROM (SELECT employee.id AS id, employee.manager_id AS manager_id,
... employee.name AS name
FROM employee
WHERE employee.manager_id IS NULL)
WHERE name LIKE ?
```

## CHAPTER 6

Building an Object Mapper

Atop the SQL expression language, SQLAlchemy provides an object-relational mapper (ORM). The purpose of an ORM is to provide a convenient way to store your application data objects in a relational database. Generally, an ORM will provide a way to define the method of storing your object in the database. This chapter focuses on the SQLAlchemy methods that do this.

Introduction to ORMs

ORMs provide methods of updating the database by using your application objects. For instance, to update a column in a mapped table in SQLAlchemy, you merely have to update the object, and SQLAlchemy will take care of making sure that the change is reflected in the database. ORMs also allow you to construct application objects based on database queries. Chapter 7 will focus on how to use SQLAlchemy's ORM to update and query objects in the database.

Design Concepts in the ORM

There are two major patterns used in the ORM you should become familiar with in order to understand how to best use the ORM. These are the *data mapper pattern* and the *unit of work pattern*.

The data mapper pattern

In the data mapper pattern (shown in Figure 6-1), database tables, views, and other "selectable" objects are mapped onto "plain old Python objects" (POPOs) by "mapper" objects. This is different from the "active record" pattern (shown in Figure 6-2), where the objects themselves are responsible for mapping themselves to database views. The data mapper pattern can, of course, be used to emulate the active record pattern by merging the mapper with the application objects.

One benefit of using the data mapper pattern as implemented in SQLAlchemy is that it allows the database design to be decoupled from the object hierarchy. In

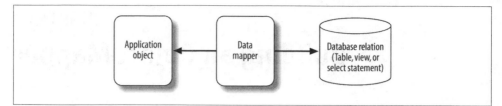

Figure 6-1. Data mapper pattern

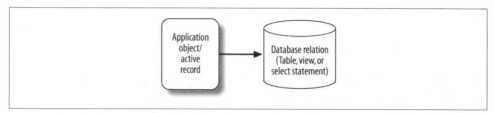

Figure 6-2. Active record pattern

SQLAlchemy, this decoupling can be nearly complete: you can define your classes in one module and your tables in another with no references from one to the other. The mapping can then be performed by a third module, which imports the other two modules and instantiates the `Mapper` objects, which do the work of mapping the selectables to your objects.

The unit of work pattern

The major second pattern used in the SQLAlchemy ORM is the unit of work pattern. In this pattern, when you make a change to an object, the database is not updated immediately. Instead, SQLAlchemy tracks changes to your objects in a `session` object, and then flushes all your changes at once in a single "unit of work." This has the advantage of generally improving performance by reducing the number of round-trips to the database.

The alternative to the unit of work pattern, of course, is to update the database as soon as a mapped object property changes. This can lead to a very "chatty" application, but it does have the advantage of keeping your objects in sync with the database, which can be handy if you wish to execute queries before flushing the objects you've modified back out to the database.

To alleviate this concern, SQLAlchemy actually provides an "autoflush" feature on the `session` object that will take care of flushing the session before any queries are performed on it. As long as you use an autoflushing `session` and execute all queries through the `session`, you generally do not need to worry about inconsistencies between your objects in memory and the database on disk.

Of course, if you use the SQL expression layer of SQLAlchemy, you *can* get your in-memory objects out-of-sync with the database, so some care needs to be taken when mixing ORM-level semantics with SQL-level semantics in the same transaction.

Declaring Object Mappers

In order to use the SQLAlchemy ORM, we need three things: a database schema defined on a MetaData object, an object model (no special preparation of the object model is required for use by SQLAlchemy), and a mapper configuration. In this section, we will use the following schema, designed to maintain information about a retail product catalog:

```
level_table = Table(❶
    'level', metadata,
    Column('id', Integer, primary_key=True),
    Column('parent_id', None, ForeignKey('level.id')),
    Column('name', String(20)))
category_table = Table(❷
    'category', metadata,
    Column('id', Integer, primary_key=True),
    Column('level_id', None, ForeignKey('level.id')),
    Column('parent_id', None, ForeignKey('category.id')),
    Column('name', String(20)))
product_table = Table(
    'product', metadata,
    Column('sku', String(20), primary_key=True),
    Column('msrp', Numeric))
product_summary_table = Table(❸
    'product_summary', metadata,
    Column('sku', None, ForeignKey('product.sku'), primary_key=True),
    Column('name', Unicode(255)),
    Column('description', Unicode))
product_category_table = Table(❹
    'product_category', metadata,
    Column('product_id', None, ForeignKey('product.sku'), primary_key=True),
    Column('category_id', None, ForeignKey('category.id'), primary_key=True))
region_table = Table(
    'region', metadata,
    Column('id', Integer, primary_key=True),
    Column('name', Unicode(255)))
store_table = Table(
    'store', metadata,
    Column('id', Integer, primary_key=True),
    Column('region_id', None, ForeignKey('region.id')),
    Column('name', Unicode(255)))
product_price_table = Table(❺
    'product_price', metadata,
    Column('sku', None, ForeignKey('product.sku'), primary_key=True),
    Column('store_id', None, ForeignKey('store.id'), primary_key=True),
    Column('price', Numeric, default=0))
```

❶ This is a "level" used in categorizing a product in a hierarchy. In our example, we will use the levels "Gender", "Department", "Class", and "Subclass".

❷ These are the individual categories within a level. In our example, for instance, within the "Gender" level, we have "Men", "Women", "Children", and "Unisex."

❸ This table contains auxiliary information about products that may or may not be present for each product.

❹ This table links the product table with the category table. A product should generally have one category per level.

❺ This table lists the retail price for each product at each store location.

The application object model in the following listing is extremely basic. In a real application, the classes would probably have additional methods defined for performing domain-specific operations:

```python
class Level(object):

    def __init__(self, name, parent=None):
        self.name = name
        self.parent = parent

    def __repr__(self):
        return '<Level %s>' % self.name

class Category(object):

    def __init__(self, name, level, parent=None):
        self.name = name
        self.level = level
        self.parent = parent

    def __repr__(self):
        return '<Category %s.%s>' % (self.level.name, self.name)

class Product(object):

    def __init__(self, sku, msrp, summary=None):
        self.sku = sku
        self.msrp = msrp
        self.summary = summary
        self.categories = []
        self.prices = []

    def __repr__(self):
        return '<Product %s>' % self.sku

class ProductSummary(object):

    def __init__(self, name, description):
        self.name = name
        self.description = description
```

```
    def __repr__(self):
        return '<ProductSummary %s>' % self.name

class Region(object):

    def __init__(self, name):
        self.name = name

    def __repr__(self):
        return '<Region %s>' % self.name

class Store(object):

    def __init__(self, name):
        self.name = name

    def __repr__(self):
        return '<Store %s>' % self.name

class Price(object):

    def __init__(self, product, store, price):
        self.product = product
        self.store = store
        self.price = price

    def __repr__(self):
        return '<Price %s at %s for $%.2f>' % (
            self.product.sku, self.store.name, self.price)
```

Basic Object Mapping

Now that we have the basic schema and object model in place, we can start exploring
how to map objects. The region_table is one of the simplest tables, so we will start
there. The following example demonstrates mapping the region_table to the Region
class, and also illustrates the alterations that SQLAlchemy performs on the Region class
during mapping:

```
>>> print dir(Region)
['__class__', '__delattr__', '__dict__', '__doc__',
... '__getattribute__', '__hash__', '__init__',
... '__module__','__new__', '__reduce__', '__reduce_ex__',
... '__repr__', '__setattr__', '__str__', '__weakref__']
>>> mapper(Region, region_table)
<sqlalchemy.orm.mapper.Mapper object at 0x2af4d7004310>
>>> print dir(Region)
['__class__', '__delattr__', '__dict__', '__doc__',
... '__getattribute__', '__hash__', '__init__', '__module__',
... '__new__', '__reduce__', '__reduce_ex__', '__repr__',
... '__setattr__', '__str__', '__weakref__',
... '_sa_attribute_manager', 'c', 'id', 'name']
>>> print Region.id
<sqlalchemy.orm.mapper._CompileOnAttr object at 0x2af4d70046d0>
>>> print Region.name
```

```
<sqlalchemy.orm.mapper._CompileOnAttr object at 0x2af4d7004790>
>>> print Region.c.id
region.id
>>> print Region.c.name
region.name
```

 It is possible to make SQLAlchemy "forget" all the mappings that have been declared by invoking the `clear_mappers()` function. This feature can be useful when prototyping various mappers within the interactive shell, as it will let you remap classes to try out different strategies.

As shown previously, the `mapper()` function has added a few attributes to our class. The attributes we're interested in are `c`, `id`, and `name`. This `c` attribute is a proxy for the `store_table`'s `c` attribute, and allows access to all the columns of the `store_table`.

The `id` and `name` attributes are actually class properties that track access to these attributes to synchronize them with the database later. These are mapped because the default behavior of the SQLAlchemy mapper is to provide a property for each column in the selectable mapped, and the `store_table` has two columns, id and name.

Note that we can still use the object just as if it had not been mapped (unless, of course, we were relying on existing properties `id` and `name`, or an existing attribute `c`):

```
>>> r0 = Region(name="Northeast")
>>> r1 = Region(name="Southwest")
>>> print r0
<Region Northeast>
>>> print r1
<Region Southwest>
```

The difference now is that these objects can be loaded or saved to the database using a `session` object (covered in more detail in the next chapter):

```
>>> Session = sessionmaker()
>>> session = Session()
>>>
>>> session.save(r0)
>>> session.save(r1)
>>> metadata.bind.echo = True
>>> print r0.id
None
>>> print r1.id
None
>>> session.flush()
2007-10-13 12:47:07,621 INFO sqlalchemy.engine.base.Engine.0x..90
... BEGIN
2007-10-13 12:47:07,623 INFO sqlalchemy.engine.base.Engine.0x..90
... INSERT INTO region (name) VALUES (?)
2007-10-13 12:47:07,623 INFO sqlalchemy.engine.base.Engine.0x..90
... ['Northeast']
2007-10-13 12:47:07,625 INFO sqlalchemy.engine.base.Engine.0x..90
... INSERT INTO region (name) VALUES (?)
```

```
2007-10-13 12:47:07,625 INFO sqlalchemy.engine.base.Engine.0x..90
... ['Southwest']
>>> print r0.id
1
>>> print r1.id
2
```

Note how SQLAlchemy automatically inserted the store names we specified into the database, and then populated the mapped id attribute based on the synthetic key value generated by the database. We can also update mapped properties once an object has been saved to the database:

```
>>> r0.name = 'Northwest'
>>> session.flush()
2007-10-13 12:47:53,879 INFO sqlalchemy.engine.base.Engine.0x..90
... UPDATE region SET name=? WHERE region.id = ?
2007-10-13 12:47:53,879 INFO sqlalchemy.engine.base.Engine.0x..90
... ['Northwest', 1]
```

Customizing Property Mapping

The basic way mapping that SQLAlchemy performs is useful, but what if we have a property or function that conflicts with the way SQLAlchemy wants to map columns? Or what if we just want to customize the columns mapped by SQLAlchemy? Fortunately, SQLAlchemy provides a rich set of ways to customize the way properties are mapped onto your classes.

Using include_properties and exclude_properties

The simplest case is where we want to restrict the properties mapped. In this case, we can use the include_properties to only map those columns specified:

```
>>> print dir(Region)
['__class__', '__delattr__', '__dict__', '__doc__',
...    '__getattribute__', '__hash__', '__init__', '__module__',
...    '__new__', '__reduce__', '__reduce_ex__', '__repr__',
...    '__setattr__', '__str__', '__weakref__']
>>> mapper(Region, region_table, include_properties=['id'])
<sqlalchemy.orm.mapper.Mapper object at 0x2ba1a7ca3310>
>>> print dir(Region)
['__class__', '__delattr__', '__dict__', '__doc__',
...    '__getattribute__', '__hash__', '__init__', '__module__',
...    '__new__', '__reduce__', '__reduce_ex__', '__repr__',
...    '__setattr__', '__str__', '__weakref__',
...    '_sa_attribute_manager', 'c', 'id']
```

We can also use exclude_properties to specify columns to be *excluded*:

```
>>> mapper(Region, region_table, exclude_properties=['id'])
<sqlalchemy.orm.mapper.Mapper object at 0x2ba1a7ca34d0>
```

Customizing the name of the mapped column

If we want to map all the columns to properties with a particular prefix, we can use the `column_prefix` keyword argument:

```
>>> mapper(Region, region_table, column_prefix='_')
<sqlalchemy.orm.mapper.Mapper object at 0x2aecf62d5310>
>>> print dir(Region)
['__class__', '__delattr__', '__dict__', '__doc__',
...    '__getattribute__', '__hash__', '__init__', '__module__',
...    '__new__', '__reduce__', '__reduce_ex__', '__repr__',
...    '__setattr__', '__str__', '__weakref__', '_id', '_name',
...    '_sa_attribute_manager', 'c']
```

We can also customize the mapped property names on a column-by-column basis using the `properties` parameter:

```
>>> mapper(Region, region_table, properties=dict(
...        region_name=region_table.c.name,
...        region_id=region_table.c.id))
<sqlalchemy.orm.mapper.Mapper object at 0x2b37165b8310>
>>> print dir(Region)
['__class__', '__delattr__', '__dict__', '__doc__',
...    '__getattribute__', '__hash__', '__init__', '__module__',
...    '__new__', '__reduce__', '__reduce_ex__', '__repr__',
...    '__setattr__', '__str__', '__weakref__',
...    '_sa_attribute_manager', 'c', 'region_id', 'region_name']
```

Using synonyms

SQLAlchemy provides certain functions and methods (covered in the next chapter) that expect mapped property names as keyword arguments. This can be cumbersome to use if we have mapped the column names to other property names (perhaps to allow for user-defined getters and setters). To alleviate the burden of using the actual property names, SQLAlchemy provides the `synonym()` function to allow a name to be used "as if" it were a real property. Suppose, for instance, that we wish to verify that all store names end in "Store". We might use the following approach:

```
>>> class Region(object):
...        def __init__(self, name):
...            self.name = name
...        def __repr__(self):
...            return '<Region %s>' % self.name
...        def _get_name(self):
...            return self._name
...        def _set_name(self, value):
...            assert value.endswith('Region'), \
...                'Region names must end in "Region"'
...            self._name = value
...        name=property(_get_name, _set_name)
...
>>> mapper(Region, region_table, column_prefix='_', properties=dict(
...        name=synonym('_name')))❶
<sqlalchemy.orm.mapper.Mapper object at 0x2b2f953ff4d0>
```

```
>>>
>>> s0 = Region('Southeast')❷
Traceback (most recent call last):
...
AssertionError: Region names must end in "Region"
>>> s0 = Region('Southeast Region')
>>> session.save(s0)
>>> session.flush()
>>> session.clear()
>>>
>>> q = session.query(Region)
>>> print q.filter_by(name='Southeast Region').first()
❸

<Region Southeast Region>
>>> print s0.name
Southeast Region
```

❶ This defines the synonym "name" to be usable in all SQLAlchemy functions where "_name" is usable.

❷ Here, we tried to create an object with an invalid name and were rejected.

❸ Using the synonym, we can still select stores by name without abusing the private attribute.

If you wish to create a property that is a true proxy for the original mapped property (so you don't have to write the getter and setter), you can use synonym(*name*, proxy=True) to define it.

Mapping subqueries

In some cases, we may wish to create a property that is a combination of a few columns or the result of a subquery. For instance, suppose we wanted to map the product_table, providing a property that will yield the average price of the product across all stores. To do this, we use the column_property() function:

```
>>> average_price = select(
...     [func.avg(product_price_table.c.price)],
...     product_price_table.c.sku==product_table.c.sku)\
...     .as_scalar() \
...     .label('average_price')
>>> print average_price
(SELECT avg(product_price.price)
FROM product_price, product
WHERE product_price.sku = product.sku) AS average_price
>>> mapper(Product, product_table, properties=dict(
...     average_price=column_property(average_price)))
<sqlalchemy.orm.mapper.Mapper object at 0x2b6b9d5336d0>
>>> metadata.bind.echo = True
>>> p = session.query(Product).get('123')
2007-10-06 18:47:27,289 INFO sqlalchemy.engine.base.Engine.0x..90.
... SELECT (SELECT avg(product_price.price)
FROM product_price
```

```
WHERE product_price.sku = product.sku) AS average_price,
... product.sku AS product_sku, product.msrp AS product_msrp
FROM product
WHERE product.sku = ? ORDER BY product.oid
 LIMIT 1 OFFSET 0
2007-10-06 18:47:27,290 INFO sqlalchemy.engine.base.Engine.0x..90.
... ['123']
>>> print p.sku, p.msrp, p.average_price
123 12.34 12.34
```

Mapping composite values

The SQLAlchemy ORM also provides for creating properties from a group of columns. To use this feature, we must create a custom class to store the composite value. That class must have a constructor that accepts column values as positional arguments (to create the object from the database result) and a method __composite_values__() that returns a list or tuple representing the state of the object in the order of the columns that map to it. The custom class should also support equality comparisons via the __eq__() and __ne__() methods.

For instance, suppose we have a mapping database that stores route segments in the following table:

```
segment_table = Table(
    'segment', metadata,
    Column('id', Integer, primary_key=True),
    Column('lat0', Float),
    Column('long0', Float),
    Column('lat1', Float),
    Column('long1', Float))
```

In this case, our application expects RouteSegments to have a beginning and an ending MapPoint object, defined as follows:

```
class RouteSegment(object):
    def __init__(self, begin, end):
        self.begin = begin
        self.end = end
    def __repr__(self):
        return '<Route %s to %s>' % (self.begin, self.end)

class MapPoint(object):
    def __init__(self, lat, long):
        self.coords = lat, long
    def __composite_values__(self):
        return self.coords
    def __eq__(self, other):
        return self.coords == other.coords
    def __ne__(self, other):
        return self.coords != other.coords
    def __repr__(self):
        return '(%s lat, %s long)' % self.coords
```

We can then map the class and use it with the composite() function:

```
>>> mapper(RouteSegment, segment_table, properties=dict(
...     begin=composite(MapPoint,
...                     segment_table.c.lat0,
... segment_table.c.long0),
...     end=composite(MapPoint,
...                   segment_table.c.lat1, segment_table.c.long1)))
<sqlalchemy.orm.mapper.Mapper object at 0x2b13e58a5450>
>>>
>>> work=MapPoint(33.775562,-84.29478)
>>> library=MapPoint(34.004313,-84.452062)
>>> park=MapPoint(33.776868,-84.389785)
>>> routes = [
...     RouteSegment(work, library),
...     RouteSegment(work, park),
...     RouteSegment(library, work),
...     RouteSegment(library, park),
...     RouteSegment(park, library),
...     RouteSegment(park, work)]
>>> for rs in routes:
...     session.save(rs)
...
>>> session.flush()
>>>
>>> q = session.query(RouteSegment)
>>> print RouteSegment.begin==work
segment.lat0 = ? AND segment.long0 = ?
>>> q = q.filter(RouteSegment.begin==work)
>>> for rs in q:
...     print rs
...
<Route (33.775562 lat, -84.29478 long) to (34.004313 lat, -84.452062
... long)>
<Route (33.775562 lat, -84.29478 long) to (33.776868 lat, -84.389785
... long)>
```

By default, SQLAlchemy generates an equality comparator that generates SQL to compare all mapped columns for use in methods such as `filter()`, shown previously. If you want to provide custom comparison operators, you can do so by implementing a subclass of `PropComparator`:

```
class MapPointComparator(PropComparator):
    def __lt__(self, other):
        return and_(*[a<b for a, b in
                      zip(self.prop.columns,
                          other.__composite_values__())])

mapper(RouteSegment, segment_table, properties=dict(
    begin=composite(MapPoint,
                    segment_table.c.lat0, segment_table.c.long0,
                    comparator=MapPointComparator),
    end=composite(MapPoint,
                  segment_table.c.lat1, segment_table.c.long1,
                  comparator=MapPointComparator)))
```

Eager versus deferred loading

In some cases, it may not be efficient to retrieve all properties of an object at object creation time. For instance, if the table being mapped has a BLOB column that is needed only infrequently in the mapped object, it may be more efficient to retrieve that column only when the property is accessed. In SQLAlchemy, this is referred to as "deferred column loading," and is accomplished by mapping a property to the `deferred()` function.

In our product catalog schema, for instance, suppose we have an image stored for each product in a BLOB column:

```
product_table = Table(
    'product', metadata,
    Column('sku', String(20), primary_key=True),
    Column('msrp', Numeric),
    Column('image', BLOB))
```

In this case, we can map the `image` column as a deferred column:

```
mapper(Product, product_table, properties=dict(
    image=deferred(product_table.c.image)))
```

Now, if we select a product, we can observe that SQLAlchemy delays loading the deferred column until its mapped property is actually accessed:

```
>>> metadata.bind.echo=True
>>> q = session.query(Product)
>>> prod=q.get_by(sku='123')
2007-10-08 11:27:45,582 INFO sqlalchemy.engine.base.Engine.0x..d0
... SELECT product.sku AS product_sku, product.msrp AS product_msrp
FROM product
WHERE product.sku = ? ORDER BY product.oid
 LIMIT 1 OFFSET 0
2007-10-08 11:27:45,583 INFO sqlalchemy.engine.base.Engine.0x..d0
... ['123']
>>> print prod.image
2007-10-08 11:27:45,589 INFO sqlalchemy.engine.base.Engine.0x..d0
... SELECT product.image AS product_image
FROM product
WHERE product.sku = ?
2007-10-08 11:27:45,589 INFO sqlalchemy.engine.base.Engine.0x..d0
... [u'123']
abcdef
```

We can also mark multiple deferred columns to be members of a "group" of deferred columns, so that they are all loaded when any column in the group is accessed:

```
product_table = Table(
    'product', metadata,
    Column('sku', String(20), primary_key=True),
    Column('msrp', Numeric),
    Column('image1', Binary),
    Column('image2', Binary),
    Column('image3', Binary))
```

```
mapper(Product, product_table, properties=dict(
    image1=deferred(product_table.c.image, group='images'),
    image2=deferred(product_table.c.image, group='images'),
    image3=deferred(product_table.c.image, group='images')))
```

If the default deferred behavior is not desired, columns can be individually deferred or undeferred at query creation time by using the defer() and undefer() functions along with the options() method of the Query object (described more completely in the next chapter).

Mapping Arbitrary Selectables

It is worth noting that, although we have been mapping tables in our examples, it is possible to map any "selectable" object in SQLAlchemy. This includes tables, and the result of the select(), *join(), union*(), intersect*(), and except*() functions or methods. For instance, we may wish to map the result of joining the product table with the product summary table to a single object:

```
q = product_table.join(
    product_summary_table,
    product_table.c.sku==product_summary_table.c.sku).alias('full_product')

class FullProduct(object): pass

mapper(FullProduct, q)
```

Other mapper( ) Parameters

The mapper() function takes a number of keyword arguments, listed next.

entity_name=None
> A string to associate with a nonprimary mapper (see the non_primary parameter description for more detail) that allows it to be distinguished from the primary mapper in session methods such as save() and query().

always_refresh=False
> Whenever a query returns an object corresponding to an in-memory object, overwrite the in-memory object's fields with the fields from the query if this flag is True. This will overwrite any changes to the in-memory object, and so using the populate_existing() method on Query objects is preferred over this parameter.

allow_column_override=False
> Allow a relation() property to be defined with the same name as a mapped column (the column will not be mapped in this case). Otherwise, the name conflict will generate an exception.

allow_null_pks=False
> When using a composite primary key in the mapped selectable, this flag allows some (but not all) of the primary key columns to be NULL. Otherwise, any NULL

value in any primary key column will cause the row to be skipped when constructing objects.

batch=True

Allow the save operations of multiple object to be batched together for efficiency (for instance, saving all the sku columns of multiple Products). If False, each object will be completely created in the database before moving on to the next object.

column_prefix=None

A string that will be used to prefix all automatically mapped column property names. This is ignored on all explicitly named properties.

concrete=False

If True, indicates the use of concrete table inheritance (covered in detail in Chapter 8).

extension=None

Either a MapperExtension or a list of MapperExtensions to be applied on all operations on this mapper (covered in detail later in this chapter in the section "Extending Mappers").

inherits=None

Another mapper that will serve as the "parent" when using mapper inheritance (covered in detail in Chapter 8).

inherit_condition=None

The method of joining tables in joined table inheritance (covered in detail in Chapter 8).

inherit_foreign_keys=None

The "foreign" side of the inherit_condition parameter.

order_by=None

The default ordering for entities when selecting from this mapper.

non_primary=False

When True, specifies that this is a nonprimary mapper. For any mapped class, only one primary mapper can be registered. When you create an instance of the class and save it to the database, the primary mapper *alone* determines how that object will be saved. Nonprimary mappers are useful for loading objects through a different way than the primary mapper (e.g., from a different table, with a different set of columns, etc). Any number of non_primary mappers may be defined for a class.

polymorphic_on=None

Column that identifies which class/mapper should be used when using inheritance for a particular row (covered in detail in Chapter 8).

polymorphic_identity=None

Value stored in the polymorphic_on parameter to identify this mapper in an inheritance relationship (covered in detail in Chapter 8).

`polymorphic_fetch='union'`

> The method used to fetch subclasses using joined-table inheritance, either 'union', 'select', or 'deferred' (covered in detail in Chapter 8).

`properties=None`

> Dictionary of properties to be mapped onto the class (in addition to automatically mapped properties).

`include_properties=None`

> List of properties to map onto the class (columns in the mapped table but not referenced in this list will *not* be mapped automatically).

`exclude_properties=None`

> List of properties not to map onto the class (columns in the mapped table will be mapped automatically *unless* they are in this list).

`primary_key=None`

> List of columns that define the primary key for the selectable being mapped. (By default, this is the primary key of the table being mapped, but this behavior can be overridden with this parameter.)

`select_table=None`

> The selectable used to select instances of the mapped class. Generally used with polymorphic loading (covered in detail in Chapter 8).

`version_id_col=None`

> An integer column on the mapped selectable that is used to keep a version ID of the data in that row. Each save will increment this version number. If the version number is changed between the time when the object is selected and when it is flushed, then a `ConcurrentModificationError` is thrown.

Declaring Relationships Between Mappers

Although the features that SQLAlchemy provides for mapping tables and other selectables to classes are powerful in their own right, SQLAlchemy also allows you to model relationships between tables as simple Python lists and properties using the `relation()` function in the `properties` parameter of the `mapper()` function.

Basic Relationships

The three main relationships modeled by SQLAlchemy are 1:N, M:N, and 1:1 (which is actually a special case of 1:N). In a 1:N relationship, one table (the "N" side) generally has a foreign key to another table (the "1" side). In M:N, two tables (the "primary" tables) are related via a scondary, "join" table that has foreign keys into both primary tables. A 1:1 relationship is simply a 1:N relationship where there is only one "N"-side row with a foreign key to any particular "1"-side row.

1:N relations

To model each type of relationship, SQLAlchemy uses the **relation()** function in the
properties dict of the mapper. In many cases, SQLAlchemy is able to infer the proper
join condition for 1:N relations. For instance, since the stores in our data model are
members of regions (a 1:N relationship region:store), we can model this on our
Region class as follows:

```
>>> mapper(Store, store_table)
<sqlalchemy.orm.mapper.Mapper object at 0x2b794eb2f610>
>>> mapper(Region, region_table, properties=dict(
...     stores=relation(Store)))
❶

<sqlalchemy.orm.mapper.Mapper object at 0x2b794eb3af90>
>>> rgn = session.query(Region).get(1)
2007-10-13 12:59:47,876 INFO sqlalchemy.engine.base.Engine.0x..90
... SELECT region.id AS region_id, region.name AS region_name
FROM region
WHERE region.id = ? ORDER BY region.oid
 LIMIT 1 OFFSET 0
2007-10-13 12:59:47,877 INFO sqlalchemy.engine.base.Engine.0x..90
... [1]
>>> s0 = Store(name='3rd and Juniper')
>>> rgn.stores.append(s0)❷
2007-10-13 13:00:06,339 INFO sqlalchemy.engine.base.Engine.0x..90
... SELECT store.id AS store_id, store.region_id AS store_region_id,
... store.name AS store_name
FROM store
WHERE ? = store.region_id ORDER BY store.oid
2007-10-13 13:00:06,339 INFO sqlalchemy.engine.base.Engine.0x..90
... [1]
>>> session.flush()❸
2007-10-13 13:00:14,344 INFO sqlalchemy.engine.base.Engine.0x..90
... INSERT INTO store (region_id, name) VALUES (?, ?)
2007-10-13 13:00:14,345 INFO sqlalchemy.engine.base.Engine.0x..90
... [1, '3rd and Juniper']
```

❶ SQLAlchemy is able to infer the 1:N relation type by the foreign key relationship
between **region_table** and **store_table**.

❷ Adding a store to the region is as simple as appending on to the property. Generally,
when working at the ORM level, it is not necessary to worry about foreign keys. The
SELECT statement is necessary for SQLAlchemy to retrieve the inital contents of
the "stores" property.

❸ SQLAlchemy automatically infers that a new store must be inserted with the
region_id properly set.

In some cases, SQLAlchemy is unable to infer the proper join condition (for instance,
when there are multiple foreign key relations between the two tables). In this case, we
can simply use the **primaryjoin** parameter to the **relation()** function:

```
mapper(Region, region_table, properties=dict(
    stores=relation(Store,
                    primaryjoin=(store_table.c.region_id
                                 ==region_table.c.id))))
```

M:N relations

It is often useful to model many-to-many (M:N) type relations between objects. In the database, this is accomplished by the use of an association or join table. In the following schema, the relation between the `product_table` and the `category_table` is a many-to-many:

```
category_table = Table(
    'category', metadata,
    Column('id', Integer, primary_key=True),
    Column('level_id', None, ForeignKey('level.id')),
    Column('parent_id', None, ForeignKey('category.id')),
    Column('name', String(20)))
product_table = Table(
    'product', metadata,
    Column('sku', String(20), primary_key=True),
    Column('msrp', Numeric))
product_category_table = Table(
    'product_category', metadata,
Column('product_id', None, ForeignKey('product.sku'),
... primary_key=True),
Column('category_id', None, ForeignKey('category.id'),
... primary_key=True))
```

In SQLAlchemy, we can model this relationship with the `relation()` function and the `secondary` parameter:

```
>>> mapper(Category, category_table, properties=dict(
...        products=relation(Product,
... secondary=product_category_table)))
<sqlalchemy.orm.mapper.Mapper object at 0xee6810>
>>> mapper(Product, product_table, properties=dict(
...        categories=relation(Category,
... secondary=product_category_table)))
<sqlalchemy.orm.mapper.Mapper object at 0xee6d10>
>>>
>>> session.query(Product).get('123').categories
2007-10-15 20:06:17,375 INFO sqlalchemy.engine.base.Engine.0x..d0
... SELECT category.id AS category_id, category.level_id AS
... category_level_id, category.parent_id AS category_parent_id,
... category.name AS category_name
FROM category, product_category
WHERE ? = product_category.product_id AND category.id =
... product_category.category_id ORDER BY product_category.oid
2007-10-15 20:06:17,375 INFO sqlalchemy.engine.base.Engine.0x..d0
... [u'123']
[]
```

As in the case of the 1:N join, we can also explicitly specify the join criteria by using the `primaryjoin` (the join condition between the table being mapped and the join table) and the `secondaryjoin` (the join condition between the join table and the table being related to) parameters:

```
mapper(Category, category_table, properties=dict(
    products=relation(Product, secondary=product_category_table,
primaryjoin=(product_category_table.c.category_id
                                == category_table.c.id),
    secondaryjoin=(product_category_table.c.product_id
                                == product_table.c.sku))))
mapper(Product, product_table, properties=dict(
    categories=relation(Category, secondary=product_category_table,
primaryjoin=(product_category_table.c.product_id
                                == product_table.c.sku),
    secondaryjoin=(product_category_table.c.category_id
                                == category_table.c.id))))
```

1:1 relations

SQLAlchemy also supports 1:1 mappings as a type of 1:N mappings. This is modeled in our schema with the `product_table` and the `product_summary_table`:

```
product_table = Table(
    'product', metadata,
    Column('sku', String(20), primary_key=True),
    Column('msrp', Numeric))
product_summary_table = Table(
    'product_summary', metadata,
    Column('sku', None, ForeignKey('product.sku'), primary_key=True),
    Column('name', Unicode(255)),
    Column('description', Unicode))
```

Note in particular the foreign key relationship between `product_table` and `product_summary_table`. This relationship *allows*, in SQL, many `product_summary_table` rows to exist for one `product_table` row. If left to its own devices, then, SQLAlchemy will assume that this is a 1:N join:

```
>>> mapper(ProductSummary, product_summary_table)
<sqlalchemy.orm.mapper.Mapper object at 0xeee150>
>>> mapper(Product, product_table, properties=dict(
...     summary=relation(ProductSummary)))
<sqlalchemy.orm.mapper.Mapper object at 0xef0410>
>>>
>>> prod = session.query(Product).get('123')
>>> print prod.summary
[]
```

To avoid this, we simply specify `uselist=False` to the `relation()` function:

```
>>> mapper(ProductSummary, product_summary_table)
<sqlalchemy.orm.mapper.Mapper object at 0xef5c90>
>>> mapper(Product, product_table, properties=dict(
...     summary=relation(ProductSummary, uselist=False)))
<sqlalchemy.orm.mapper.Mapper object at 0xef88d0>
>>>
>>> prod = session.query(Product).get('123')
```

```
>>> print prod.summary
None
```

Using BackRefs

In most cases, when mapping a relation between two tables, we want to create a property on *both* classes. We can certainly do this in SQLAlchemy by using two `relation()` calls, one for each mapper, but this is verbose and potentially leads to the two properties becoming out-of-sync with each other. To eliminate these problems, SQLAlchemy provides the `backref` parameter to the `relation()` function:

```
>>> mapper(ProductSummary, product_summary_table)
<sqlalchemy.orm.mapper.Mapper object at 0xfbba10>
>>> mapper(Product, product_table, properties=dict(
...     summary=relation(ProductSummary, uselist=False,
... backref='product')))
<sqlalchemy.orm.mapper.Mapper object at 0xee7dd0>
>>>
>>> prod = session.query(Product).get('123')
>>> prod.summary = ProductSummary(name="Fruit", description="Some
... Fruit")
>>> print prod.summary
<ProductSummary Fruit>
>>> print prod.summary.product
<Product 123>
>>> print prod.summary.product is prod
True
```

Note in particular that SQLAlchemy automatically updated the `backref` property. This is particularly useful in many-to-many (M:N) relations. For instance, to model an M:N relation, we could use the `relation()` function twice, but the two properties would not remain synchronized with each other. Note the *incorrect* behavior in the following example:

```
>>> mapper(Level, level_table, properties=dict(
...     categories=relation(Category, backref='level')))
<sqlalchemy.orm.mapper.Mapper object at 0x1044d90>
>>> mapper(Category, category_table, properties=dict(
...     products=relation(Product,
... secondary=product_category_table)))
<sqlalchemy.orm.mapper.Mapper object at 0x104a8d0>
>>> mapper(Product, product_table, properties=dict(
...     categories=relation(Category,
... secondary=product_category_table)))
<sqlalchemy.orm.mapper.Mapper object at 0x104aed0>
>>> lvl = Level(name='Department')
>>> cat = Category(name='Produce', level=lvl)
>>> session.save(lvl)
>>> prod = session.query(Product).get('123')
>>> print prod.categories
[]
>>> print cat.products
[]
```

```
>>> prod.categories.append(cat)
>>> print prod.categories
[<Category Department.Produce>]
>>> print cat.products
[]
```

If we declare a backref on the products property, however, the two lists *are* kept in sync:

```
>>> mapper(Level, level_table, properties=dict(
...     categories=relation(Category, backref='level')))
<sqlalchemy.orm.mapper.Mapper object at 0x107cf90>
>>> mapper(Category, category_table, properties=dict(
...     products=relation(Product, secondary=product_category_table,
... backref='categories')))
<sqlalchemy.orm.mapper.Mapper object at 0x107c350>
>>> mapper(Product, product_table)
<sqlalchemy.orm.mapper.Mapper object at 0x104f110>
>>> lvl = Level(name='Department')
>>> cat = Category(name='Produce', level=lvl)
>>> session.save(lvl)
>>> prod = session.query(Product).get('123')
>>> print prod.categories
[]
>>> print cat.products
[]
>>> prod.categories.append(cat)
>>> print prod.categories
[<Category Department.Produce>]
>>> print cat.products
[<Product 123>]
```

Rather than specifying just the backref's name, we can also use the SQLAlchemy-provided backref() function. This function allows us to pass along arguments to the relation that is created by the backref. For instance, if we wanted to declare the product property on the ProductSummary class rather than declaring the summary property on the Product class, we could use backref() with uselist=False as follows:

```
mapper(ProductSummary, product_summary_table, properties=dict(
    product=relation(Product,
                     backref=backref('summary', uselist=False))))
mapper(Product, product_table)
```

Using a Self-Referential Mapper

It is sometimes useful to have a relation() map from one object to another object of the same class. This is referred to as *self-referential* mapping. For instance, in our schema, each row of the level_table has a parent_id column referring to another level_table row:

```
level_table = Table(
    'level', metadata,
    Column('id', Integer, primary_key=True),
```

```
Column('parent_id', None, ForeignKey('level.id')),
Column('name', String(20)))
```

To specify the parent-child relationship between different levels, we can use the
`relation()` function with a little extra work. When there is a relation specified with a
self-referential foreign key constraint, SQLAlchemy assumes that the relation will be a
1·N relation. If we want to get only the "children" property working, then the mapper
setup is as simple as the following:

```
mapper(Level, level_table, properties=dict(
    children=relation(Level)))
```

However, we would also like to get the backref to the parent working as well. For this,
we need to specify the "remote side" of the backref. In the case of the "parent" attribute,
the "local side" is the `parent_id` column, and the "remote side" is the `id` column. To
specify the remote side of a relation (or backref), we use the `remote_side` parameter:

```
>>> mapper(Level, level_table, properties=dict(
...     children=relation(Level,
...                       backref=backref('parent',
...
... remote_side=[level_table.c.id]))))
<sqlalchemy.orm.mapper.Mapper object at 0x1050990>
>>>
>>> l0 = Level('Gender')
>>> l1 = Level('Department', parent=l0)
>>> session.save(l0)
>>> session.flush()
2007-10-19 10:23:53,861 INFO sqlalchemy.engine.base.Engine.0x..50
... INSERT INTO level (parent_id, name) VALUES (?, ?)
2007-10-19 10:23:53,862 INFO sqlalchemy.engine.base.Engine.0x..50
... [None, 'Gender']
2007-10-19 10:23:53,875 INFO sqlalchemy.engine.base.Engine.0x..50
... INSERT INTO level (parent_id, name) VALUES (?, ?)
2007-10-19 10:23:53,876 INFO sqlalchemy.engine.base.Engine.0x..50
... [1, 'Department']
```

We could, of course, specify the relation "in reverse" as well:

```
mapper(Level, level_table, properties=dict(
    parent=relation(Level, remote_side=[level_table.c.parent_id],
                    backref='children')))
```

Note that a list is used for the `remote_side` parameter to allow for compound foreign
keys in the relation.

Cascading Changes to Related Objects

It is often the case, particularly in 1:N relations, that you want to cascade the changes
on one object to another "child" object. For instance, in the previous schema, if we
delete a row from the `product_table`, we would also want to delete it from the
`product_summary_table`. In many cases, this can be handled natively by the database
using `ON DELETE CASCADE` in SQL or the `ondelete` parameter in the `Table()` definition.

In some cases, however, the underlying database may not support cascading deletes natively. For circumstances such as these, SQLAlchemy provides the `cascade` parameter to `relation()`s and `backref()`s.

The cascade parameter is specified as a string composed of a comma-separated list of keywords that specify which session operations should cascade onto the related objects. In the following list, the "parent" object is the one that has the relation as a property. The "child" object is the object that it is related to. For instance, in the following relation, the Region object is the "parent", and the related `Store` objects are the "children".

```
mapper(Region, region_table, properties=dict(
    stores=relation(Store)))
```

All of the cascade values in the following list refer to various functions that are performed by the `Session` object (covered in more detail in Chapter 7). The default value for the `cascade` parameter on a relation is `"save-update,merge"`.

`all`
> Specifies that all options should be enabled except `delete-orphan`:.

`delete`
> When the parent object is marked for deletion via `session.delete()`, mark the child(ren) as well.

`save-update`
> When the parent object is attached to the session, attach the child(ren) as well. (Attachment to a session generally happens by calling the `save()`, `update()`, or `save_or_update()` methods on the `Session` object.)

`refresh-expire`
> When the parent object is refreshed (reloaded from the database) or expired (marked as expired, to be refreshed if any properties are subsequently read), refresh or expire the child(ren) as well.

`merge`
> When the parent object is merged, then merge the child(ren) as well. Merging is the process of taking an object and copying its state onto a persistent instance of that object that is managed by the session.

`expunge`
> When the parent object is expunged from the session (removing all references to the object from the session, the opposite of `save_or_update()`), expunge the child(ren) as well.

`delete-orphan`
> When the child object is removed from the relation (by reassigning a 1:1 or N:1 relation or by removing it from the list in a 1:N or M:N relation), mark the child object for deletion. (This operation is referred to as "orphaning" the child object by removing its relation to its parent.)

Other relation( ) and backref( ) Parameters

The `relation(argument, secondary=None, **kwargs)` and `backref(name, **kwargs)` functions also take a number of other parameters, specified in the following list of arguments. `relation()` and `backref()` take the same keyword arguments.

`backref` (`relation( )` *only*)

Either the name of the property to be used for the reverse relationship, or an invocation of the `backref()` function to customize the backreference further.

`cascade`

String of comma-separated cascade values (for more detail, see the list of cascade values in the preceding section).

`collection_class`

The class or function used to build a list-holding object (used to store 1:N and M:N relations). See the section "Using custom collections in relations" for more detail.

`foreign_keys`

List of columns that are used as the "foreign keys" in the relation, if no actual foreign keys are present. Always used in conjunction with explicit `primaryjoin` and/or `secondaryjoin` parameters.

`join_depth=None`

When non-`None`, this limits the depth an eager-loading join will traverse with a self-referential mapper. The `join_depth` specifies the maximum number of times the same `mapper` can be present along a join branch before eager loading is stopped. The default value of `None` stops the traversal of an eager join when it encounters the first duplicate `mapper`.

`lazy=True`

Specifies how related items should be loaded. The options are:

`True` (*default*)

Load items when the property is first accessed.

`False`

Load the items eagerly when the parent is fetched, using a JOIN or LEFT OUTER JOIN.

`None`

SQLAlchemy will never automatically load the related items. This is used for write-only properties or properties that are populated in some other way.

`'dynamic'`

Returns a `Query` object when reading the property and supports writes only through the `append()` and `remove()` methods. This option allows partial results to be fetched lazily. This option is mainly used in backrefs. To use dynamic loading on a forward relation, use the `dynamic_loader()` function in place of `relation()`.

order_by

> List of ClauseElements specifying the ordering that should be applied when loading a 1:N or M:N relation.

passive_deletes=False

> When True, indicates that the database will automatically cascade deletes (either by deleting the child row or by setting its foreign key to NULL, whichever is appropriate). This prevents the default SQLAlchemy behavior of loading related objects from the database to either set them to deleted or to set their foreign key column to NULL.

post_update=False

> If True, this property will be handled by a separate statement whenever inserting, updating, or deleting the parent row. If False, SQLAlchemy will attempt to update the row along with all its relations in a single statement, something that is impossible to do when there is a cyclical set of foreign key relationships.
>
> Attempting to insert, update, or delete such a cyclical set will raise a "cyclical dependency" exception when flush()ing the session. Setting post_update to True on one of the relations in the cycle will "break" it and allow flushing to proceed.

primaryjoin

> The ClauseElement that specifies how to join the parent row to the child row (in a 1:N, N:1, or 1:1 relation) or the association table row (in an M:N relation). If not specified, SQLAlchemy will infer a relationship based on the foreign key relationships between the tables involved in the relation.

remote_side

> In a self-referential relationship, the column or columns that form the "remote side" (i.e., the "child side") of the relationship.

secondary

> In an M:N relationship, this argument specifies the join table used to create the relation. Note that, if you are using SQLAlchemy's ability to do M:N relationships, the join table should *only* be used to join the two tables together, not to store auxiliary properties. If you need to use the intermediate join table to store additional properties of the relation, you should use two 1:N relations instead.

secondaryjoin

> The ClauseElement that specifies how to join the association table row to the child row in an M:N relation. If not specified, SQLAlchemy will infer a relationship based on the foreign key relationships between the tables involved in the relation.

uselist=True

> If False, forces SQLAlchemy to use a scalar to represent a 1:N relationship (thus modeling a 1:1 relationship).

viewonly=False

> If True, tells SQLAlchemy that the relation is suitable only for read operations. This allows greater flexibility in the join conditions (normally, these must be fairly

straightforward in order for SQLAlchemy to determine how to persist the relation). Updates to a relation marked as `viewonly` will not have any effect on the flush process.

Using custom collections in relations

When you specify a `relation()` that implements a one-to-many or many-to-many join, SQLAlchemy uses a collection to implement the property on the mapped object. By default, this collection is a list. In order to implement appropriate `cascade` and `backref` behavior, however, SQLAlchemy must *instrument* the class, tracking additions and removals of objects to and from the collection. This happens via the `CollectionAdapter` class, which is used by SQLAlchemy to link the class that implements the collection with the attribute on the mapped object.

To complicate matters further, SQLAlchemy provides the `collection_class` parameter, which allows you to customize the implementation of list-like relationships. If you specify a `collection_class` value of the built-in types of `list`, `dict`, `set`, or any subclass of these types, SQLAlchemy will automatically apply the appropriate instrumentation to track changes. For instance, if we wish to use a set to track the changes to the `stores` attribute in a `Region`, we could simply write the following:

```
mapper(Region, region_table, properties=dict(
    stores=relation(Store, collection_class=set)))
```

In some cases, SQLAlchemy can even instrument custom collection classes that are *not* derived from Python's built-in collection types by inspecting the class definition and determining whether it is `list`-like, `set`-like, or `dict`-like. This inference is not perfect, however, so SQLAlchemy provides two methods to override it. The first is the `__emulates__` class attribute. If you supply a built-in type as the value for this attribute, SQLAlchemy will assume that your custom collection class is "like" the type you name. So, to implement a collection that is `set`-like but includes a `list`-like `append()` method, we could do the following:

```
class SetAndListLike(object):
    __emulates__ = set
    def __init__(self):
        self._c = set()
    def append(self, o):
        self._c.add(o)
    def remove(self, o):
        self._c.remove(o)
    def __iter__(self):
        return iter(self._c)
```

The second method for overriding the `collection_class` inference mechanism is by using the SQLAlchemy-provided collection decorators, which are available as attributes of the `collections` class in the *sqlalchemy.orm.collections* module. In the previous example, for instance, SQLAlchemy will correctly infer the usage of `remove()` and `__iter__()`, but because `append()` is not normally used in `set`-like objects, it will not be

instrumented. To force SQLAlchemy to instrument this method, we can use
`collection.appender`:

```
from sqlalchemy.orm.collections import collection

class SetAndListLike(object):
    __emulates__ = set
    def __init__(self):
        self._c = set()
    @collection.appender
    def append(self, o):
        self._c.add(o)
    def remove(self, o):
        self._c.remove(o)
    def __iter__(self):
        return iter(self._c)
```

The following decorators are available for manually instrumenting your custom collection class:

`appender(cls, fn)`

> This decorator marks the decorated function as a "collection appender." The decorated function should take one positional argument: the value to add to the collection.

`remover(cls, fn)`

> This decorator marks the decorated function as a "collection remover." The decorated function should take one positional argument: the value to remove from the collection.

`iterator(cls, fn)`

> This decorator marks the decorated function as a "collection iterator." The decorated function should take no arguments and return an iterator over all collection members.

`internally_instrumented(cls, fn)`

> This decorator prevents other decorators from being applied to the decorated function. This is useful to prevent "recognized" method names such as `append()` from being automatically decorated.

`on_link(cls, fn)`

> This decorator marks the decorated function as a "linked to attribute" event handler. This event handler is called when the collection class is linked to the `CollectionAdapter` that, in turn, is linked to the relation attribute. The decorated function should take one positional argument: the `CollectionAdapter` being linked (or `None` if the adapter is being unlinked). This might be useful if you wish to perform some setup on the mapped class or relation when your custom collection is initially linked.

`adds(cls, arg)`

This decorator factory is used to create decorators that function as "collection appenders." The one argument to the factory is an indicator of *which* parameter to the decorated function should be added to the collection. This argument may be specified as either an integer (representing the position number of a positional argument) or a string (indicating the name of the parameter).

`replaces(cls, arg)`

This decorator factory is used to create decorators that function as "collection replacers." The one argument to the factory is an indicator of *which* parameter to the decorated function should be added to the collection. This argument may be specified as either an integer (representing the position number of a positional argument) or a string (indicating the name of the parameter). The return value from the decorated function, if any, is used as the value to be removed from the function.

`removes(cls, arg)`

This decorator factory is used to create decorators that function as "collection removers." The one argument to the factory is an indicator of *which* parameter to the decorated function should be removed from the collection. This argument may be specified as either an integer (representing the position number of a positional argument) or a string (indicating the name of the parameter).

`removes_return(cls)`

This decorator factory is used to create decorators that function as "collection removers." The value that is returned from the decorated function is the value that SQLAlchemy will consider to be removed from the collection. This is useful for implementing a `list`-like `pop()` method, for instance.

One common use case is using a `dict` to represent a relation. This presents a problem over using `sets` and `lists`, however, as `dicts` require key values. The `sqlalchemy.orm.collections` module provides the following helpers for just this purpose:

`column_mapped_collection(mapping_spec)`

Return a collection class that will be keyed by the `mapping_spec`, which may be either a column from the related table, or a list of columns from the related table.

`attribute_mapped_collection(attr_name)`

Return a collection class that will be keyed by the `attr_name`, which is the name of an attribute on the related class.

`mapped_collection(keyfunc)`

Return a collection class that will be keyed by the value returned from the supplied `keyfunc` function. `keyfunc` takes as its single parameter the related object and returns a key value.

To use a dictionary that is keyed by the store name in our `Region` class, for instance, we could either use the column:

```
mapper(Region, region_table, properties=dict(
    stores=relation(Store,
collection_class=column_mapped_collection(store_table.c.name)))
```

or the attribute:

```
mapper(Region, region_table, properties=dict(
    stores=relation(Store,
collection_class=attribute_mapped_collection('name')))
```

If you wish to determine the key value to be used in some other way, you can also use the SQLAlchemy-supplied `MappedCollection` class as base class for your custom dict-like classes. `MappedCollection` takes a `keyfunc` parameter in its constructor just like the `mapped_collection()` function.

Extending Mappers

Although the mapper function—combined with the various property creation functions—is extremely powerful, it is sometimes useful to extend the functionality of a mapper. To that end, SQLAlchemy provides the `MapperExtension` class, which can be extended to provide mapper behavior modification via a series of hooks. Multiple `MapperExtension`s can be registered on a mapper, allowing a chain of responsibility for modifying the mapper behavior. `MapperExtension`s are registered either in the `mapper()` function call via the `extension` parameter, or by using an `extension()` argument to the `option()` method in queries (covered in Chapter 7).

Each hook should return either `orm.EXT_CONTINUE` or `orm.EXT_STOP`. (Any other value will be interpreted by SQLAlchemy as `orm.EXT_STOP`.) If `orm.EXT_CONTINUE` is returned, processing continues, either to the next `MapperExtension` or by the mapper itself. If `orm.EXT_STOP` is returned, then the mapper will not call any other extensions in the chain.

Some of the useful hooks in `MapperExtension` are described in the following list:

before_delete(self, mapper, connection, instance)
    Called with an object instance before that instance is deleted.

before_insert(self, mapper, connection, instance)
    Called with an object instance before that instance is inserted.

before_update(self, mapper, connection, instance)
    Called with an object instance before that instance is updated.

after_delete(self, mapper, connection, instance)
    Called with an object instance after that instance is deleted.

after_insert(self, mapper, connection, instance)
    Called with an object instance after that instance is inserted.

after_update(self, mapper, connection, instance)
    Called with an object instance after that instance is updated.

`append_result(self, mapper, selectcontext, row, instance, result, **flags)`

 Called just before an object instance is appended to a result list. Returning anything other than `EXT_CONTINUE` will prevent the instance from being appended to the result.

`create_instance(self, mapper, selectcontext, row, class_)`

 Called when a new object is about to be created from a row. If `None` is returned, normal object creation will take place. Any other value is presumed to be the object instance created by the `MapperExtension`.

`get(self, query, *args, **kwargs)`

 Overrides the `get()` method of the `Query` object if anything other than `EXT_CONTINUE` is returned.

`get_session(self)`

 Called to retrieve a `Session` instance with which to register a new object.

`load(self, query, *args, **kwargs)`

 Used to override the `load()` method of the `Query` object, if anything other than `EXT_CONTINUE` is returned.

`populate_instance(self, mapper, selectcontext, row, instance, **flags)`

 Called when a new object is about to have its attributes populated. If `EXT_CONTINUE` is returned, normal attribute population will take place. Any other value will prevent attribute population by SQLAlchemy.

`translate_row(self, mapper, context, row)`

 Called before rows are converted to instances, allowing the row to be transformed. The new row (or the original, unmodified row) must be returned from this method.

`instrument_class(self, mapper, class_)`

 Called at class instrumentation time.

`init_instance(self, mapper, class_, oldinit, instance, args, kwargs)`

 Called when initializing an instance (as part of the constructor call).

`init_failed(self, mapper, class_, oldinit, instance, args, kwargs)`

 Called when instance initialization fails (when the constructor raises an unhandled exception).

ORM Partitioning Strategies

Sometimes you want to use the ORM to map objects that may exist in multiple databases. SQLAlchemy provides support for "vertical" partitioning (placing different kinds of objects or different tables in different databases) as well as "horizontal" partitioning, also called "sharding" (partitioning the rows of a single table across multiple databases).

Vertical Partitioning

In vertical partitioning, different mapped classes are retrieved from different database servers. In the following example, we create product_table in one in-memory sqlite database and product_summary_table in another:

```
engine1 = create_engine('sqlite://')
engine2 = create_engine('sqlite://')

metadata = MetaData()

product_table = Table(
    'product', metadata,
    Column('sku', String(20), primary_key=True),
    Column('msrp', Numeric))
product_summary_table = Table(
    'product_summary', metadata,
Column('sku', None, ForeignKey('product.sku'), primary_key=True),
    Column('name', Unicode(255)),
    Column('description', Unicode))

product_table.create(bind=engine1)
product_summary_table.create(bind=engine2)

stmt = product_table.insert()
engine1.execute(
    stmt,
    [dict(sku="123", msrp=12.34),
     dict(sku="456", msrp=22.12),
     dict(sku="789", msrp=41.44)])
stmt = product_summary_table.insert()
engine2.execute(
    stmt,
    [dict(sku="123", name="Shoes", description="Some Shoes"),
     dict(sku="456", name="Pants", description="Some Pants"),
     dict(sku="789", name="Shirts", description="Some Shirts")])
```

Now, we can create and map the Product and ProductSummary classes:

```
class Product(object):
    def __init__(self, sku, msrp, summary=None):
        self.sku = sku
        self.msrp = msrp
        self.summary = summary
    def __repr__(self):
        return '<Product %s>' % self.sku

class ProductSummary(object):
    def __init__(self, name, description):
        self.name = name
        self.description = description
    def __repr__(self):
        return '<ProductSummary %s>' % self.name

clear_mappers()
```

```
mapper(ProductSummary, product_summary_table, properties=dict(
    product=relation(Product,
                     backref=backref('summary', uselist=False))))
mapper(Product, product_table)
```

Finally, we configure the session to load the `Product` class from `engine1` and `ProductSummary` from `engine2`:

```
>>> Session = sessionmaker(binds={Product:engine1,
...                               ProductSummary:engine2})
>>> session = Session()
>>> engine1.echo = engine2.echo = True
>>> session.query(Product).all()
2007-11-17 14:32:20,890 INFO sqlalchemy.engine.base.Engine.0x..90
... BEGIN
2007-11-17 14:32:20,895 INFO sqlalchemy.engine.base.Engine.0x..90
... SELECT product.sku AS product_sku, product.msrp AS product_msrp
FROM product ORDER BY product.oid
2007-11-17 14:32:20,895 INFO sqlalchemy.engine.base.Engine.0x..90 []
[<Product 123>, <Product 456>, <Product 789>]
>>> session.query(ProductSummary).all()
2007-11-17 14:32:20,900 INFO sqlalchemy.engine.base.Engine.0x..10
... BEGIN
2007-11-17 14:32:20,901 INFO sqlalchemy.engine.base.Engine.0x..10
... SELECT product_summary.sku AS product_summary_sku,
... product_summary.name AS product_summary_name,
... product_summary.description AS product_summary_description
FROM product_summary ORDER BY product_summary.oid
2007-11-17 14:32:20,902 INFO sqlalchemy.engine.base.Engine.0x..10 []
[<ProductSummary Shoes>, <ProductSummary Pants>, <ProductSummary
... Shirts>]
```

Note that the appropriate engine is invoked depending on which class is being queried, completely transparently to the user.

Horizontal Partitioning

In horizontal partitioning, or "sharding," the database schema (or part of it) is replicated across multiple databases ("shards"). This essentially means that some rows of a mapped table will be loaded from one database and some from another. To use sharding, you must provide functions that identify which database to access in various situations. These arguments are passed to the `sessionmaker()` function, along with a `class_` parameter specifying that we will be creating a `ShardedSession`:

```
Session = sessionmaker(class_=ShardedSession)
```

The first function that must be provided is the `shard_chooser(mapper, instance, clause=None)` function. This function is responsible for returning a "shard ID" that should contain the row for the given mapper and instance. The ID may be based off of the instance's properties, or it may simply be the result of a round-robin selection scheme. If it is *not* based on attributes of the instance, the `shard_chooser()` should modify the instance in some way to mark it as participating in the returned shard.

The next function that must be provided is the id_chooser(query, ident) function. This function, when presented with a query and a tuple of identity values (the primary key of the mapped class), should return a list of shard IDs where the objects sought by the query might reside. In a round-robin implementation, all of the shard IDs might be returned. In other implementations, the shard ID might be inferred from the ident parameter.

The final function that must be provided when using sharding is the query_chooser(query) function, which should return a list of shard IDs where results for a given query might be found. Note that both id_chooser() and query_chooser() may simply return a list of all the shard IDs, in which case each shard will be searched for the results of the query.

In the following example, we will create a sharded implementation of the product database where products are stored according to the first digit of their SKU. If the first digit is even, the products are stored in engine1; otherwise they are stored in engine2. All other types of objects will be stored in engine2:

```
engine1 = create_engine('sqlite://')
engine2 = create_engine('sqlite://')

metadata = MetaData()

product_table = Table(
    'product', metadata,
    Column('sku', String(20), primary_key=True),
    Column('msrp', Numeric))
metadata.create_all(bind=engine1)
metadata.create_all(bind=engine2)

class Product(object):
    def __init__(self, sku, msrp):
        self.sku = sku
        self.msrp = msrp
    def __repr__(self):
        return '<Product %s>' % self.sku

clear_mappers()
product_mapper = mapper(Product, product_table)

def shard_chooser(mapper, instance, clause=None):
    if mapper is not product_mapper:
        return 'odd'
    if (instance.sku
        and instance.sku[0].isdigit()
        and int(instance.sku[0]) % 2 == 0):
        return 'even'
    else:
        return 'odd'

def id_chooser(query, ident):
    if query.mapper is not product_mapper:
        return ['odd']
```

```
    if (ident \
        and ident[0].isdigit()
        and int(ident[0]) % 2 == 0):
        return ['even']
    return ['odd']

def query_chooser(query):
    return ['even', 'odd']

Session = sessionmaker(class_=ShardedSession)
session = Session(
    shard_chooser=shard_chooser,
    id_chooser=id_chooser,
    query_chooser=query_chooser,
    shards=dict(even=engine1,
                odd=engine2))
```

Now we can create some products, save them to the database, observe their partitioning using the SQL layer, and observe that the session's `Query` object is able to correctly merge results from both databases:

```
>>> products = [ Product('%d%d%d' % (i,i,i), 0.0)
...                 for i in range(10) ]
>>> for p in products:
...     session.save(p)
...
>>> session.flush()
>>>
>>> for row in engine1.execute(product_table.select()):
...     print row
...
(u'000', Decimal("0"))
(u'222', Decimal("0"))
(u'444', Decimal("0"))
(u'666', Decimal("0"))
(u'888', Decimal("0"))
>>> for row in engine2.execute(product_table.select()):
...     print row
...
(u'111', Decimal("0"))
(u'333', Decimal("0"))
(u'555', Decimal("0"))
(u'777', Decimal("0"))
(u'999', Decimal("0"))
>>> for row in engine1.execute(product_table.select()):
...     print row
...
>>> for row in engine2.execute(product_table.select()):
...     print row
...
>>> session.query(Product).all()
[<Product 000>, <Product 222>, <Product 444>, <Product 666>,
... <Product 888>, <Product 111>, <Product 333>, <Product 555>,
... <Product 777>, <Product 999>]
```

## CHAPTER 7

Querying and Updating at the ORM Level

This chapter introduces the SQLAlchemy `Session` object. You will learn how to use the `Session` to perform queries and updates of mapped classes, as well as how to customize the `Session` class and create a "contextual" session that simplifies session management.

The SQLAlchemy ORM Session Object

SQLAlchemy manages all querying and updating of objects in the ORM with `Session` objects. The `Session` is responsible for implementing the unit of work pattern of synchronization between in-memory objects and database tables. Sessions also provide a rich interface for querying the database based on object attributes rather than the underlying SQL database structure.

Creating a Session

The first step in creating a session is to obtain a `Session` object from SQLAlchemy. One way to do this is to directly instantiate the `sqlalchemy.orm.session.Session` class. However, this constructor for the SQLAlchemy-provided `Session` has a number of keyword arguments, making instantiating `Session`s in this manner verbose and tedious. In order to alleviate this burden, SQLAlchemy provides the `sessionmaker()` function, which returns a subclass of `orm.session.Session` with default arguments set for its constructor.

Once you have this customized `Session` class, you can instantiate it as many times as necessary in your application without needing to retype the keyword arguments (which in many applications will not change between `Session` instantiations). If you wish to override the defaults supplied to `sessionmaker`, you can do so at `Session` instantiation time. You can also modify the default arguments bound to a particular `Session` subclass by calling the class method `Session.configure()`:

```
# Create a Session class with the default
#    options
Session = sessionmaker(bind=engine)

# Create an unbound Session class
Session = sessionmaker()

# Bind the Session class once the engine
#    is available
Session.configure(bind=engine)
```

The sessionmaker() and the associated Session subclass's configure class method and constructor take the following keyword arguments:

bind=None

> The database Engine or Connection to which to bind the session.

binds=None

> Optional dictionary that provides more detailed binding information. The keys to this dictionary can be mapped classes, mapper() instances, or Tables. The values in the dictionary indicate which Engine or Connectable to use for a given mapped class, overriding the values set in the bind parameter.

autoflush=True

> When True, the Session will automatically be flush()ed before executing any queries against the session. This ensures that the results returned from the query match the operations that have been done in-memory in the unit-of-work.

transactional=False

> When True, the Session will automatically use transactions. To commit a set of changes, simply use the Session's commit() method. To revert changes, use the rollback() method. Using transactional=True, it is never necessary to explicitly begin() a transaction on a Session. It is, however, necessary to explicitly call commit() at the end of your transaction.

twophase=False

> This tells SQLAlchemy to use two-phase commits on all transactions (on databases that support two-phase commits, currently MySQL and PostgreSQL, soon to include Oracle), which is useful when dealing with multiple database instances. In this case, after flush()ing changes to all databases but before issuing a COMMIT, SQLAlchemy issues a PREPARE to each database, allowing the entire transaction to be rolled back if an error is raised during any of the PREPARE executions.

echo_uow=False

> When True, instructs the Session to log all unit-of-work operations. This is the equivalent of setting a log level of logging.DEBUG for the 'sqlalchemy.orm.unitofwork' logger.

extension=None

> Optional `SessionExtension` that receives various session events, similar to the `MapperExtension`. (`SessionExtensions` are covered in more detail later in this chapter in "Extending Sessions.")

weak_identity_map=True

> The default value uses weak references in the identity map maintained by the session, allowing objects that are a) no longer referenced outside the session and b) have no pending changes to be automatically garbage-collected. If this is set to `False`, then a regular Python `dict` is used, and objects will remain in the `Session`'s identity map until they are explicitly removed using the `Session` methods `expunge()`, `clear()`, or `purge()`.

Saving Objects to the Session

Once you have a `Session` instance, you can begin persisting in-memory objects. This is accomplished quite simply by calling the **save()** method on the `Session` object. Suppose we have the following schema and mapping:

```
from sqlalchemy import *
from sqlalchemy.orm import *

engine = create_engine('sqlite://')
metadata = MetaData(engine)

product_table = Table(
    'product', metadata,
    Column('sku', String(20), primary_key=True),
    Column('msrp', Numeric))

class Product(object):
    def __init__(self, sku, msrp, summary=None):
        self.sku = sku
        self.msrp = msrp
        self.summary = summary
        self.categories = []
        self.prices = []
    def __repr__(self):
        return '<Product %s>' % self.sku

mapper(Product, product_table)
```

To save two products to the database, we can do the following. Note that the `echo_uow` property on the session as well as the `echo` property on the `Engine` are `True` in order to display exactly what SQLAlchemy is doing in response to our **flush()** call:

```
>>> Session = sessionmaker(bind=engine, echo_uow=True)
>>> engine.echo = True
>>> session = Session()
>>>
>>> p1 = Product('123', 11.22)
>>> p2 = Product('456', 33.44)
```

```
>>> session.save(p1)
>>> session.save(p2)
>>> session.flush()
2007-10-28 16:55:05,117 INFO
... sqlalchemy.orm.unitofwork.UOWTransaction.0x..90 Task dump:

UOWTask(0xb4e7d0, Product/product/None) (save/update phase)
   |- Save Product@0xb4e750
   |- Save Product@0xb4e690
   |----


2007-10-28 16:55:05,118 INFO sqlalchemy.engine.base.Engine.0x..90
... BEGIN
2007-10-28 16:55:05,119 INFO sqlalchemy.engine.base.Engine.0x..90
... INSERT INTO product (sku, msrp) VALUES (?, ?)
2007-10-28 16:55:05,119 INFO sqlalchemy.engine.base.Engine.0x..90
... ['123', '11.22']
2007-10-28 16:55:05,120 INFO sqlalchemy.engine.base.Engine.0x..90
... INSERT INTO product (sku, msrp) VALUES (?, ?)
2007-10-28 16:55:05,120 INFO sqlalchemy.engine.base.Engine.0x..90
... ['456', '33.44']
2007-10-28 16:55:05,121 INFO
... sqlalchemy.orm.unitofwork.UOWTransaction.0x..90 Execute Complete
```

Object States with a Session

Objects can have various states as they relate to `Session`s. These states are defined as follows:

Transient
> The object exists in memory only. It is not attached to a session, and it has no representation in the database. A *Transient* object has no relationship to the ORM other than the fact that its class has an associated `mapper()`.

Pending
> A *Pending* object has been marked for insertion into the database at the next `flush()` operation. *Transient* objects become *Pending* when they are `save()`d to the `Session`.

Persistent
> The object is present in both the session and the database. *Persistent* objects are created either by `flush()`ing *Pending* objects or by querying the database for existing instances.

Detached
> The object has a corresponding record in the database, but is not attached to any session. *Detached* objects cannot issue any SQL automatically to load related objects or attributes, unlike *Persistent* objects. An object becomes detached if it is explicitly `expunge()`d from the session.

We can actually save large graphs of objects to the database by using the default cascade value `'save-update'` on our `relation()` objects. For instance, consider the additional schema and mapping:

```python
level_table = Table(
    'level', metadata,
    Column('id', Integer, primary_key=True),
    Column('parent_id', None, ForeignKey('level.id')),
    Column('name', String(20)))

category_table = Table(
    'category', metadata,
    Column('id', Integer, primary_key=True),
    Column('level_id', None, ForeignKey('level.id')),
    Column('parent_id', None, ForeignKey('category.id')),
    Column('name', String(20)))

product_category_table = Table(
    'product_category', metadata,
Column('product_id', None, ForeignKey('product.sku'),
... primary_key=True),
Column('category_id', None, ForeignKey('category.id'),
... primary_key=True))

class Product(object):
    def __init__(self, sku, msrp, summary=None):
        self.sku = sku
        self.msrp = msrp
        self.summary = summary
        self.categories = []
        self.prices = []
    def __repr__(self):
        return '<Product %s>' % self.sku

class Level(object):
    def __init__(self, name, parent=None):
        self.name = name
        self.parent = parent
    def __repr__(self):
        return '<Level %s>' % self.name

class Category(object):
    def __init__(self, name, level, parent=None):
        self.name = name
        self.level = level
        self.parent = parent
    def __repr__(self):
        return '<Category %s.%s>' % (self.level.name, self.name)

# Clear the mappers so we can re-map the Product class
#     with an additional property
clear_mappers()

mapper(Product, product_table, properties=dict(
    categories=relation(Category, secondary=product_category_table,
```

```
                        backref='products')))

    mapper(Level, level_table, properties=dict(
        children=relation(Level, backref='parent'),
        categories=relation(Category, backref='level')))

    mapper(Category, category_table, properties=dict(
        children=relation(Category, backref='parent')))
```

Now we can create a product hierarchy and assign some categories *just as if there were no database*, and the `Session` will infer the appropriate operations to persist the entire data model:

```
>>> department = Level('Department')
>>> tops = Category('Tops', level=department)
>>> bottoms = Category('Bottoms', level=department)
>>>
>>> class_ = Level('Class', parent=department)
>>> shirts = Category('Shirts', level=class_, parent=tops)
>>> pants = Category('Pants', level=class_, parent=bottoms)
>>>
>>> subclass = Level('SubClass', parent=class_)
>>> tshirts = Category('T-Shirts', level=subclass, parent=shirts)
>>> dress_shirts = Category('Dress Shirts', level=subclass,
... parent=shirts)
>>> slacks = Category('Slacks', level=subclass, parent=pants)
>>> denim = Category('Denim', level=subclass, parent=pants)
>>>
>>> # Create two more products
... p3 = Product('111', 55.95)
>>> p4 = Product('222', 15.95)
>>> p3.categories=[denim, pants, bottoms]
>>> p4.categories=[tshirts, shirts, tops]
```

Now that we have created all the objects and specified the relations between them, we can save *one* object to the `Session`, and all related objects will be saved as well (this is due to the default `'save-update'` value of the `cascade` parameter in all the `relations()` created). In this example, the `department` object is connected to all the other objects through various `relation()`s, so it is sufficient to save it alone. Once this is done, we can flush the changes out to the database. For the purposes of brevity, we will use a fresh session with `echo_uow` set to `False`:

```
>>> session = Session(echo_uow=False)
>>> session.save(department)
>>> session.flush()
2007-10-28 18:41:10,042 INFO sqlalchemy.engine.base.Engine.0x..90
... BEGIN
2007-10-28 18:41:10,043 INFO sqlalchemy.engine.base.Engine.0x..90
... INSERT INTO product (sku, msrp) VALUES (?, ?)
2007-10-28 18:41:10,043 INFO sqlalchemy.engine.base.Engine.0x..90
... ['111', '55.95']
2007-10-28 18:41:10,045 INFO sqlalchemy.engine.base.Engine.0x..90
... INSERT INTO product (sku, msrp) VALUES (?, ?)
2007-10-28 18:41:10,045 INFO sqlalchemy.engine.base.Engine.0x..90
```

```
... ['222', '15.95']
2007-10-28 18:41:10,047 INFO sqlalchemy.engine.base.Engine.0x..90
... INSERT INTO level (parent_id, name) VALUES (?, ?)
2007-10-28 18:41:10,047 INFO sqlalchemy.engine.base.Engine.0x..90
... [None, 'Department']
2007-10-28 18:41:10,049 INFO sqlalchemy.engine.base.Engine.0x..90
... INSERT INTO level (parent_id, name) VALUES (?, ?)
2007-10-28 18:41:10,049 INFO sqlalchemy.engine.base.Engine.0x..90
... [1, 'Class']
2007-10-28 18:41:10,053 INFO sqlalchemy.engine.base.Engine.0x..90
... INSERT INTO level (parent_id, name) VALUES (?, ?)
2007-10-28 18:41:10,053 INFO sqlalchemy.engine.base.Engine.0x..90
... [2, 'SubClass']
2007-10-28 18:41:10,057 INFO sqlalchemy.engine.base.Engine.0x..90
... INSERT INTO category (level_id, parent_id, name) VALUES (?, ?,
... ?)
2007-10-28 18:41:10,057 INFO sqlalchemy.engine.base.Engine.0x..90
... [1, None, 'Bottoms']
2007-10-28 18:41:10,059 INFO sqlalchemy.engine.base.Engine.0x..90
... INSERT INTO category (level_id, parent_id, name) VALUES (?, ?,
... ?)
2007-10-28 18:41:10,059 INFO sqlalchemy.engine.base.Engine.0x..90
... [1, None, 'Tops']
2007-10-28 18:41:10,060 INFO sqlalchemy.engine.base.Engine.0x..90
... INSERT INTO category (level_id, parent_id, name) VALUES (?, ?,
... ?)
2007-10-28 18:41:10,060 INFO sqlalchemy.engine.base.Engine.0x..90
... [2, 1, 'Pants']
2007-10-28 18:41:10,062 INFO sqlalchemy.engine.base.Engine.0x..90
... INSERT INTO category (level_id, parent_id, name) VALUES (?, ?,
... ?)
2007-10-28 18:41:10,063 INFO sqlalchemy.engine.base.Engine.0x..90
... [2, 2, 'Shirts']
2007-10-28 18:41:10,065 INFO sqlalchemy.engine.base.Engine.0x..90
... INSERT INTO category (level_id, parent_id, name) VALUES (?, ?,
... ?)
2007-10-28 18:41:10,065 INFO sqlalchemy.engine.base.Engine.0x..90
... [3, 4, 'T-Shirts']
2007-10-28 18:41:10,066 INFO sqlalchemy.engine.base.Engine.0x..90
... INSERT INTO category (level_id, parent_id, name) VALUES (?, ?,
... ?)
2007-10-28 18:41:10,066 INFO sqlalchemy.engine.base.Engine.0x..90
... [3, 4, 'Dress Shirts']
2007-10-28 18:41:10,068 INFO sqlalchemy.engine.base.Engine.0x..90
... INSERT INTO category (level_id, parent_id, name) VALUES (?, ?,
... ?)
2007-10-28 18:41:10,068 INFO sqlalchemy.engine.base.Engine.0x..90
... [3, 3, 'Slacks']
2007-10-28 18:41:10,069 INFO sqlalchemy.engine.base.Engine.0x..90
... INSERT INTO category (level_id, parent_id, name) VALUES (?, ?,
... ?)
2007-10-28 18:41:10,070 INFO sqlalchemy.engine.base.Engine.0x..90
... [3, 3, 'Denim']
2007-10-28 18:41:10,071 INFO sqlalchemy.engine.base.Engine.0x..90
... INSERT INTO product_category (product_id, category_id) VALUES
```

```
... (?, ?)
2007-10-28 18:41:10,072 INFO sqlalchemy.engine.base.Engine.0x..90
... [['222', 2], ['111', 1], ['111', 8], ['222', 4], ['111', 3],
... ['222', 5]]
```

Updating Objects in the Session

If we wish to update *Persistent* or *Pending* objects, we can simply modify them in-memory and rely on the `Session` to figure out the changes required in the database. This even works for related objects. For instance, if we decide to recategorize the product with sku "111", we would simply update the list of categories:

```
>>> p3.categories = [ slacks, pants, bottoms ]
2007-10-28 18:48:31,534 INFO sqlalchemy.engine.base.Engine.0x..90
... SELECT product.sku AS product_sku, product.msrp AS product_msrp
FROM product, product_category
WHERE ? = product_category.category_id AND product.sku =
... product_category.product_id ORDER BY product_category.oid
2007-10-28 18:48:31,534 INFO sqlalchemy.engine.base.Engine.0x..90
... [7]
>>> session.flush()
2007-10-28 18:48:31,554 INFO sqlalchemy.engine.base.Engine.0x..90
... DELETE FROM product_category WHERE product_category.product_id =
... ? AND product_category.category_id = ?
2007-10-28 18:48:31,555 INFO sqlalchemy.engine.base.Engine.0x..90
... ['111', 8]
2007-10-28 18:48:31,558 INFO sqlalchemy.engine.base.Engine.0x..90
... INSERT INTO product_category (product_id, category_id) VALUES
... (?, ?)
2007-10-28 18:48:31,558 INFO sqlalchemy.engine.base.Engine.0x..90
... ['111', 7]
```

Note in particular that SQLAlchemy has inferred the minimum change necessary to update the relationship. Also note that SQLAlchemy allowed us to assign a normal Python list for a `relation()`-type property. This is in contrast to some other ORMs, which require you to use specialized add/remove functions to change object relationships. One caveat with SQLAlchemy is that you are still required to only use the `remove()` and `append()` list when using dynamic relation loaders (declared with `dynamic_loader()` or `lazy='dynamic'`). This is due to the fact that SQLAlchemy never implicitly loads the entire list of related objects into memory and so cannot deduce how to update the database if you use other methods of modifying the property.

Embedding SQL expressions in a flush

One feature that can be particularly useful in performing atomic updates to an object is the ability to assign an SQL expression (from the SQL expression language) to a mapped property on an object. For instance, consider a banking application where there is a need to deduct a certain amount from the balance. In many cases, it is unsafe and inefficient to SELECT the balance and then UPDATE it to the previous balance minus some amount. It would be better to simply deduct the amount atomically in one UPDATE statement. So, if we have the following (partial) schema and mapping:

```
account_table = Table(
    'account', metadata,
    Column('id', Integer, primary_key=True),
    Column('balance', Numeric))

class Account(object): pass

mapper(Account, account_table)
```

we could deduct a certain amount from an account balance atomically by doing something like the following:

```
>>> # Create the table for testing purposes
>>> account_table.create()
2007-10-28 19:21:29,498 INFO sqlalchemy.engine.base.Engine.0x..90
CREATE TABLE account (
        id INTEGER NOT NULL,
        balance NUMERIC(10, 2),
        PRIMARY KEY (id)
)


2007-10-28 19:21:29,498 INFO sqlalchemy.engine.base.Engine.0x..90 {}
2007-10-28 19:21:29,498 INFO sqlalchemy.engine.base.Engine.0x..90
... COMMIT
>>> # Create an account for testing purposes
>>> a = Account()
>>> a.balance = 100.00
>>> session.save(a)
>>> session.flush()
2007-10-28 19:21:29,581 INFO sqlalchemy.engine.base.Engine.0x..90
... INSERT INTO account (balance) VALUES (?)
2007-10-28 19:21:29,582 INFO sqlalchemy.engine.base.Engine.0x..90
... ['100.0']
>>>
>>> a.balance = Account.c.balance - 50.0
>>> session.flush()
2007-10-28 19:21:29,700 INFO sqlalchemy.engine.base.Engine.0x..90
... UPDATE account SET balance=(account.balance - ?) WHERE
... account.id = ?
2007-10-28 19:21:29,700 INFO sqlalchemy.engine.base.Engine.0x..90
... ['50.0', 1]
```

Deleting Objects from the Session

To delete an object from the session, simply use the Session's delete() method:

```
>>> session.delete(p3)
>>> session.flush()
2007-10-28 18:58:51,150 INFO sqlalchemy.engine.base.Engine.0x..90
... DELETE FROM product_category WHERE product_category.product_id =
... ? AND product_category.category_id = ?
```

```
2007-10-28 18:58:51,150 INFO sqlalchemy.engine.base.Engine.0x..90
... [['111', 1], ['111', 3], ['111', 7]]
2007-10-28 18:58:51,152 INFO sqlalchemy.engine.base.Engine.0x..90
... DELETE FROM product WHERE product.sku = ?
2007-10-28 18:58:51,153 INFO sqlalchemy.engine.base.Engine.0x..90
... ['111']
```

Notice that SQLAlchemy automatically removed the corresponding entries in the `product_category_table`. This is because we declared that to be the **secondary** parameter of a many-to-many `relation()`. This is a special feature of M:N relations. In 1:N relations, unless you tell SQLAlchemy how to cascade a delete on the parent object, it will not assume that the delete should be cascaded. To cascade `delete()`s onto the child objects, simply specify `cascade='delete'` (or `'all'`) in the `relation()` function call.

Flushing, Committing, and Rolling Back Session Changes

We have already seen the basic usage of the `flush()` Session method. `flush()` can also take an optional parameter `objects`, which specifies a list of objects to be flushed. If this is omitted, all modified objects are flushed.

SQLAlchemy also provides support for managing transactions on a `Session` basis via the `begin()`, `commit()`, and `rollback()` methods, and via the `transactional=True` parameter to the `Session` constructor. `begin()` begins a transaction, `commit()` commits it, and `rollback()` rolls back to the state of the database at the last `begin()`.

Specifying `transactional=True` lets SQLAlchemy know that all operations on this `Session` are intended to be in the context of a transaction, and so there is no need to issue an explicit `begin()`. SQLAlchemy also supports the use of SAVEPOINTs on supported databases (currently MySQL and PostgreSQL, soon to include Oracle) via the `begin_nested()` method. In this case, the `commit()` and `rollback()` methods apply only to the last "nested" transaction, so you can roll back "part" of a transaction.

Other Session Methods

Sessions have several utilities other than `save()` and `delete()` for dealing with objects that they manage. These methods, as well as `save()`, `delete()`, and a few query-related methods (covered in detail later in this chapter, in "Querying at the ORM Level"), are documented here:

`save(self, obj, entity=None)`
> Save the given object to the session. This operation cascades to related objects according to the `'save-update'` cascade rule.
>
> If an `entity` name is specified, then use the named nonprimary `mapper()` to persist the object.

`delete(self, obj)`
> Mark the given object for deletion at the next `flush()`.

`expire(self, obj)`

Mark the given object as no longer up-to-date. This causes any mapped attributes to be refetched from the database the next time they are accessed. This operation cascades to related objects according to the `'refresh-expire'` cascade rule.

`refresh(self, obj)`

Reload the object from the database with a fresh query. This operation cascades to related objects according to the `'refresh-expire'` cascade rule.

`merge(self, obj, entity=None )`

Copy the state of the given object onto a persistent object with the same database identity. This will either load an existing *Persistent* instance from the database, modify one in memory, or save a copy of the given `obj`. In none of these cases does the object passed in become associated with the `Session`. This operation cascades to related objects according to the `'merge'` cascade rule.

If an `entity` name is specified, then use the named nonprimary `mapper()` to load or save the *Persistent* object.

`expunge(self, obj)`

Remove all references to `obj` from the `Session`. This operation cascades to related objects according to the `'expunge'` cascade rule.

`update(self, obj, entity=None)`

Bring a given *Detached* `obj` into this session. This operation cascades to related objects according to the `'save-or-update'` cascade rule.

If an `entity` name is specified, then use the named nonprimary `mapper()` to load or save the *Detached* object.

`get(self, class_, ident, **kwargs)`

Return a *Persistent* instance of the object with the given `class_` and `identifier`. (An object identifier is either the primary key value if there is only one primary key in the underlying table, or a tuple of primary keys in the case of a composite primary key.) If an `entity_name` is specified as part of `kwargs`, then use the named nonprimary mapper to map the class. The other `kwargs` are passed unchanged to the underlying `query()` used to retrieve the object.

`load(self, class_, ident, **kwargs)`

This is the same as the `get()` method with one exception: if the object was already in the `Session`, the session will overwrite any pending changes with fresh values from the database.

`query(self, mapper_or_class, *addtl_entities, **kwargs)`

Return a new `Query` object corresponding to this `Session` and the given `mapper_or_class`.

`close(self)`

Clear the session and end any transactions in progress. This restores the `Session` object to a "pristine" state, exactly the same as when it was initially instantiated.

`execute(self, clause, params=None, mapper=None, **kwargs)`
> This method is a thin wrapper around the underlying engine or connection's `execute()` method. (The `clause`, `params`, and `kwargs` parameters are passed through unmodified, for instance.) It is useful for executing SQL-level queries and updates within the same transactional environment as your ORM queries and updates. If the `mapper` parameter is specified, that mapper is used to determine the engine on which to execute the query.

`identity_map`
> The identity mapping between (`class,identity`) tuples and objects in the session. Note that *Persistent* objects have an `_instance_key` attribute attached to them, which is their `Session` identity.

`new`
> A collection of all *Pending* objects added to the `Session` since the last `flush()`.

`dirty`
> A collection of all *Persistent* objects that have changes detected.

`deleted`
> A collection of all *Persistent* objects that have been marked for deletion via the `Session delete()` method.

Extending Sessions

Similar to the `MapperExtension` covered in Chapter 6, `SessionExtension`s can be used to hook into session operations. Unlike `MapperExtension`s, `SessionExtension`s cannot modify the process that they "hook into" easily, making `SessionExtension`s more useful for recording `Session` operations than influencing them directly. `SessionExtension`s are installed via the `extension` parameter to the `Session` constructor.

The various methods that a subclass of `SessionExtension` can implement are described here:

`before_commit(self, session)`
> Called just before a commit is executed.

`after_commit(self, session)`
> Called just after a commit is executed.

`after_rollback(self, session)`
> Called just after a rollback has occurred.

`before_flush(self, session, flush_context, objects)`
> Called just before the flush process starts. The `objects` parameter is the optional list of objects passed to the `Session`'s `flush()` method.

`after_flush(self, session, flush_context)`
> Called just after the flush process completes, but before any `commit()`. The session's properties at this point still show their pre-flush state.

```
after_flush_postexec(self, session, flush_context)
```
Called just after the flush process completes, as well as after any automatic
`commit()` occurs. (If no explicit transaction is specified, all `flush()`es generate their
own transactions.) The `session`'s properties at this point show their final, post-
flush state.

Querying at the ORM Level

Saving and updating objects via SQLAlchemy's ORM interface isn't very useful without
the ability to retrieve objects from the database. This is where the `Session`'s `query()`
method comes in handy. To retrieve an iterator over all the objects of a particular type
in the database, simply specify either the class you wish to query or its mapper:

```
>>> query = session.query(Product)
>>> print query
SELECT product.sku AS product_sku, product.msrp AS product_msrp
FROM product ORDER BY product.oid
>>> for obj in query:
...     print obj
...
2007-11-16 16:19:42,669 INFO sqlalchemy.engine.base.Engine.0x..90
... SELECT product.sku AS product_sku, product.msrp AS product_msrp
FROM product ORDER BY product.oid
2007-11-16 16:19:42,669 INFO sqlalchemy.engine.base.Engine.0x..90 []
<Product 123>
<Product 456>
<Product 222>
```

Notice here that the query is *generative*, as were the SQL-layer queries mentioned in
Chapter 5. This means that SQLAlchemy will not actually execute the query on the
database until the results are iterated over. You can also retrieve all the results as a list
by calling the `all()` method on the query object:

```
>>> query.all()
2007-11-16 16:21:35,349 INFO sqlalchemy.engine.base.Engine.0x..90
... SELECT product.sku AS product_sku, product.msrp AS product_msrp
FROM product ORDER BY product.oid
2007-11-16 16:21:35,349 INFO sqlalchemy.engine.base.Engine.0x..90 []
[<Product 123>, <Product 456>, <Product 222>]
```

Because retrieving the entire collection of mapped objects isn't very useful, SQLAlchemy provides various methods to modify the query object. Note that all of these
methods actually generate and return a new query object rather than modifying the
existing query object. The most useful of these methods are `filter()` and
`filter_by()`. These methods work, as their names imply, by restricting the set of objects
returned from the query. For instance, to retrieve all the products with an MSRP between $10 and $20, we could use `filter()` as follows:

```
>>> session.bind.echo = False
>>> query = query.filter(Product.msrp > 10.00)
>>> query = query.filter(Product.msrp < 20.00)
```

```
>>> for product in query:
...     print product.sku, product.msrp
...
123 11.22
222 15.95
```

Note that we can use mapped properties just like column objects in SQL expressions. SQLAlchemy also provides access to the c attribute (and all the attached columns) from the mapper's underlying selectable. In addition to this, SQLAlchemy provides a number of methods on mapped properties to facilitate the construction of complex queries. Some of these methods are summarized in the following lists.

The following are methods on mapped columns:

asc(self)
: Return a clause representing the mapped column in ascending order.

between(self, cleft, cright)
: Generate a BETWEEN clause with the specified left and right values (*column* BETWEEN *cleft* AND *cright*).

concat(self, other)
: Generate a clause that concatenates the value of the column with the value given.

desc(self)
: Generate a clause representing the mapped column in ascending order.

distinct(self)
: Generate a clause that limits the result set to rows with distinct values for this column.

endswith(self, other)
: Generate a clause (using LIKE) that implements the Python endswith() string method.

in_(self, other)
: Generate an IN clause with other as the righthand side. other may be either a sequence of literal values or a selectable.

like(self, other)
: Generate a LIKE clause with other as the righthand side.

startswith(self, other)
: Generate a clause (using LIKE) that implements the Python startswith() string method.

The following are methods on mapped relations:

any(self, criterion=None, **kwargs)
: Generate a clause that will be true if any of the related objects satisfy the given criterion. A filter_by()-style criterion (a conjunction of equality constraints) is generated if kwargs is nonempty.

contains(self, other)
> Generate a clause that will be true if the specified object is in the list of related objects.

has(self, criterion=None, **kwargs)
> For scalar-style relations, generate a clause that will be true if the related object satisfies the given criterion. A filter_by()-style criterion (a conjunction of equality constraints) is generated if kwargs is nonempty.

The filter() method, in fact, takes any valid SQL expression, allowing you to build up complex queries fairly simply. Also note that the two filters were applied as a conjunction: both criteria had to be satisfied to produce an object.

The filter_by() method allows more convenient filtering when the filter criteria are all equality constraints. For instance, to retrieve the products with an MSRP of $11.22, we could use the following query:

```
>>> query = session.query(Product)
>>> query = query.filter_by(msrp=11.22)
>>> print query.all()
[<Product 123>]
```

Note that we now specify the filter criteria as keyword arguments to filter_by(). The query then searches for mapped properties with the given name and applies appropriate filtering to the returned query.

The SQLAlchemy Query object also supports applying offsetting and limiting to a query via the offset() and limit() methods, as well as the slicing operator:

```
>>> query = session.query(Product)
>>> print query.offset(2)
SELECT product.sku AS product_sku, product.msrp AS product_msrp
FROM product ORDER BY product.oid
 LIMIT -1 OFFSET 2
>>> print query.limit(3)
SELECT product.sku AS product_sku, product.msrp AS product_msrp
FROM product ORDER BY product.oid
 LIMIT 3 OFFSET 0
>>> print query[1:2]
SELECT product.sku AS product_sku, product.msrp AS product_msrp
FROM product ORDER BY product.oid
 LIMIT 1 OFFSET 1
```

In many cases, we want to retrieve only one object from the database. The Query object provides three different ways to do this:

get(ident)
> Retrieve an object by its identity (the primary key of the mapped selectable). If there is no object identified by that key, return None. get() is also available as a method on the Session object.

first()

Retrieve the first result from the query. If there are no results, return None. This is
equivalent to *query*.all()[0].

one()

Retrieve the first result from the query, raising an exception unless the query returns
exactly one result. This is implemented by executing the query with a limit of 2. If
either 0 or 2 rows are returned, an exception is raised. Otherwise, the single object
is returned.

ORM Querying with Joins

The true power of the SQLAlchemy ORM query system is really only realized when
using it to join across the relations defined in the mapper() configuration. Joins can be
performed across mapped properties by using the join() method on the Query object.
Once a new class has been joined to the query, all its properties are available for use in
the filter() and filter_by() methods:

```
>>> query = session.query(Product)
>>> query = query.join('categories')
>>> query = query.filter_by(name='T-Shirts')
>>> print query.all()
[<Product 222>]
>>> print query
SELECT product.sku AS product_sku, product.msrp AS product_msrp
FROM product JOIN product_category ON product.sku =
... product_category.product_id JOIN category ON category.id =
... product_category.category_id
WHERE category.name = ? ORDER BY product.oid
```

SQLAlchemy also allows you to join across multiple property "hops." For instance, if
we wish to see all the products with some categorization under the "Class" level, we
could do the following:

```
>>> query = session.query(Product)
>>> query = query.join(['categories', 'level'])
>>> query = query.filter_by(name='Class')
>>> print query
SELECT product.sku AS product_sku, product.msrp AS product_msrp
FROM product JOIN product_category ON product.sku =
... product_category.product_id JOIN category ON category.id =
... product_category.category_id JOIN level ON level.id =
... category.level_id
WHERE level.name = ? ORDER BY product.oid
>>> print query.all()
[<Product 222>]
```

Note that filter_by() used the Level's name property, rather than the Category's name
property, when performing the filter. SQLAlchemy keeps track of a "joinpoint," the
last class referenced in an ORM join, and applies any filter_by() criteria to

that joinpoint until the joinpoint changes. To manually reset the joinpoint to the "root" class, simply call the reset_joinpoint() method.

Any new join() calls will also reset the joinpoint to the root of the query. To disable this behavior (and continue joining from the current joinpoint), simply specify from_joinpoint=True in the call to join().

As you may have noticed, the join() method constructs inner joins. SQLAlchemy also provides an outerjoin() method for constructing left outer joins. So, if we wanted to get a list of all products that have no "Class" categorization or have a "Class" of "Pants," we could execute the following query:

```
>>> query = session.query(Product)
>>> query = query.outerjoin('categories')
>>> query = query.filter(or_(Category.c.name=='Pants',
...                          Category.c.name==None))
>>> print query
SELECT product.sku AS product_sku, product.msrp AS product_msrp
FROM product LEFT OUTER JOIN product_category ON product.sku =
... product_category.product_id LEFT OUTER JOIN category ON
... category.id = product_category.category_id
WHERE category.name = ? OR category.name IS NULL ORDER BY
... product.oid
>>> print query.all()
[<Product 123>, <Product 456>]
```

When constructing complex queries using joins, it is often useful to join to the same table twice. In this case, we can specify that the join() method use an alias for the table being joined:

```
>>> query = session.query(Product)
>>> query = query.join('categories')
>>> query = query.filter_by(name='T-Shirts')
>>> query = query.join('categories', aliased=True)
>>> query = query.filter_by(name='Shirts')
>>> print query
SELECT product.sku AS product_sku, product.msrp AS product_msrp
FROM product JOIN product_category ON product.sku =
... product_category.product_id JOIN category ON category.id =
... product_category.category_id JOIN product_category AS
... product_category_1 ON product.sku =
... product_category_1.product_id JOIN category AS category_2 ON
... category_2.id = product_category_1.category_id
WHERE category.name = ? AND category_2.name = ? ORDER BY product.oid
>>> print query.all()
[<Product 222>]
```

One of the more powerful features of the SQLAlchemy ORM is that it allows properties to be defined as either "lazily" loaded or "eagerly" loaded (via the lazy parameter to the relation() function). It is often useful, however, to customize the load strategy of various properties on a query-by-query basis. To facilitate this, SQLAlchemy provides the options() method on the Query object and various functions, including eagerload(name), lazyload(name), and eagerload_all(name) to customize the loading strategy of relations on a query-by-query basis. `eagerload()` and `lazyload()` each change the default loading strategy for the named property. `eagerload_all()` makes an entire "property chain" eager-loaded.

For instance, suppose we are generating a table of all the products in the system, along with their categorization and the level name. If we use the default lazy loading approach, we will execute one query per object to read its categories and one query per category to read its levels:

```
>>> session.bind.echo=True
>>> query = session.query(Product)
>>> session.clear()
>>> for prod in query:
...     print prod.sku, prod.categories
...
2007-11-16 17:30:08,356 INFO sqlalchemy.engine.base.Engine.0x..90
... SELECT product.sku AS product_sku, product.msrp AS product_msrp
FROM product ORDER BY product.oid
2007-11-16 17:30:08,357 INFO sqlalchemy.engine.base.Engine.0x..90 []
1232007-11-16 17:30:08,360 INFO sqlalchemy.engine.base.Engine.0x..90
... SELECT category.id AS category_id, category.level_id AS
... category_level_id, category.parent_id AS category_parent_id,
... category.name AS category_name
FROM category, product_category
WHERE ? = product_category.product_id AND category.id =
... product_category.category_id ORDER BY product_category.oid
2007-11-16 17:30:08,361 INFO sqlalchemy.engine.base.Engine.0x..90
... [u'123']
[]
4562007-11-16 17:30:08,364 INFO sqlalchemy.engine.base.Engine.0x..90
... SELECT category.id AS category_id, category.level_id AS
... category_level_id, category.parent_id AS category_parent_id,
... category.name AS category_name
FROM category, product_category
WHERE ? = product_category.product_id AND category.id =
... product_category.category_id ORDER BY product_category.oid
2007-11-16 17:30:08,365 INFO sqlalchemy.engine.base.Engine.0x..90
... [u'456']
[]
2222007-11-16 17:30:08,367 INFO sqlalchemy.engine.base.Engine.0x..90
... SELECT category.id AS category_id, category.level_id AS
... category_level_id, category.parent_id AS category_parent_id,
... category.name AS category_name
FROM category, product_category
WHERE ? = product_category.product_id AND category.id =
... product_category.category_id ORDER BY product_category.oid
2007-11-16 17:30:08,368 INFO sqlalchemy.engine.base.Engine.0x..90
... [u'222']
2007-11-16 17:30:08,371 INFO sqlalchemy.engine.base.Engine.0x..90
... SELECT level.id AS level_id, level.parent_id AS level_parent_id,
... level.name AS level_name
FROM level
WHERE level.id = ? ORDER BY level.oid
2007-11-16 17:30:08,371 INFO sqlalchemy.engine.base.Engine.0x..90
```

```
... [1]
2007-11-16 17:30:08,373 INFO sqlalchemy.engine.base.Engine.0x..90
... SELECT level.id AS level_id, level.parent_id AS level_parent_id,
... level.name AS level_name
FROM level
WHERE level.id = ? ORDER BY level.oid
2007-11-16 17:30:08,374 INFO sqlalchemy.engine.base.Engine.0x..90
... [2]
2007-11-16 17:30:08,380 INFO sqlalchemy.engine.base.Engine.0x..90
... SELECT level.id AS level_id, level.parent_id AS level_parent_id,
... level.name AS level_name
FROM level
WHERE level.id = ? ORDER BY level.oid
2007-11-16 17:30:08,381 INFO sqlalchemy.engine.base.Engine.0x..90
... [3]
[<Category Department.Tops>, <Category Class.Shirts>, <Category
... SubClass.T-Shirts>]
```

If we eagerly load the `categories` property, however, we execute only a single query:

```
>>> session.clear()
>>> query = session.query(Product)
>>> query = query.options(eagerload_all('categories.level'))
>>> for prod in query:
...     print prod.sku, prod.categories
...
2007-11-16 17:30:09,392 INFO sqlalchemy.engine.base.Engine.0x..90
... SELECT category_1.id AS category_1_id, category_1.level_id AS
... category_1_level_id, category_1.parent_id AS
... category_1_parent_id, category_1.name AS category_1_name,
... level_2.id AS level_2_id, level_2.parent_id AS
... level_2_parent_id, level_2.name AS level_2_name, product.sku AS
... product_sku, product.msrp AS product_msrp
FROM product LEFT OUTER JOIN product_category AS product_category_3
... ON product.sku = product_category_3.product_id LEFT OUTER JOIN
... category AS category_1 ON category_1.id =
... product_category_3.category_id LEFT OUTER JOIN level AS level_2
... ON level_2.id = category_1.level_id ORDER BY product.oid,
... product_category_3.oid, level_2.oid
2007-11-16 17:30:09,393 INFO sqlalchemy.engine.base.Engine.0x..90 []
123 []
456 []
222 [<Category Department.Tops>, <Category Class.Shirts>, <Category
... SubClass.T-Shirts>]
```

The `options()` method can also be used with a variety of other options. Notice how the eager/lazy loading can also be specified on the mapper itself. From SQLAlchemy's point of view, the `options()` method is changing the view of the mapper that the query is based on. Thus other options can be specified that "morph" the mapper as well. These options are summarized here:

extension(ext)

Add the `MapperExtension` ext into the beginning of the list of extensions that will be called in the context of the query.

eagerload(name)

> Set the load strategy on the named `relation()` property to be eager (equivalent to specifying `lazy=False` in the `mapper()` call). For mapped column properties, use `undefer()` instead.

eagerload_all(name)

> `name` is a string containing a list of dot-separated names that represent a chain of `relation()` properties to be eager loaded. For mapped column properties, use `undefer()` instead.

lazyload(name)

> Set the load strategy on the named `relation()` property to be lazy (equivalent to specifying `lazy=True` in the `mapper()` call). For mapped column properties, use `defer()` instead.

noload(name)

> Set the load strategy on the named property to be nonloading (equivalent to specifying `lazy=None` in the `mapper()` calls).

contains_alias(alias)

> Indicates to the query that the main table in the underlying select statement has been aliased to the given `alias` (which is a string or `Alias` object).

contains_eager(key, alias=None, decorator=None)

> Indicates that an attribute (the **key** parameter) will be eagerly loaded. This is used in conjunction with feeding SQL result sets directly into the `instances()` method on queries (covered next in "Customizing the Select Statement in ORM Queries"). The `alias` parameter is the alias (either a string or an `Alias` object) representing aliased columns in the query. The `decorator` parameter, mutually exclusive of `alias`, is a function used to preprocess rows before passing them to the eager-loading handler. This can be used to do arbitrary processing on the row before it passes to the eager loader.

defer(name)

> Convert the named column property into a deferred column (lazily loaded). For `relation()`s, use `lazyload()` instead.

undefer(name)

> Convert the named column property into a deferred column (eagerly loaded). For `relation()`s, use `eagerload()` or `eagerload_all()` instead.

undefer_group(name)

> Convert the named deferred group of column properties into an undeferred group.

Note that the addition of the `eagerload_all()` option (and all other options) is completely transparent; the only difference in the code that uses the results of such a query is in its performance.

Customizing the Select Statement in ORM Queries

Although SQLAlchemy is quite flexible in the types of queries it can generate at the ORM level, it is sometimes necessary to either modify the generated query or to even replace it entirely while still generating SQLAlchemy ORM objects. One of the simplest query modifications is replacing the underlying selectable using the select_from() method. For instance, if we wish to manually perform some joins and then select from the joined table, we can do so as follows:

```
>>> joined_product = product_table.join(product_category_table)
>>> joined_product = joined_product.join(category_table)
>>> query = session.query(Product).select_from(joined_product)
>>> query = query.filter(category_table.c.name=='T-Shirts')
>>> print query
SELECT product.sku AS product_sku, product.msrp AS product_msrp
FROM product JOIN product_category ON product.sku =
... product_category.product_id JOIN category ON category.id =
... product_category.category_id
WHERE category.name = ? ORDER BY product.oid
>>> print query.all()
[<Product 222>]
```

If we wish to completely replace the SQL underlying the query object, we can do so with the from_statement() method. When using from_statement(), it's important to make certain that all the necessary columns are returned by the underlying query. If a mapped column is omitted, then the mapped property will be set to None:

```
>>> session.clear()
>>> stmt = select([product_table.c.sku])
>>> query = session.query(Product).from_statement(stmt)
>>> for prod in query:
...     print prod, prod.msrp
...
<Product 123> None
<Product 456> None
<Product 222> None
```

Using from_statement() also interferes with SQLAlchemy's eager-loading mechanism because SQLAlchemy has no way of tacking on its LEFT OUTER JOINs to retrieve the eagerly loaded objects. To support this condition, SQLAlchemy provides the contains_eager() mapper option, which allows you to make SQLAlchemy aware of the LEFT OUTER JOINs that have already been added to the underlying SQL:

```
>>> session.clear()
>>> joined_product = product_table.outerjoin(product_category_table)
>>> joined_product = joined_product.outerjoin(category_table)
>>> stmt = select([product_table, category_table],
...               from_obj=[joined_product])
>>> query = session.query(Product).from_statement(stmt)
>>> query = query.options(contains_eager('categories'))
>>> session.bind.echo = True
>>> for prod in query:
...     print prod, [c.name for c in prod.categories ]
```

```
...
2007-11-17 09:52:13,730 INFO sqlalchemy.engine.base.Engine.0x..90
... SELECT product.sku AS product_sku, product.msrp AS product_msrp,
... category.id AS category_id, category.level_id AS
... category_level_id, category.parent_id AS category_parent_id,
... category.name AS category_name
FROM product LEFT OUTER JOIN product_category ON product.sku =
... product_category.product_id LEFT OUTER JOIN category ON
... category.id = product_category.category_id LEFT OUTER JOIN level
... ON level.id = category.level_id
2007-11-17 09:52:13,731 INFO sqlalchemy.engine.base.Engine.0x..90 []
<Product 123> []
<Product 456> []
<Product 222> [u'Tops', u'Shirts', u'T-Shirts']
```

It is also possible to eagerly load where the LEFT OUTER JOIN is with an alias. In this case, simply supply the alias (either as a string or as an **Alias** object) to the contains_eager() alias parameter:

```
>>> session.clear()
>>> alias = category_table.alias('cat1')
>>> joined_product = product_table.outerjoin(product_category_table)
>>> joined_product = joined_product.outerjoin(alias)
>>> stmt = select([product_table, alias],
...                from_obj=[joined_product])
>>> query = session.query(Product).from_statement(stmt)
>>> query = query.options(contains_eager('categories',
... alias='cat1'))
>>> session.bind.echo = True
>>> for prod in query:
...     print prod, [c.name for c in prod.categories ]
...
2008-01-27 19:51:55,567 INFO sqlalchemy.engine.base.Engine.0x..90
... SELECT product.sku AS product_sku, product.msrp AS product_msrp,
... cat1.id AS cat1_id, cat1.level_id AS cat1_level_id,
... cat1.parent_id AS cat1_parent_id, cat1.name AS cat1_name
FROM product LEFT OUTER JOIN product_category ON product.sku =
... product_category.product_id LEFT OUTER JOIN category AS cat1 ON
... cat1.id = product_category.category_id
2008-01-27 19:51:55,567 INFO sqlalchemy.engine.base.Engine.0x..90 []
<Product 123> []
<Product 456> []
<Product 222> [u'Tops', u'Shirts', u'T-Shirts']
```

SQLAlchemy also supports creating objects from SQL where the main table is aliased to another name. In this case, you must use the contains_alias() mapper option. Again, you can pass either a string name of the alias or the **Alias** object itself:

```
>>> alias = product_table.alias()
>>> stmt = alias.select()
>>> query = session.query(Product).from_statement(stmt)
>>> query = query.options(contains_alias(alias))
>>> print query.all()
[<Product 123>, <Product 456>, <Product 222>]
```

We can also use the `from_statement()` method with string-based queries. In this case, it is a good idea to use bind parameters for performance and to avoid SQL injection attacks. Bind parameters for SQLAlchemy are always specified using the *:name* notation, and they are bound to particular values using the `params()` method of the `Query` object:

```
>>> query = session.query(Product)
>>> query - query.from_statement('SELECT * FROM product WHERE
... sku=:sku')
>>> query = query.params(sku='123')
>>> print query.all()
[<Product 123>]
```

Up until now, we have been using the `Query` object to generate a sequence of mapped objects. In some cases, we may want a query to retrieve several objects per "row," where the objects retrieved may either be fully mapped ORM objects or simple SQL columns. SQLAlchemy supports this via the `add_entity()` and `add_column()` `Query` methods:

```
>>> query = session.query(Product)
>>> query = query.add_entity(Category)
>>> query =
... query.filter(Product.sku==product_category_table.c.product_id)
>>> query =
... query.filter(Category.id==product_category_table.c.category_id)
>>> for row in query:
...     print row
...
(<Product 222>, <Category Department.Tops>)
(<Product 222>, <Category Class.Shirts>)
(<Product 222>, <Category SubClass.T-Shirts>)
>>> query = query.add_column(category_table.c.level_id)
>>> for row in query:
...     print row
...
(<Product 222>, <Category Department.Tops>, 1)
(<Product 222>, <Category Class.Shirts>, 2)
(<Product 222>, <Category SubClass.T-Shirts>, 3)
```

If you know *a priori* what objects you wish to construct, you can create the query initially with this knowledge, rather than using the `add_entity()` method:

```
>>> query = session.query(Product, Category)
>>> query =
... query.filter(Product.sku==product_category_table.c.product_id)
>>> query =
... query.filter(Category.id==product_category_table.c.category_id)
>>> for row in query:
...     print row
...
(<Product 222>, <Category Department.Tops>)
(<Product 222>, <Category Class.Shirts>)
(<Product 222>, <Category SubClass.T-Shirts>)
```

Other Query Methods

The Query object has a number of other methods that allow great flexibility. Some useful Query methods are summarized here:

add_column(self, column, id=None)
    Add the named column to the query, making the query return a tuple including the named column. id, if supplied, specifies that the column will be correlated with the id parameter given to a matching join() or outerjoin() method.

add_entity(self, entity, alias=None, id=None)
    Add a class or mapper to the query, making the query return a tuple including the given entity. If alias is supplied, the entity will be aliased using the given alias. If id is supplied, the entity will be selected from the join() or outerjoin() in the query with a matching id parameter.

all(self)
    Retrieve a list of results from the query (simply returns list(self)).

autoflush(self, setting)
    Sets the autoflushing behavior of the query (True or False). If the query is auto-flushing, the session will be flushed before the query is executed, guaranteeing that in-memory objects are consistent with query results. The default autoflush behavior of the query is inherited from the session.

apply_avg(self, col)
    Apply the SQL AVG() function to the given column and return the resulting query.

apply_max(self, col)
    Apply the SQL MAX() function to the given column and return the resulting query.

apply_min(self, col)
    Apply the SQL MIN() function to the given column and return the resulting query.

apply_sum(self, col)
    Apply the SQL SUM() function to the given column and return the resulting query.

avg(self, col)
    Execute the SQL AVG() function against the given column and return the result.

count(self)
    Execute the SQL COUNT() function against this query and return the result. (count() takes other parameters, but they are deprecated in SQLAlchemy 0.4.)

distinct(self)
    Apply a SQL DISTINCT modifier to the query and return the resulting query.

filter(self, criterion)
    Apply the given SQL filtering criterion to the query and return the resulting query. All filters are conjoined (combined using the SQL AND operator).

`filter_by(self, **kwargs)`

Apply equality filtering criteria to the query and return the result. The criteria are constructed based on the name, value pairs supplied to the `kwargs` parameter.

`first(self)`

Execute the query and return the first result, or `None` if the query has no results.

`from_statement(self, statement)`

Replace the underlying statement used by the query with the given statement, which may be either a string of SQL or a query constructed using the SQL expression language.

`get(self, ident, reload=False, lockmode=None)`

Retrieve an object based on the given identity from the session. If the object is not currently loaded in the session, it will be loaded. If `reload` is `True`, the object will be refreshed, regardless of whether it is in the session. If `lockmode` is specified, the object will be loaded with the given `lockmode`. The locking mode is based around the idea of SELECT...FOR UPDATE and related constructs. The `lockmode` value is inserted after the FOR keyword.

`group_by(self, criterion)`

Apply a SQL GROUP BY clause to the query and return the resulting query. This is generally useful in ORM queries only when you are grouping by the main class and aggregating over some related class. For instance, if a `Product` had many `Recommendation`s, you might group by the product's sku and add a `having()` clause to return products with three or more recommendations.

`having(self, criterion)`

Apply a SQL HAVING clause to the query and return the resulting query.

`instances(self, cursor)`

Return a list of mapped instances corresponding to rows in the given `cursor` (generally a `ResultProxy`). `instances()` takes other parameters, but they are deprecated in SQLAlchemy 0.4.

`join(self, prop, id=None, aliased=False, from_joinpoint=False)`

Create a join of this query based on a mapped property `prop` and return the resulting query. `prop` can be either a string property name or a list of string property names specifying a join path. If `id` is specified, it should be a string for use in matching `add_column()` or `add_entity()` id parameters. If `aliased` is `True`, the joined entity will be aliased in the underlying query. If `from_joinpoint` is `True`, the join will be from the last-joined entity. Otherwise, it will be from the "root" entity of the query. This method is typically used to add a filter based on some related class.

`limit(self, limit)`

Apply a LIMIT modifier to the query and return the resulting query. Note that SQLAlchemy generates appropriate SQL to make the LIMIT apply to the *objects* generated, not the rows. This is done to return the specified number of *objects* even in the presence of JOINs.

`load(self, ident, raiseerr=True, lockmode=None)`
> Return an instance of the object based on the given **ident**, refreshing the object from the database. This is similar to `get()` with `reload=True`, but will raise an error if the object is not found in the database.

`max(self, col)`
> Execute the `SQL MAX()` function against the given column and return the result.

`min(self, col)`
> Execute the `SQL MIN()` function against the given column and return the result.

`offset(self, offset)`
> Apply an OFFSET modifier to the query and return the resulting query. Note that SQLAlchemy generates appropriate SQL to make the OFFSET apply to the objects generated, not the rows, in order to skip the specified number of *objects* even in the presence of JOINs.

`one(self)`
> Return the first result of the query, raising an exception if the query does not return exactly one result.

`options(self, *args)`
> Return a new query with the mapper options (such as `eagerload()`, etc.) listed in `args` applied.

`order_by(self, criterion)`
> Apply a SQL ORDER BY modifier to the query and return the resulting query.

`outerjoin(self, prop, id=None, aliased=False, from_joinpoint=False)`
> Create a LEFT OUTER JOIN of this query based on a mapped property **prop** and return the resulting query. **prop** can be either a string property name or a list of string property names specifying a join path. If **id** is specified, it should be a string for use in matching `add_column()` or `add_entity()` id parameters. If **aliased** is True, the joined entity will be aliased in the underlying query. If `from_joinpoint` is True, the join will be from the last-joined entity. Otherwise, it will be from the "root" entity of the query. This method is typically used to add a filter based on some related class.

`params(self, *args, **kwargs)`
> Add values for bind parameters that exist in the underlying query. The binding dictionary may be passed as keyword arguments or as a `dict` in the first positional argument.

`populate_existing(self)`
> Return a query that will refresh all objects loaded. Normally, when a query executes, it will not modify any objects already in memory. This option changes that behavior.

`query_from_parent(cls, instance, property, **kwargs)` (classmethod)
> Create a new `Query` object that returns objects with a relationship to a given object **instance** through the named **property**. The **kwargs** are passed along unmodified to

the `Query` constructor. This is mainly used internally to SQLAlchemy, to construct queries for lazily loaded properties.

reset_joinpoint(self)
> Reset the joinpoint of the query to the "root" mapper. This affects subsequent calls to `filter_by()` and possibly to `join()` and `outerjoin()`.

sum(self, col)
> Execute the SQL `SUM()` function against the given column and return the result.

with_lockmode(self, mode)
> Return a new `Query` object using the specified locking mode.

with_parent(self, instance, property=None)
> Add a join criterion based on a relationship to a mapped `instance` via the named `property`. If `property` is not supplied, SQLAlchemy attempts to infer an appropriate `property`.

__getitem__(self, item) (indexing)
> If `item` is a slice object, apply appropriate OFFSET and LIMIT modifers to the query to emulate the Python slicing operation. If `item` is an integer, apply an appropriate OFFSET with a LIMIT of 1, execute the query, and return the result.

__iter__(self) (iteration)
> Returns an iterator that will build mapped objects from the query.

Contextual or Thread-Local Sessions

Although the SQLAlchemy ORM is extremely flexible and powerful, it can be somewhat repetitive in some cases. One of these cases is constructing the `Session` object. Fortunately, SQLAlchemy provides the ability to manage sessions for you in such a way that a `Session` object can be shared among various parts of your application without explicitly passing it around as a parameter. This is useful in web frameworks in particular, where you generally want all the code servicing a given web request to use the same `Session` object. SQLAlchemy achieves implicit `Session` object sharing via "contextual" sessions.

The idea of a contextual session is that there is one session that is available in a given "context," where the default context is the thread. When you need a session, rather than constructing one yourself, you simply ask SQLAlchemy for the session that is appropriate to the current context. You can generate a contextual `Session` object by using the `scoped_session()` function:

```
>>> Session = scoped_session(sessionmaker(
...     bind=engine, autoflush=True, transactional=True))
>>>
>>> session = Session()
>>> session2 = Session()
>>> session is session2
```

As mentioned earlier, the default context is the current thread. To override this and supply a different context, simply pass a scopefunc parameter to the scoped_session() function. scopefunc should be a callable that returns a key that uniquely identifies the context. By default, the scopefunc is the get_ident() function from the thread module.

The contextual Session class also supplies class methods for all the Session instance methods. These class methods simply proxy to the contextual Session object. This means that we can use scoped_session() to declare the contextual Session class globally and use it anywhere we would normally need a Session object, without explicitly constructing the Session object. So, if we want to save a new Product to the contextual Session *object*, we can simply save it to the (globally declared) contextual Session *class*:

```
>>> prod = Product(sku='333', msrp=44.55)
>>> Session.save(prod)
>>> Session.flush()
```

To use contextual sessions effectively, they must be periodically "cleared out" of the objects they manage, or else they will grow beyond all reasonable bounds. In the context of a web framework, for instance, the contextual session should be cleared between requests. This can be accomplished by using either the close() method, which frees all resources maintained by the contextual session, or the remove() method, which actually removes the session from the current context altogether. close() should be used when the current context is "permanent," as in web servers that use a never-shrinking pool of threads to handle requests. remove() should be used if the context may "go away," as the session object will be "leaked" if the context is not reused. This is the appropriate choice in web frameworks, which may stop threads that previously handled requests.

Using Contextual Sessions with Mappers and Classes

The contextual session allows us to dispense with explicit references to sessions in many cases by instrumenting our mapped classes with a query() *and* modifying the mapped class's constructor to automatically save() it to the session when it is created. This very nice feature is accomplished by using the contextual Session's mapper() method rather than the mapper() function when defining our object mappers. So, where previously our mappers were declared as follows:

```
mapper(Product, product_table, properties=dict(
    categories=relation(Category, secondary=product_category_table,
                        backref='products')))

mapper(Level, level_table, properties=dict(
    children=relation(Level, backref='parent'),
    categories=relation(Category, backref='level')))

mapper(Category, category_table, properties=dict(
    children=relation(Category, backref='parent')))
```

we can now declare them like this (assuming that Session has already been declared globally as a contextual Session):

```
Session.mapper(Product, product_table, properties=dict(
    categories=relation(Category, secondary=product_category_table,
                        backref='products')))

Session.mapper(Level, level_table, properties=dict(
    children=relation(Level, backref='parent'),
    categories=relation(Category, backref='level')))

Session.mapper(Category, category_table, properties=dict(
    children=relation(Category, backref='parent')))
```

Once we have mapped the classes as shown, we can use the mapped classes themselves to perform session-like functions:

```
>>> Product.query().all()
[<Product 123>, <Product 456>, <Product 222>, <Product 333>]
>>> prod = Product('444', msrp=55.66)
>>> Product.query().all()
[<Product 123>, <Product 456>, <Product 222>, <Product 333>,
... <Product 444>]
```

Using the contextual session mapper() method also gives us one other benefit: a reasonably usable default constructor. This constructor allows us to provide values for any of the properties defined in the mapped class via keyword arguments. So, if we omitted the Product constructor and used Session.mapper() to map it, we could initialize products as follows:

```
>>> p = Product(sku='555', msrp=22.11)
```

## CHAPTER 8

Inheritance Mapping

In this chapter, you will learn the different methods of mapping object-oriented inheritance to relational database tables. You will learn how to use different methods of inheritance mapping with SQLAlchemy, as well as how to use inheritance in the presence of mapped relations between classes.

Overview of Inheritance Mapping

No object-relational mapper would be complete without some method of mapping object-oriented inheritance hierarchies to SQL tables, and so SQLAlchemy provides rich support for modeling inheritance. Inheritance is typically modeled in SQL in one of three ways: *single table inheritance*, *concrete table inheritance*, or *joined table inheritance*.

For the purposes of illustrating SQLAlchemy's support for the various types of inheritance modeling, we will use a simple inheritance hierarchy that models products, including clothing products and accessories. This hierarchy is illustrated in Figure 8-1 and is implemented by the following Python code:

```python
class Product(object):
    def __init__(self, sku, msrp):
        self.sku = sku
        self.msrp = msrp
    def __repr__(self):
        return '<%s %s>' % (
            self.__class__.__name__, self.sku)

class Clothing(Product):
    def __init__(self, sku, msrp, clothing_info):
        Product.__init__(self, sku, msrp)
        self.clothing_info = clothing_info

class Accessory(Product):
    def __init__(self, sku, msrp, accessory_info):
        Product.__init__(self, sku, msrp)
        self.accessory_info = accessory_info
```

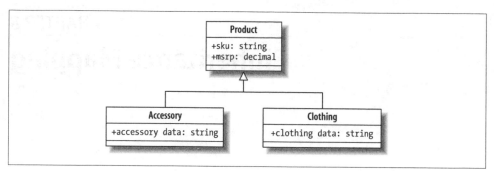

Figure 8-1. Sample inheritance hierarchy

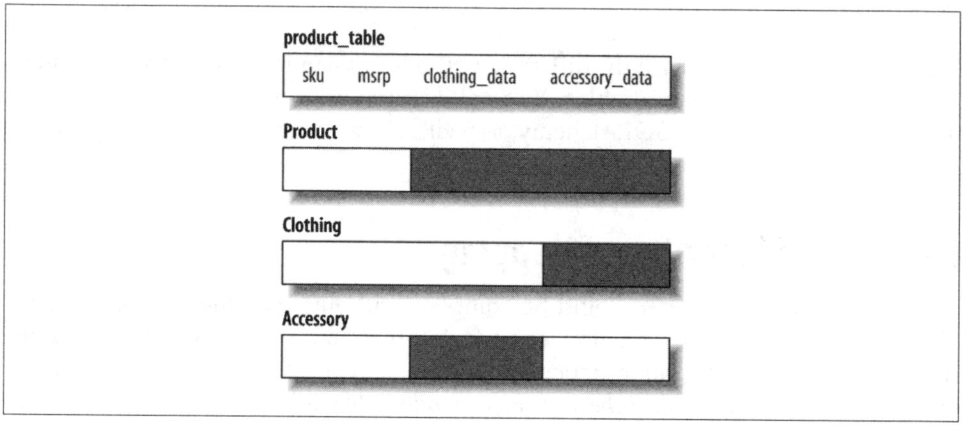

Figure 8-2. Single table inheritance mapping (unmapped columns masked)

Single Table Inheritance Mapping

In single table inheritance, a single table is used to represent all the different types in the class hierarchy, as shown in Figure 8-2.

In our preceding example, this table might be defined as follows:

```
product_table = Table(
    'product', metadata,
    Column('sku', String(20), primary_key=True),
    Column('msrp', Numeric),
    Column('clothing_info', String),
    Column('accessory_info', String),
    Column('product_type', String(1), nullable=False))
```

Notice that we have constructed a table that contains columns for all of the attributes across the entire hierarchy we wish to model. This means that we incur some overhead for all of the classes in the hierarchy in each row. Although this doesn't cause too many problems with the simple hierarchy we are using in this example, the space overhead can become significant with larger and more attribute-rich hierarchies.

Also note that we have introduced a new column, the 'product_type' column. This column holds the "polymorphic identity" of each row, so named because it allows SQLAlchemy to return the appropriate class from a query on the parent object. The polymorphic identity is used by SQLAlchemy to determine what type of object is contained in the row. SQLAlchemy supports using any data type desired to hold this information; here we use a single character. 'P' will represent a Product (the parent class), 'C' will represent a Clothing product, and 'A' will represent an Accessory product.

To map this table onto our inheritance hierarchy, we will use some new keyword arguments to the mapper() function, namely polymorphic_on, inherits, and polymorphic_identity:

```
mapper(
    Product, product_table,
    polymorphic_on=product_table.c.product_type,
    polymorphic_identity='P')

mapper(Clothing, inherits=Product,
       polymorphic_identity='C')

mapper(Accessory, inherits=Product,
       polymorphic_identity='A')
```

The polymorphic_on parameter identifies which column contains the polymorphic identity of each row. The polymorphic_identity parameter identifies the value that should be present in that column to tell SQLAlchemy to use this particular mapper, and the inherits parameter tells SQLAlchemy to retrieve all other parameters and properties from the named mapper.

Once we have defined the mappers, we can insert some data and perform some queries:

```
>>> # Create some products
... products = [
...     # Some parent class products
...     Product('123', 11.22),
...     Product('456', 33.44),
...     # Some clothing
...     Clothing('789', 123.45, "Nice Pants"),
...     Clothing('111', 125.45, "Nicer Pants"),
...     # Some accessories
...     Accessory('222', 24.99, "Wallet"),
...     Accessory('333', 14.99, "Belt") ]
>>>
>>> Session = sessionmaker()
>>> session = Session()
>>> for p in products: session.save(p)
...
>>> session.flush()
>>> session.clear()
```

```
>>>
>>> metadata.bind.echo = True
>>>
>>> print session.query(Product).all()
2007-11-19 14:35:55,244 INFO sqlalchemy.engine.base.Engine.0x..90
... SELECT product.sku AS product_sku, product.msrp AS product_msrp,
... product.clothing_info AS product_clothing_info,
... product.accessory_info AS product_accessory_info,
... product.product_type AS product_product_type
FROM product ORDER BY product.oid
2007-11-19 14:35:55,245 INFO sqlalchemy.engine.base.Engine.0x..90 []
[<Product 123>, <Product 456>, <Clothing 789>, <Clothing 111>,
... <Accessory 222>, <Accessory 333>]
>>> print session.query(Clothing).all()
2007-11-19 14:35:55,259 INFO sqlalchemy.engine.base.Engine.0x..90
... SELECT product.sku AS product_sku, product.msrp AS product_msrp,
... product.clothing_info AS product_clothing_info,
... product.accessory_info AS product_accessory_info,
... product.product_type AS product_product_type
FROM product
WHERE product.product_type IN (?) ORDER BY product.oid
2007-11-19 14:35:55,259 INFO sqlalchemy.engine.base.Engine.0x..90
... ['C']
[<Clothing 789>, <Clothing 111>]
>>> print session.query(Accessory).all()
2007-11-19 14:35:55,274 INFO sqlalchemy.engine.base.Engine.0x..90
... SELECT product.sku AS product_sku, product.msrp AS product_msrp,
... product.clothing_info AS product_clothing_info,
... product.accessory_info AS product_accessory_info,
... product.product_type AS product_product_type
FROM product
WHERE product.product_type IN (?) ORDER BY product.oid
2007-11-19 14:35:55,274 INFO sqlalchemy.engine.base.Engine.0x..90
... ['A']
[<Accessory 222>, <Accessory 333>]
```

Note in particular that SQLAlchemy generated appropriate queries (through filtering based on product_type) based on whether we were selecting from a parent class or a child class.

Also note how SQLAlchemy was able to create appropriate objects based on the polymorphic identity column (which SQLAlchemy generated itself when flushing the instances). If we inspect the table at the SQL level, we will see the 'type_' column populated just as we expect:

```
>>> metadata.bind.echo = False
>>> for row in product_table.select().execute():
...     print row
...
(u'123', Decimal("11.22"), None, None, u'P')
(u'456', Decimal("33.44"), None, None, u'P')
(u'789', Decimal("123.45"), u'Nice Pants', None, u'C')
(u'111', Decimal("125.45"), u'Nicer Pants', None, u'C')
(u'222', Decimal("24.99"), None, u'Wallet', u'A')
(u'333', Decimal("14.99"), None, u'Belt', u'A')
```

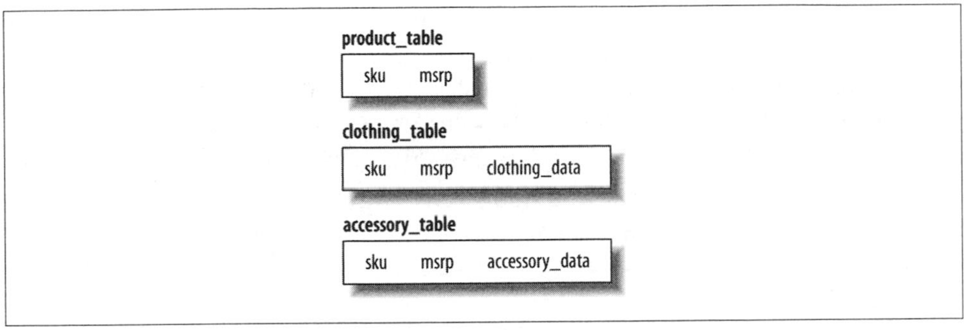

Figure 8-3. Concrete table inheritance mapping

Aside from the space overhead, there is one problem in using single table inheritance mapping: the mapper will try to map *all* the columns of the single table unless you manually specify columns to map at each level of the inheritance hierarchy via the `include_columns` or `exclude_columns` arguments to the mapper. For instance, if we try to get the `clothing_info` for a nonclothing product, SQLAlchemy will not complain:

```
>>> print session.query(Accessory)[0].clothing_info
None
```

This problem is alleviated in the concrete table and joined table inheritance mappings, which each use a different table for each class in the hierarchy.

Concrete Table Inheritance Mapping

In concrete table inheritance mapping, we use a separate table for each class in the inheritance hierarchy, with each table containing all the columns necessary to represent the object in its entirety, as shown in Figure 8-3.

So, for the product hierarchy in our example, we would define the following tables in this way:

```
product_table = Table(
    'product', metadata,
    Column('sku', String(20), primary_key=True),
    Column('msrp', Numeric))

clothing_table = Table(
    'clothing', metadata,
    Column('sku', String(20), primary_key=True),
    Column('msrp', Numeric),
    Column('clothing_info', String))

accessory_table = Table(
    'accessory', metadata,
    Column('sku', String(20), primary_key=True),
    Column('msrp', Numeric),
    Column('accessory_info', String))
```

Note that in concrete table inheritance, each table contains exactly the amount of data that is required to implement its class; there is no wasted space, unlike single table inheritance. Also note that there is no longer a need for the "polymorphic identity" column, as SQLAlchemy knows that `Clothing` objects are created from the `clothing_table`, `Accessory` objects from the `accessory_table`, etc.

The mapper configuration is likewise straightforward:

```
mapper(Product, product_table)
mapper(Clothing, clothing_table)
mapper(Accessory, accessory_table)
```

In fact, as far as SQLAlchemy is concerned, we aren't modeling inheritance at all! We've just persisted three classes which happen to have an inheritance relationship that is completely ignored by SQLAlchemy. Unfortunately, in doing so, we have lost the ability to query polymorphically. For instance, we may wish to retrieve the Product with sku '222'. Without some extra work, we'd have to query each of the classes in the inheritance hierarchy. Luckily, SQLAlchemy provides support for polymorphic loading if we do a little extra work in the mapper configuration.

The first thing we need to do is get a selectable that yields something like what the single table select yielded. SQLAlchemy provides a utility function `polymorphic_union()` which provides just such a selectable. To use it, we simply supply a `dict` object whose keys are the old polymorphic identities and whose values are the tables in the inheritance hierarchy:

```
>>> punion = polymorphic_union(
...     dict(P=product_table,
...          C=clothing_table,
...          A=accessory_table),
...     'type_')
>>>
>>> print punion
SELECT accessory.sku, CAST(NULL AS TEXT) AS clothing_info,
... accessory.msrp, accessory.accessory_info, 'A' AS type_
FROM accessory UNION ALL SELECT product.sku, CAST(NULL AS TEXT) AS
... clothing_info, product.msrp, CAST(NULL AS TEXT) AS
... accessory_info, 'P' AS type_
FROM product UNION ALL SELECT clothing.sku, clothing.clothing_info,
... clothing.msrp, CAST(NULL AS TEXT) AS accessory_info, 'C' AS
... type_
FROM clothing
>>>
```

Now, we have a nicely labeled selectable that can be selected from, just as in the single table inheritance. To complete the mapping, we need to let the mappers know about the union and the inheritance relationship:

```
mapper(
    Product, product_table, select_table=punion,
    polymorphic_on=punion.c.type_,
    polymorphic_identity='P')
mapper(Clothing, clothing_table, inherits=Product,
```

```
        polymorphic_identity='C',
        concrete=True)
mapper(Accessory, accessory_table, inherits=Product,
        polymorphic_identity='A',
        concrete=True)
```

Here, we have specified a different table for selects (the `polymorphic_union( )` result) and let SQLAlchemy know to use concrete table inheritance in the child classes. Otherwise, the mapper configuration is identical to the single table inheritance. Now, assuming we have created the objects in the database as we did previously, we can perform polymorphic loads as follows:

```
>>> session.query(Product).get('222')
2007-11-19 15:13:55,727 INFO sqlalchemy.engine.base.Engine.0x..50
... SELECT p_union.accessory_info AS p_union_accessory_info,
... p_union.type_ AS p_union_type_, p_union.sku AS p_union_sku,
... p_union.clothing_info AS p_union_clothing_info, p_union.msrp AS
... p_union_msrp
FROM (SELECT accessory.sku AS sku, CAST(NULL AS TEXT) AS
... clothing_info, accessory.msrp AS msrp, accessory.accessory_info
... AS accessory_info, 'A' AS type_
FROM accessory UNION ALL SELECT product.sku AS sku, CAST(NULL AS
... TEXT) AS clothing_info, product.msrp AS msrp, CAST(NULL AS TEXT)
... AS accessory_info, 'P' AS type_
FROM product UNION ALL SELECT clothing.sku AS sku,
... clothing.clothing_info AS clothing_info, clothing.msrp AS msrp,
... CAST(NULL AS TEXT) AS accessory_info, 'C' AS type_
FROM clothing) AS p_union
WHERE p_union.sku = ? ORDER BY p_union.oid
2007-11-19 15:13:55,737 INFO sqlalchemy.engine.base.Engine.0x..50
... ['222']
<Accessory 222>
```

Joined Table Inheritance Mapping

Joined table inheritance is perhaps the closest to directly mapping the inheritance hierarchy to the database. In joined table inheritance mapping, as in concrete table inheritance mapping, a distinct table is used to map each class. Unlike concrete inheritance mapping, however, each table contains only the columns the attributes added, allowing the row in the "parent" table to take care of inherited attributes, as shown in Figure 8-4.

The total set of attributes required to represent an instance are then retrieved by joining along the inheritance hierarchy. In our product database, this would have the following declaration:

```
product_table = Table(
    'product', metadata,
    Column('sku', String(20), primary_key=True),
    Column('msrp', Numeric),
    Column('product_type', String(1), nullable=False))
```

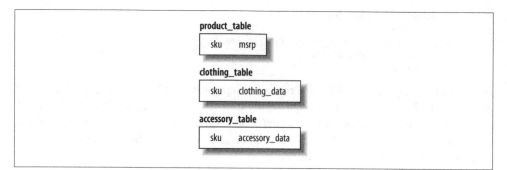

Figure 8-4. Joined table inheritance mapping

```
clothing_table = Table(
    'clothing', metadata,
    Column('sku', None, ForeignKey('product.sku'),
           primary_key=True),
    Column('clothing_info', String))

accessory_table = Table(
    'accessory', metadata,
    Column('sku', None, ForeignKey('product.sku'),
           primary_key=True),
    Column('accessory_info', String))
```

Notice that we have reintroduced the `'product_type'` polymorphic identity column from single table inheritance mapping. In joined table inheritance, this column is only required on the "root" table of the inheritance hierarchy, again to let SQLAlchemy know what type of object to create in a polymorphic load.

The mappers we build are almost identical to the ones we used in the single table inheritance mapping, except that each mapper references a distinct table, whereas all the mappers shared a table in the single-table inheritance case:

```
mapper(
    Product, product_table,
    polymorphic_on=product_table.c.product_type,
    polymorphic_identity='P')

mapper(Clothing, clothing_table, inherits=Product,
       polymorphic_identity='C')

mapper(Accessory, accessory_table, inherits=Product,
       polymorphic_identity='A')
```

We can now perform polymorphic selects just as before:

```
>>> metadata.bind.echo = True
>>> session.query(Product).all()
2007-11-19 19:51:11,985 INFO sqlalchemy.engine.base.Engine.0x..d0
... SELECT product.sku AS product_sku, product.msrp AS product_msrp,
... product.product_type AS product_product_type
FROM product ORDER BY product.oid
```

```
2007-11-19 19:51:11,985 INFO sqlalchemy.engine.base.Engine.0x..d0 []
2007-11-19 19:51:11,989 INFO sqlalchemy.engine.base.Engine.0x..d0
... SELECT accessory.sku AS accessory_sku, accessory.accessory_info
... AS accessory_accessory_info
FROM accessory
WHERE ? = accessory.sku
2007-11-19 19:51:11,990 INFO sqlalchemy.engine.base.Engine.0x..d0
... [u'222']
2007-11-19 19:51:11,991 INFO sqlalchemy.engine.base.Engine.0x..d0
... SELECT accessory.sku AS accessory_sku, accessory.accessory_info
... AS accessory_accessory_info
FROM accessory
WHERE ? = accessory.sku
2007-11-19 19:51:11,991 INFO sqlalchemy.engine.base.Engine.0x..d0
... [u'333']
2007-11-19 19:51:11,993 INFO sqlalchemy.engine.base.Engine.0x..d0
... SELECT clothing.sku AS clothing_sku, clothing.clothing_info AS
... clothing_clothing_info
FROM clothing
WHERE ? = clothing.sku
2007-11-19 19:51:11,993 INFO sqlalchemy.engine.base.Engine.0x..d0
... [u'789']
2007-11-19 19:51:11,994 INFO sqlalchemy.engine.base.Engine.0x..d0
... SELECT clothing.sku AS clothing_sku, clothing.clothing_info AS
... clothing_clothing_info
FROM clothing
WHERE ? = clothing.sku
2007-11-19 19:51:11,995 INFO sqlalchemy.engine.base.Engine.0x..d0
... [u'111']
[<Product 123>, <Product 456>, <Clothing 789>, <Clothing 111>,
... <Accessory 222>, <Accessory 333>]
```

As you can see, the various types of products are selected from their tables appropriately. Note, however, that the single query() call yielded not one, but *five* SELECT statements. This is due to the fact that SQLAlchemy must perform an auxiliary query for each row that represents a child object. The next section shows how we can improve performance in this situation.

Optimizing Performance with Joined Table Inheritance Mapping

As shown previously, the default query strategy for joined table inheritance mapping requires one query to the database to retrieve the "parent" row, and one additional query to retrieve each "child" row. Although this is bandwidth-efficient for small fetches (since only the columns that are actually required are returned from the database), the latency of additional queries can incur significant performance overheads, especially when retrieving large result sets.

There are two main strategies for addressing these performance concerns: deferring the child table loads and using a join with the select_table parameter to the mapper( ) function.

Using deferred loading

If the child attributes will not be accessed, or will not be accessed frequently, then the child table's select statements can be deferred until a mapped attribute is accessed. In the previous example, for instance, if we were displaying a table with only the sku and msrp columns, we could eliminate the extra selects by using the polymorphic_fetch parameter to the mapper( ) function:

```
mapper(
    Product, product_table,
    polymorphic_on=product_table.c.product_type,
    polymorphic_identity='P',
    polymorphic_fetch='deferred')

mapper(Clothing, clothing_table, inherits=Product,
    polymorphic_identity='C')

mapper(Accessory, accessory_table, inherits=Product,
    polymorphic_identity='A')
```

Now, when we iterate over all the Products, we see that the auxiliary queries have been eliminated:

```
>>> session.clear()
>>> session.query(Product).all()
2007-11-19 21:25:44,320 INFO sqlalchemy.engine.base.Engine.0x..d0
... SELECT product.sku AS product_sku, product.msrp AS product_msrp,
... product.product_type AS product_product_type
FROM product ORDER BY product.oid
2007-11-19 21:25:44,321 INFO sqlalchemy.engine.base.Engine.0x..d0 []
[<Product 123>, <Product 456>, <Clothing 789>, <Clothing 111>,
... <Accessory 222>, <Accessory 333>]
```

If we access one of the child attributes, then the secondary select executes to retrieve that value:

```
>>> prod=session.get(Product, '789')
>>> print prod.clothing_info
2007-11-19 21:27:11,856 INFO sqlalchemy.engine.base.Engine.0x..d0
... SELECT clothing.sku AS clothing_sku, clothing.clothing_info AS
... clothing_clothing_info
FROM clothing
WHERE ? = clothing.sku
2007-11-19 21:27:11,856 INFO sqlalchemy.engine.base.Engine.0x..d0
... [u'789']
Nice Pants
```

Using select_table

Although using deferred polymorphic fetching alleviates some of the performance problems with joined table inheritance, it still does not help in the case where you need attributes from the child table. In this case, you can simply use the select_table parameter with the mapper(), similar to the way we used it with concrete table inheritance and the polymorphic_union() function. In this case, however, because of the foreign key relationships between parent and child tables, we can simply use an outerjoin():

```
pjoin = product_table
pjoin = pjoin.outerjoin(clothing_table)
pjoin = pjoin.outerjoin(accessory_table)

mapper(
    Product, product_table,
    polymorphic_on=product_table.c.product_type,
    polymorphic_identity='P',
    select_table=pjoin)

mapper(Clothing, clothing_table, inherits=Product,
        polymorphic_identity='C')

mapper(Accessory, accessory_table, inherits=Product,
        polymorphic_identity='A')
```

Now, when we iterate over all Products, we have access to all attributes of all child classes in a single query:

```
>>> session.clear()
>>> for prod in session.query(Product):
...     if hasattr(prod, 'clothing_info'):
...         print '%s : %s' % (prod, prod.clothing_info)
...     elif hasattr(prod, 'accessory_info'):
...         print '%s : %s' % (prod, prod.accessory_info)
...     else:
...         print prod
...
2007-11-19 21:35:11,193 INFO sqlalchemy.engine.base.Engine.0x..d0
... SELECT product.sku AS product_sku, clothing.sku AS clothing_sku,
... accessory.sku AS accessory_sku, product.msrp AS product_msrp,
... product.product_type AS product_product_type,
... clothing.clothing_info AS clothing_clothing_info,
... accessory.accessory_info AS accessory_accessory_info
FROM product LEFT OUTER JOIN clothing ON product.sku = clothing.sku
... LEFT OUTER JOIN accessory ON product.sku = accessory.sku ORDER
... BY product.oid
2007-11-19 21:35:11,194 INFO sqlalchemy.engine.base.Engine.0x..d0 []
<Product 123>
<Product 456>
<Clothing 789> : Nice Pants
<Clothing 111> : Nicer Pants
<Accessory 222> : Wallet
<Accessory 333> : Belt
```

Relations and Inheritance

In the cases of single table and joined table inheritance mapping, relations "just work" in SQLAlchemy. In particular, it is possible for a mapped class to declare a relation to a class that is part of an inheritance hierarchy (a "polymorphic class"), and have that relation comprise instances of various child classes. This setup is shown in the following listing, where inventory information is added to our schema:

```
store_table = Table(
    'store', metadata,
    Column('id', Integer, primary_key=True),
    Column('name', String))

inventory_table = Table(
    'inventory', metadata,
    Column('store_id', None, ForeignKey('store.id')),
    Column('product_id', None, ForeignKey('product.sku')),
    Column('quantity', Integer, default=0)

class Store(object): pass

class Inventory(object): pass

mapper(Store, store_table, properties=dict(
    inventory=relation(Inventory, backref='store')))

mapper(Inventory, inventory_table, properties=dict(
    product=relation(Product, backref='inventory')))
```

It is also possible to declare relations on a polymorphic class at any level of the inheritance hierarchy, and those relations will be inherited by the child classes. In the previous example, for instance, the `Clothing` and `Accessory` classes inherit the `backref` to their `Inventory` records.

In concrete table inheritance, mapping relations to a "parent class" is more difficult because there is no unique table to join to. For instance, it is possible to implement one-to-many and one-to-one joins where the polymorphic class has a foreign key into another table. As an example, if we introduced a "vendor" table identifying the manufacturer of all products, we could relate it to the `Product` hierarchy as follows:

```
vendor_table = Table(
    'vendor', metadata,
    Column('id', Integer, primary_key=True),
    Column('name', String))

product_table = Table(
    'product', metadata,
    Column('sku', String(20), primary_key=True),
    Column('msrp', Numeric),
    Column('vendor_id', None, ForeignKey('vendor.id'))

clothing_table = Table(
    'clothing', metadata,
    Column('sku', String(20), primary_key=True),
    Column('msrp', Numeric),
    Column('vendor_id', None, ForeignKey('vendor.id'),
    Column('clothing_info', String))

accessory_table = Table(
```

```
        'accessory', metadata,
        Column('sku', String(20), primary_key=True),
        Column('msrp', Numeric),
        Column('vendor_id', None, ForeignKey('vendor.id')),
        Column('accessory_info', String))

punion = polymorphic_union(
    dict(P=product_table,
         C=clothing_table,
         A=accessory_table),
    'type_')

mapper(
    Product, product_table, select_table=punion,
    polymorphic_on=punion.c.type_,
    polymorphic_identity='P')

mapper(Clothing, clothing_table, inherits=Product,
       polymorphic_identity='C',
       concrete=True)

mapper(Accessory, accessory_table, inherits=Product,
       polymorphic_identity='A',
       concrete=True)

class Vendor(object): pass

mapper(Vendor, vendor_table, properties=dict(
    products=relation(Product)))
```

The main limitation with relations and concrete table inheritance mapping is that relations *from* the polymorphic classes (rather than *to* them, as shown previously) are not inherited and must therefore be configured individually for each mapper. This includes all many-to-many relations, as the secondary join condition (and probably the secondary table as well) is different depending on which child class is being related to.

Nonpolymorphic Inheritance

All of the inheritance relationships shown so far were implemented using SQLAlchemy's polymorphic loading. If polymorphic loading is not desired, either because of its overhead or because you always know what types of classes you will be fetching, it is possible to use nonpolymorphic loading by omitting all of the `polymorphic_*` parameters from the mappers.

Nonpolymorphic loading will always return the type of object being selected in the case of a query (never the child class, as polymorphic loading does). Relations to nonpolymorphic classes also apply only to the actual class being mapped, not to its descendants. Polymorphic loading is much more flexible than nonpolymorphic loading, and therefore should probably be selected unless the performance overhead is prohibitive.

## CHAPTER 9

Elixir: A Declarative Extension to SQLAlchemy

This chapter describes Elixir, a module developed to automate some of the more common tasks in SQLAlchemy by providing a declarative layer atop "base" or "raw" SQLAlchemy. This chapter also describes the various extensions to Elixir that provide features such as encryption and versioning.

Introduction to Elixir

The Elixir module was developed as a declarative layer on top of SQLAlchemy, implementing the "active record" pattern described in Chapter 6. Elixir goes out of its way to make all of the power of SQLAlchemy available, while providing sensible default behavior with significantly less code than "raw" SQLAlchemy. This chapter describes versions 0.4 and 0.5 of Elixir, corresponding to the 0.4 version of SQLAlchemy. Differences between versions 0.4 and 0.5 are discussed in the upcoming sidebar, "Differences Between Elixir 0.4 and 0.5."

So, what exactly does Elixir *do*? Well, consider a simple product database. In SQLAlchemy, we might set up the products, stores, and prices with the following code:

```
product_table = Table(
    'product', metadata,
    Column('sku', String(20), primary_key=True),
    Column('msrp', Numeric))
store_table = Table(
    'store', metadata,
    Column('id', Integer, primary_key=True),
    Column('name', Unicode(255)))
product_price_table = Table(
    'product_price', metadata,
Column('sku', None, ForeignKey('product.sku'), primary_key=True),
Column('store_id', None, ForeignKey('store.id'), primary_key=True),
    Column('price', Numeric, default=0))
```

```
class Product(object):
    def __init__(self, sku, msrp):
        self.sku = sku
        self.msrp = msrp
        self.prices = []
    def __repr__(self):
        return '<Product %s>' % self.sku

class Store(object):
    def __init__(self, name):
        self.name = name
    def __repr__(self):
        return '<Store %s>' % self.name

class Price(object):
    def __init__(self, product, store, price):
        self.product = product
        self.store = store
        self.price = price
    def __repr__(self):
        return '<Price %s at %s for $%.2f>' % (
            self.product.sku, self.store.name, self.price)

mapper(Product, product_table, properties=dict(
    prices=relation(Price, backref='product')))
mapper(Store, store_table, properties=dict(
    prices=relation(Price, backref='store')))
mapper(Price, product_price_table)
```

In Elixir, the corresponding setup is much simpler:

```
class Product(Entity):
    sku=Field(String(20), primary_key=True)
    msrp=Field(Numeric)
    prices=OneToMany('Price')

    def __repr__(self):
        return '<Product %s>' % self.sku

class Store(Entity):
    name=Field(Unicode(255))
    prices=OneToMany('Price')

    def __repr__(self):
        return '<Store %s>' % self.name

class Price(Entity):
    price=Field(Numeric, default=0)
    product=ManyToOne('Product')
    store=ManyToOne('Store')

    def __repr__(self):
        return '<Price %s at %s for $%.2f>' % (
            self.product.sku, self.store.name, self.price)
```

Differences Between Elixir 0.4 and 0.5

The main difference between Elixir versions 0.4 and 0.5 is in the way your entities get transformed into SQLAlchemy tables and mappers. In version 0.4, Elixir introduced the idea of "autosetup," where entities were "set up" when they were first accessed. Under 0.4, you could delay the setup of an entity by specifying autosetup=False in the using_options() DSL statement. In this case, you would need to manually set up the entity at some point before using it by calling either setup_all(), which will set up all entities defined, or setup_entities(entities), which will set up all the entities in the entities list.

In version 0.5, entities do *not* use autosetup by default, so you are responsible for manually applying either setup_all() or setup_entities() once all your entities have been defined. If you would still like to use autosetup, you can either specify autosetup=True for each entity in its using_options() statement or specify that all entities should use autosetup via:

    elixir.options_defaults['autosetup'] = True

In version 0.5, autosetup is not only not the default, but also "is not recommended" according to the official Elixir documentation. So, using setup_all() is probably the most "future-proof" way of defining your model.

There are several interesting things to notice in the Elixir listing. First, note that the declaration of the tables has been moved *inside* the class definitions, and that the classes are derived from Elixir's Entity class. This is in keeping with Elixir's "active record" model, where the mapped classes are responsible for "remembering" the necessary data for persisting themselves. Second, notice that we didn't declare any primary keys for the store or the price tables. If no primary key is declared, then Elixir will autogenerate an integer primary key with a sequence providing default values. Third, notice that the relationships were declared according to their behavior in the ORM (OneToMany, ManyToOne), and that no foreign key information was included in the model. Elixir will, based on the types of relationships declared, automatically generate foreign key columns as well as any auxiliary tables required for ManyToMany joins.

Because of the various types of assumptions Elixir makes about table layout, it is suited mainly for "blue sky" development, where there is no need to maintain an existing legacy database, and where the primary schema definition exists in Python, not in SQL. It is possible to use Elixir where Elixir does not provide the primary schema definition, but it's easy to shoot yourself in the foot if you're not aware of the assumptions Elixir makes about the schema, particularly when dealing with auto-generated tables and columns.

Installing Elixir

Elixir, like SQLAlchemy, is best installed using SetupTools and *easy_install*. Assuming you have already installed SetupTools and SQLAlchemy as described in Chapter 2, you can install Elixir on Unix-like systems—including Linux, BSD, and OS X—as follows:

```
$ sudo easy_install -UZ Elixir
```

On Windows, the command is similar:

```
c:\>easy_install -UZ Elixir
```

To verify that Elixir is installed properly, open up an interactive Python interpreter, import the module, and verify its version:

```
>>> import elixir
>>> elixir.__version__
'0.4.0'
```

And that's all there is to it. Elixir is installed!

Using Elixir

Elixir has two syntaxes for defining your classes: an attribute-based syntax (shown previously) and a "domain specific language" (DSL) syntax. Both have similar power; which one you use is mostly a matter of personal style. The DSL-based syntax may be phased out in the future, as it is no longer the "default" syntax, but it is not currently deprecated, so it is covered in this chapter. If we were to define the product database using the DSL syntax, for instance, we would write the following (with the methods for each class omitted for clarity):

```python
from elixir import *

metadata.bind = 'sqlite://'

class Product(Entity):
    has_field('sku', String(20), primary_key=True)
    has_field('msrp', Numeric)
    has_many('prices', of_kind='Price')

class Store(Entity):
    has_field('name', Unicode(255))
    has_many('prices', of_kind='Price')

class Price(Entity):
    has_field('price', Numeric, default=0)
    belongs_to('product', of_kind='Product')
    belongs_to('store', of_kind='Store')
```

There is a rough correspondence between the functionality of the attribute-based syntax for defining entities and the DSL syntax. The attribute-based classes are listed in Table 9-1 along with their corresponding DSL function. Note that the mapping from

---

attribute-based syntax to DSL syntax is not perfect; consult the rest of this chapter for the specific differences.

Table 9-1. Correspondence between attribute-based syntax and DSL syntax

Attribute class	DSL function
Field	has_field
ColumnProperty, GenericProperty	has_property
ManyToOne	belongs_to
OneToMany	has_many
OneToOne	has_one
ManyToMany	has_and_belongs_to_many

 Unlike SQLAlchemy, Elixir currently requires that your entities be defined in a module (or in several modules) and imported; they cannot be defined at the interactive Python prompt. This is due partly to the fact that Elixir uses the module name in determining how to "autoname" the tables it creates.

In all of the following examples, we will show the attribute-based syntax first, followed by the DSL syntax.

Fields and Properties

In Elixir, most columns are defined via the Field( ) class (attribute syntax) and/or the has_field() statement (DSL syntax). The Field constructor has only one required argument, its type. There are also some optional arguments parsed by Elixir. Any remaining arguments are passed along to the SQLAlchemy Column constructor. The Elixir-parsed optional keyword arguments are described here:

required
> Specifies whether the field can be set to None (corresponds to the inverse of the nullable option in the Column constructor). Defaults to False unless this is a primary key column, in which case it defaults to True.

colname
> The name of the column to be used for this field. By default it will be the same as the name used for the attribute.

deferred
> If True, use deferred loading on the underlying Column object. If set to a string value, add the underlying Column to the named deferred loading column group.

synonym
> Specifies a synonym value for the field. This is equivalent to using the synonym() function in SQLAlchemy.

Like the Field constructor, the has_field() statement passes along unrecognized keyword arguments to the Column constructor. has_field() takes two required arguments: the name of the field being defined and its type. Elixir also supports the following optional arguments:

through
> The name of a relation to go through to get the field. This uses the *association proxy* SQLAlchemy extension, which is described in Chapter 11. This allows proxying fields from a related class onto the class being mapped. The relation must be with only one object, of course, via ManyToOne / belongs_to() or OneToOne / has_one().

attribute
> The name of the attribute on the related object used in conjunction with the through parameter. If this is omitted, the name of the current field will be used.

With the through and attribute arguments to has_field(), we can proxy a related class's attribute as follows:

```
class Price(Entity):
    has_field('price', Numeric, default=0)
    belongs_to('product', of_kind='Product')
    belongs_to('store', of_kind='Store')
    has_field('store_name', through='store', attribute='name')
    has_field('sku', through='product')
```

Using this definition of the Price entity and the definitions of Product and Store used previously (all saved in a module named *model.py*), let's import the model, create the database, and see what Elixir does in the background:

```
>>> from elixir import *
>>> from model import *
>>>
>>> create_all() ❶
>>>
>>> stores = [ Store('Main Store'),
...            Store('Secondary Store') ]
>>> products = [
...     Product('123', 11.22),
...     Product('456', 33.44),
...     Product('789', 123.45) ]
>>> prices = [ Price(product=product, store=store, price=10.00)
...            for product in products
...            for store in stores ]
>>>
>>> session.flush() ❷
```

❶ This will create all the tables used to implement the entities defined up to this point.

---

❷ Elixir provides a thread-local contextual session where all the entities are defined.

Now, to access the `store_name` attribute on a price, we can do the following:

```
>>> metadata.bind.echo = True
>>> price = Price.get(1)
2007-11-20 17:44:46,141 INFO sqlalchemy.engine.base.Engine.0x..90
... SELECT model_price.id AS model_price_id, model_price.price AS
... model_price_price, model_price.product_sku AS
... model_price_product_sku, model_price.store_id AS
... model_price_store_id
FROM model_price
WHERE model_price.id = ? ORDER BY model_price.oid
2007-11-20 17:44:46,141 INFO sqlalchemy.engine.base.Engine.0x..90
... [1]
>>> price.store_name
2007-11-20 17:44:49,229 INFO sqlalchemy.engine.base.Engine.0x..90
... SELECT model_store.id AS model_store_id, model_store.name AS
... model_store_name
FROM model_store
WHERE model_store.id = ? ORDER BY model_store.oid
2007-11-20 17:44:49,230 INFO sqlalchemy.engine.base.Engine.0x..90
... [1]
u'Main Store'
```

Two things are important to note here. The first is that our `has_field()` statement did indeed create a "proxy" statement to the `Store` entity's `name` field. The second is Elixir's naming convention. By default, tables created to implement entities have names generated by combining the module name with the entity name.

Elixir deferred properties

In some cases, you may need to have access to the underlying table to define an `Entity`'s properties, particularly when creating properties that correspond to calculated SQL values that were handled by SQLAlchemy's `column_property()` function. This presents a problem in Elixir, as the underlying `Table` objects have not been created when the `Field`s are being defined. Elixir solves this problem by allowing fields to be created in a "deferred" manner. Elixir supports this in the attribute-based syntax via the `GenericProperty` and `ColumnProperty` classes, and in the DSL syntax via the `has_property()` statement.

Each of these methods of defining deferred properties takes a callable, which will be passed the underlying `Table` object's `c` attribute and should return a property to be added to the `Entity`'s mapper. In the case of `ColumnProperty`, rather than returning a property object, you simply return a `ClauseElement`, which will be wrapped in a SQLAlchemy `column_property()`:

```
class Product(Entity):
    has_field('sku', String(20), primary_key=True)
    has_field('msrp', Numeric)

    # Using has_property DSL
```

```
has_property(
    'sale_price1',
    lambda c: column_property(c.msrp * 0.9))

# Using GenericProperty attribute
sale_price2 = GenericProperty(
    lambda c: column_property(c.msrp * 0.8))

# Using ColumnProperty attribute
sale_price2 = ColumnProperty(
    lambda c: c.msrp * 0.8)
```

Relations

Relations with Elixir are extremely similar to relations using "bare" SQLAlchemy, except that in Elixir, relations are defined by their cardinality (one to many, one to one, etc.) rather than inferred by foreign key relationships. In fact, Elixir will automatically *create* the foreign key columns necessary to implement the relations as defined.

Related Entity Names

In all of the relations supported by Elixir, you must "name" the Entity to which you are relating the mapped Entity. If the related Entity is in the same module as the Entity being mapped, simply use the name of the Entity. Otherwise, you need to give a module path to the other entity. If you defined Entity1 in *package/model1.py* and Entity2 in *package/model2.py*, and Entity2 needs a ManyToOne relationship to Entity1, you would define Entity2 as follows:

```
class Entity2(Entity):
    entity1=ManyToOne('package.model1.Entity')
```

Attribute-based syntax

In the attribute-based syntax, relationships are declared via the ManyToOne, OneToMany, OneToOne, and ManyToMany classes. Each of these class constructors takes one required argument, a string specifying the name of the class being related to. Each also supports some arguments unique to Elixir and pass any unrecognized arguments along to the underlying SQLAlchemy relation() function. Note that the OneToMany and OneToOne relationships require a corresponding ManyToOne relationship in order to set up the foreign key column used to relate the classes.

 Elixir automatically generates a few arguments of its own to pass to the relation() function, so they should not be provided to the relation-creating classes unless you are trying to override the value provided by Elixir. These arguments are uselist, remote_side, secondary, primaryjoin, and secondaryjoin.

The ManyToOne optional parameters are listed here:

---

inverse

> Specifies the inverse property on the related class corresponding to this property. Generally this is not required unless there are multiple relationships between this class and the related class. Note that this does *not* set up the inverse relationship; the inverse relationship must be defined in the related class.

colname

> The name of the foreign key column to be created. The default is *entity_key*, where *entity* is the related `Entity` and *key* is the name of the related entity's primary key.

required

> If `True`, specifies that the generated foreign key column has a `nonnull` constraint. Defaults to `False`.

primary_key

> If `True`, specifies that the generated foreign key column participates in the primary key of this `Entity`. Defaults to `False`.

column_kwargs

> A `dict` containing additional keyword arguments to be passed to the foreign key's `Column` constructor.

use_alter

> If `True`, add the `ForeignKeyConstraint` after the table has been created using an ALTER TABLE constraint. This is useful, for instance, when creating entities with circular foreign key dependencies.

ondelete

> Value for the `ForeignKeyConstraint`'s `ondelete` parameter.

onupdate

> Value for the `ForeignKeyConstraint`'s `onupdate` parameter.

constraint_kwargs

> A `dict` containing additional keyword arguments to be passed to the `ForeignKeyConstraint`'s constructor.

The following list contains the `OneToMany` constructor's optional parameters:

inverse

> Specifies the inverse property on the related class corresponding to this property. Generally, this is not required unless there are multiple relationships between this class and the related class. Note that this does *not* set up the inverse relationship; the inverse relationship must be defined in the related class.

order_by

> Either a string or a list of strings specifying the field names used to sort the contents of the generated list of related items. If a field is prefixed by a minus ('-'), the list will be sorted in descending order on that field.

The following is the `OneToOne` constructor's optional parameter:

inverse

> Specifies the inverse property on the related class corresponding to this property. Generally this is not required unless there are multiple relationships between this class and the related class. Note that this does *not* set up the inverse relationship; the inverse relationship must be defined in the related class.

The ManyToMany constructor takes the following optional parameters:

inverse

> Specifies the inverse property on the related class corresponding to this property. Generally this is not required unless there are multiple relationships between this class and the related class. Note that this does *not* set up the inverse relationship; the inverse relationship must be defined in the related class.

tablename

> Specifies a custom name for the intermediate "join table" used in the relationship. By default, the join table is named based on the entity names being joined.

remote_side

> A list of columns or column names specifying which columns in the join table are used to key the remote side of a self-referential relationship.

local_side

> A list of columns or column names specifying which columns in the join table are used to key the local side of a self-referential relationship.

order_by

> Either a string or a list of strings specifying field names used to sort the contents of the generated list of related items. If a field is prefixed by a minus ('-'), the list will be sorted in descending order on that field.

Note that no feature in Elixir corresponds to the SQLAlchemy backref parameter on relation()s. This means that if you want the back reference, you must explicitly declare it in the class to which it is related.

DSL syntax

In the DSL syntax, relationships are declared via the belongs_to( ), has_many(), has_one(), and has_and_belongs_to_many() statements. Each of these functions takes two required arguments. The first is the name of the relation being defined. (This will be the name of the attribute in the mapped class.) The second argument, which must be declared using the of_kind keyword argument, is the name of the Entity being related to.

Like the has_field() statement, all the DSL relation statements take the optional parameters through and via in order to proxy attributes of the related class(es) to the mapped class. See the earlier section "Fields and Properties" for more information on these parameters.

All of the keyword arguments supported in the attribute-based syntax are also supported in the DSL syntax. Refer to Table 9-1 earlier in this chapter for the correspondence between attribute-based classes and DSL statements.

Inheritance

Inheritance in Elixir is handled via either the single table inheritance mapping or the joined table inheritance mapping supported by SQLAlchemy (and described in detail in Chapter 8). Elixir also supports specifying whether polymorphic or nonpolymorphic loading should be used with the mapped classes. Both the inheritance method (joined table or single table) and whether the loader should be polymorphic are specified via the DSL statement using_options(). There is currently no corresponding attribute-based syntax for specifying options on entities. So, to create the Product, Clothing, and Accessory hierarchy described in Chapter 8 in Elixir as a joined table ("multiple") and polymorphic hierarchy, we would write the following (with methods omitted for clarity):

```
class Product(Entity):
    using_options(inheritance='multi', polymorphic=True)
    sku=Field(String(20), primary_key=True)
    msrp=Field(Numeric)

class Clothing(Product):
    using_options(inheritance='multi', polymorphic=True)
    clothing_info=Field(String)

class Accessory(Product):
    using_options(inheritance='multi', polymorphic=True)
    accessory_info=Field(String)
```

The with_options() statement takes a number of other options, described here:

inheritance
> Specifies the type of inheritance used: either 'single' for single table inheritance mapping or 'multi' for joined ("multiple") table inheritance mapping. Concrete table inheritance mapping is not supported in Elixir. Defaults to 'single'.

polymorphic
> Specifies whether the polymorphic loader should be used in an inheritance hierarchy. Defaults to False.

metadata
> Specifies a custom MetaData to be used for this Entity. Defaults to the global elixir.metadata. You can also specify a custom MetaData on a per-module basis by defining the module-global variable __metadata__.

autoload
> Automatically loads field definitions from an existing database table. The default is False.

tablename
> Use the specified table name. This can be either a string or a callable that takes one parameter (the entity being defined) and returns a string. The default name is autogenerated by Elixir.

shortnames
> If True, rather than naming the underlying Table based on the full module path to the entity, use the lowercased Entity name without any module path information. Defaults to False.

auto_primarykey
> If this is a string, it will be used as the name of the primary key column automatically generated by Elixir (which will be an Integer column with a corresponding sequence). If this is True, allows Elixir to autocreate a primary key (with an auto-generated name) if none is defined in the Entity. If False, this disallows autocreation of the primary key column.

version_id_col
> If this is a string, it will be used as the name of a version ID column (see Chapter 6 for the corresponding mapper() option version_id in SQLAlchemy). If this is True, it uses an autogenerated name for a version_id_col. The default is False.

order_by
> The default ordering on this Entity, given as a string or list of strings representing the field names to sort by. If a field is prefixed by a minus ('-'), the list will be sorted in descending order on that field.

session
> Use the specified contextual session for this Entity. The default is to use the globally-defined elixir.session, a contextual thread-local Session. You can also specify a custom Session on a per-module basis by defining the module-global variable __session__.

autosetup
> If set to True, the underlying Table and mapper() will be set up for the Entity when they are first required (via access to the Entity's c, table, mapper, or query attributes) or when the MetaData's create_all() method is called. If set to False, you must explicitly set up the Entity either via the setup_all() or the setup_entities(entities) Elixir functions. This defaults to True in version 0.4 of Elixir, and to False in version 0.5.

allowcoloverride
> If True, allows a relation to be defined with the same name as a mapped column (the column will not be mapped in this case). If False, the name conflict will generate an exception. Corresponds to the SQLAlchemy mapper() option allow_column_override. Defaults to False.

Querying Using Elixir

One of the nice things about Elixir is that the `Entity` base class contains a rich set of methods that can be used instead of the normal SQLAlchemy `Session` and `Query` methods. In fact, each `Entity` contains a class-level attribute named `query` that returns a query on the mapped class. It is also unnecessary to explicitly `save()` entities to the `Session`, as they are automatically `save()`d when they are created.

To retrieve a mapped object from its identity (primary key), simply use the `get()` method. (In "base" SQLAlchemy, this would be accomplished by `Session.get(class_, id)`.)

```
>>> Product.get('123')
<Product 123>
```

Elixir also adds the `get_by()` method for retrieving a single instance based on nonprimary key columns. (The corresponding query in SQLAlchemy is a `filter_by()` followed by `one()`.)

```
>>> Product.get_by(msrp=33.44)
<Product 456>
```

Of course, you can always access the underlying `Session` query via the `query` attribute:

```
>>> Product.query.all()
[<Product 123>, <Product 456>, <Product 789>]
```

The complete set of (nondeprecated) methods on the `Entity` class is described in the following list. Each of these methods is a proxy for the corresponding `Session` methods, covered in Chapter 7, and any arguments provided to these methods are passed along unmodified to the underlying `Session` methods:

flush(self, *args, **kwargs)
> Flush the changes to this instance to the database.

delete(self, *args, **kwargs)
> Mark this instance for deletion from the database.

expire(self, *args, **kwargs)
> Expire this instance from the `Session`.

refresh(self, *args, **kwargs)
> Reload this instance from the database, overwriting any in-memory changes.

expunge(self, *args, **kwargs)
> Expunge this instance from the `Session`.

merge(self, *args, **kwargs)
> Merge the instance with the instance in the `Session`.

save(self, *args, **kwargs)
> Save this instance to the `Session`.

update(self, *args, **kwargs)
> Bring this (detached) instance into the `Session`.

save_or_update(self, *args, **kwargs)
:   Save or update this instance, based on whether it is in the session already.

get_by(self, *args, **kwargs) (classmethod)
:   Retrieve an instance from the database based on the given keyword arguments. Equivalent to instance.query.filter_by(*args, **kwargs).one().

get(self, *args, **kwargs) (classmethod)
:   Retrieve an object from the database or the Session's identity map based on its primary key.

Elixir Extensions

In addition to its base functionality, Elixir provides a number of extensions that allow for more advanced uses.

Associable Extension

In many database schemas, there may be one table that relates to many others via a many-to-many or a many-to-one join. The *elixir.ext.associable* extension provides a convenient way to specify this pattern and to generate the appropriate association tables. This is accomplished by the associable() function, which returns a DSL statement that can be used in the definition of the related entities.

For instance, suppose we have a schema that represents brands and retailers, each of which may have multiple addresses stored in the database. This can be accomplished as follows:

```
class Address(Entity):
    has_field('street', Unicode(255))
    has_field('city', Unicode(255))
    has_field('postal_code', Unicode(10))

# Create the DSL statement.
is_addressable = associable(Address, 'addresses')

class Brand(Entity):
    has_field('name', Unicode(255)),
    has_field('description', Unicode)
    is_addressable()

class Retailer(Entity):
    has_field('name', Unicode(255)),
    has_field('description', Unicode)
    is_addressable()
```

To implement this pattern, the associable extension actually implements something like joined table inheritance mapping, where the entity being associated joins to an intermediate association table, which is in turn joined to a "virtual base class" for each

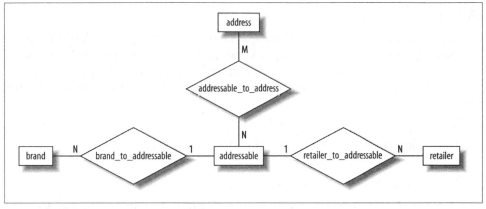

Figure 9-1. Associable table relationships

associable class. The tables created for the previous schema show this more clearly in Figure 9-1.

The `associable()` function takes one required argument, the `Entity` to be associated, as well as some optional arguments:

`plural_name=None`
> The default name to be used for the property generated by the returned DSL statement. By default, this is the lowercased name of the associable `Entity`. (This can be overridden when using the generated statement.)

`lazy=True`
> Indicates whether the property generated by the returned DSL statement should be lazy-loaded by default. (This can be overridden when using the generated statement.)

The generated DSL statement also takes some optional arguments:

`name=None`
> The name to be used for the property generated. This will use the value of the `plural_name` parameter from `associable()` if not specified here.

`uselist=True`
> Whether to use a list in the generated property (representing a `ManyToMany` relation) or a scalar attribute (representing a `ManyToOne` relation).

`lazy=True`
> Whether the property generated should be lazy-loaded by default.

The generated DSL statement, in addition to adding the named property, also adds the helper methods `select_by_property` and `select_property`, which are simply proxies for filtering the `Entity` by values in the associated `Entity`. For instance, we can return a list of all `Brands` in Albuquerque with the following query:

```
>>> Brand.select_by_addresses(city='Albuquerque')
```

Encrypted Extension

The *elixir.ext.encrypted* extension provides encrypted field support for Elixir using the Blowfish algorithm from the PyCrypto library, which must be installed separately. (PyCrypto is available from the Python Package Index via "easy_install pycrypto".) The encrypted extension provides the DSL statement `acts_as_encrypted()`, which takes the following parameters:

`for_fields=[]`
    List of field names for which encryption will be enabled

`with_secret='abcdef'`
    A secret key used to perform encryption on the listed fields

The encrypted extension is particularly useful when data must be stored on an untrusted database or as part of a defense-in-depth approach to security. For instance, you might encrypt passwords that are stored in the database. Keep in mind, however, that the source code of your application must be kept in a trusted location because it specifies the encryption key used to store the encrypted columns.

Versioned Extension

The *elixir.ext.versioned* extension provides a history and versioning for the fields in an entity. These services are provided by the `acts_as_versioned()` DSL statement. Marking an entity as versioned will apply the following operations:

- A timestamp column and a version column will be added to the versioned entity table.

- A history table will be created with the same columns as the primary entity table, including the added timestamp and version columns.

- A `versions` attribute will be added to the versioned entity that represents a `OneToMany` join to the history table.

- The instance methods `revert()`, `revert_to()`, `compare_with()`, and `get_as_of()` will be added to the versioned entity.

Whenever changes are made to a versioned entity, the version column is incremented and the previous values for all the columns are saved to the history table. Note that at the current time, relationships are not handled automatically by the versioning process (relationship changes are not tracked in the history table) and must be handled manually. The size of the history table can be managed by specifying fields *not* to include via the `ignore` option to `acts_as_versioned()`.

Using the `acts_as_versioned()` statement enables us to keep a reasonable audit trail of changes to an entity. If we set up our model as follows:

```
class Product(Entity):
    has_field('sku', String(20), primary_key=True)
    has_field('msrp', Numeric)
```

```
        acts_as_versioned()

        def __repr__(self):
            return '<Product %s, mrsp %s>' % (self.sku, self.msrp)

        @after_revert
        def price_rollback(self):
            print "Rolling back prices to %s" % self.msrp
```

we can then use the audit trail as follows:

```
>>> prod = Product(sku='123', msrp=11.22)
>>> session.flush()
>>> print prod
<Product 123, mrsp 11.22>
>>> print prod.version
1
>>> print len(prod.versions)
1
>>> prod.msrp *= 1.2
>>> session.flush()
>>> print prod
<Product 123, mrsp 13.464>
>>> print prod.version
2
>>> prod.msrp *= 1.3
>>> session.flush()
>>> print prod
<Product 123, mrsp 17.5032>
>>> print prod.version
3
>>> print prod.compare_with(prod.versions[0])
{'timestamp': (datetime.datetime(2007, 11, 21, 15, 50, 43, 951977),
... datetime.datetime(2007, 11, 21, 15, 50, 43, 893200)), 'msrp':
... (17.5032, Decimal("11.22"))}
>>> for ver in prod.versions:
...     print ver.version, ver.timestamp, ver.msrp
...
1 2007-11-21 15:50:43.893200 11.22
2 2007-11-21 15:50:43.939225 13.464
3 2007-11-21 15:50:43.951977 17.5032
>>> prod.revert()
Rolling back prices to 17.5032
>>> prod = Product.get('123')
>>> print prod
<Product 123, mrsp 17.5032>
```

The behaviors of the new methods added by acts_as_versioned() are listed here:

revert(self)

Revert the entity to the last version saved in the history table. After reverting, the instance in memory will be expired and must be refreshed to retrieve the reverted fields.

`revert_to(self, to_version)`
> Revert the entity to a particular version number saved in the history table. After reverting, the instance in memory will be expired and must be refreshed to retrieve the reverted fields.

`compare_with(self, version)`
> Compare the current field values of the entity with the values in a particular version instance. The return value from this method is a `dict` keyed by the field name with values of pairs (*named_version_value*, *current_value*). Note that instances in the entity's `versions` attribute also have a `compare_with()` method, allowing historical versions to be compared with other versions.

`get_as_of(self, dt)`
> Retrieves the most recent version of the entity that was saved before the `datetime dt`. If the current version is the most recent before `dt`, then it is returned.

The versioned extension also provides a decorator, `@after_revert`, which can be used to decorate methods in the versioned entity that should be called after the entity is reverted.

## CHAPTER 10

SqlSoup: An Automatic Mapper for SQLAlchemy

This chapter describes SqlSoup, an extension to SQLAlchemy that provides automatic mapping of introspected tables. You will learn how to use SqlSoup to map to an existing database and how to perform queries and updates. Finally, the chapter will describe the pros and cons of using SQLSoup, Elixir, or "bare" SQLAlchemy in your application.

Introduction to SqlSoup

If Elixir is ideally suited for blue sky, legacy-free development, SqlSoup is ideally suited for connecting to legacy databases. In fact, SqlSoup provides no method of *defining* a database schema through tables, classes, and mappers; it uses extensive autoloading to build the SQLAlchemy constructs (`Tables`, `classes`, and `mapper()`s) automatically from an existing database.

To illustrate the uses of SQLAlchemy in this chapter, we will use the following SQLAlchemy-created schema. Note that, unlike in previous chapters, we will be saving the test database in an on-disk SQLite database rather than using an in-memory database, to illustrate the fact that SqlSoup relies entirely on auto loading:

```
from sqlalchemy import *

engine = create_engine('sqlite:///chapter10.db')

metadata = MetaData(engine)

product_table = Table(
    'product', metadata,
    Column('sku', String(20), primary_key=True),
    Column('msrp', Numeric))
store_table = Table(
    'store', metadata,
    Column('id', Integer, primary_key=True),
    Column('name', Unicode(255)))
```

```
product_price_table = Table(
    'product_price', metadata,
Column('sku', None, ForeignKey('product.sku'), primary_key=True),
Column('store_id', None, ForeignKey('store.id'), primary_key=True),
    Column('price', Numeric, default=0))

metadata.create_all()

stmt = product_table.insert()
stmt.execute([dict(sku="123", msrp=12.34),
              dict(sku="456", msrp=22.12),
              dict(sku="789", msrp=41.44)])
stmt = store_table.insert()
stmt.execute([dict(name="Main Store"),
              dict(name="Secondary Store")])
stmt = product_price_table.insert()
stmt.execute([dict(store_id=1, sku="123"),
              dict(store_id=1, sku="456"),
              dict(store_id=1, sku="789"),
              dict(store_id=2, sku="123"),
              dict(store_id=2, sku="456"),
              dict(store_id=2, sku="789")])
```

In order to use SqlSoup, we must first create an instance of the `SqlSoup` class. This instance must be created either with an existing `MetaData` instance as its first argument, or with the same arguments as SQLAlchemy's `MetaData` class. In our case, we will pass in a database URI to use in autoloading the tables:

```
>>> from sqlalchemy.ext.sqlsoup import SqlSoup
>>> db = SqlSoup('sqlite:///chapter10.db')
```

If we wish to restrict the set of tables loaded to a particular schema (in databases that support this), we can specify it by setting the as `db.schema` attribute. Because we're using SQLite, there is no need to specify a schema.

To access the tables we've defined in the database, simply use attribute access from the `SqlSoup` instance we've created:

```
>>> print db.product.all()
[MappedProduct(sku='123',msrp=Decimal("12.34")),
... MappedProduct(sku='456',msrp=Decimal("22.12")),
... MappedProduct(sku='789',msrp=Decimal("41.44"))]

>>> print db.product.get('123')
MappedProduct(sku='123',msrp=Decimal("12.34"))
```

Note that there was no mapper or table setup required to retrieve the objects (other than when we first created the database!). The following sections describe in more detail how you can use SqlSoup.

Using SqlSoup for ORM-Style Queries and Updates

You may have noticed in the previous section that when we queried the db.product table, rather than being served with RowProxy objects as in regular SQLAlchemy, we were served with MappedProduct instances. This is because technically we're not selecting from the product table; we're selecting from the automatically created and mapped MappedProduct class, created from the product table.

The MappedProduct class provides a basic mapping of the columns of the table to the properties of the class. It also provides a query property, similar to the Elixir query property, which provides access to a session query for the MappedProduct. It also provides insert(), delete(), and update() methods for modifying the underlying data. To create a new product, for instance, we can do the following:

```
>>> newprod = db.product.insert(sku='111', msrp=22.44)
>>> db.flush()
>>> db.clear()
>>> db.product.all()
[MappedProduct(sku='123',msrp=Decimal("12.34")),
... MappedProduct(sku='456',msrp=Decimal("22.12")),
... MappedProduct(sku='789',msrp=Decimal("41.44")),
... MappedProduct(sku='111',msrp=Decimal("22.44"))]
```

You may have noticed in the previous example that we accessed the session-like methods flush() and clear() on the SqlSoup instance. SqlSoup strives to provide a rich set of functionality with a limited set of interfaces, namely the SqlSoup instance and automatically mapped classes. As such, the SqlSoup instance provides several session-like functions as well as providing access to the automatically mapped classes:

bind(attribute)
: The underlying Engine or Connectable for this SqlSoup instance.

schema(attribute)
: Use the specified schema name for auto loading and automatically mapping tables.

clear(self)
: Call the underlying contextual session's clear() method.

delete(self, *args, **kwargs)
: Call the underlying contextual session's delete() method with the specified arguments.

flush(self)
: Call the underlying contextual session's flush() method.

join(self, *args, *kwargs)
: Call SQLAlchemy's join() function with the specified arguments and return an automatically mapped object corresponding to rows of the generated join.

map(self, selectable, *kwargs)
: Automatically map an arbitrary selectable, returning the generated mapped class.

`with_labels(self, item)`
> Add labels to the columns of `item` (generally a join) based on the name of their table of origin. This is useful when mapping joins between two tables with the same column names.

You may have also noticed that the `MappedProduct` class provides some query-like methods. In fact, the `MappedProduct` class (and other automatically mapped classes) uses some `__getattr__()` magic to forward *all* unrecognized attribute and method access to its `query` attribute. Automatically mapped classes also provide some data manipulation functions for use in updating the underlying table:

`c` (attribute)
> The `c` attribute of the underlying table.

`query` (attribute)
> An ORM-based query object on the automatically mapped class.

`_table` (attribute)
> The underlying selectable to this automatically mapped object. Useful when dropping to the SQL layer in SqlSoup queries.

column_name (attribute)
> The SQLAlchemy property object of the automatically mapped column.

`delete(cls, *args, **kwargs)` (classmethod)
> Execute a `delete()` on the underlying table with the given arguments.

`insert(cls, **kwargs)` (classmethod)
> Execute an `insert()` on the underlying table with the given arguments, and return a newly constructed instance of the automatically mapped class.

`update(cls, whereclause=None, values=None, **kwargs)` (classmethod)
> Execute an `update()` on the underlying table with the given arguments.

SqlSoup and Relations

The short story on SqlSoup and SQLAlchemy `relation()`s is that they are not supported. Although SqlSoup can make reasonable assumptions about how to automatically map columns to classes, inferring the correct relations, relation names, and relation options is currently beyond its capabilities. SqlSoup does, however, fully support manually creating joins between tables and mapping the resulting selectable object. This feature is covered next in "Joins with SqlSoup."

Joins with SqlSoup

The SqlSoup object provides a `join()` method, described briefly in the list under the section "Using SqlSoup for ORM-Style Queries and Updates," earlier in this chapter. This method is actually just a thin wrapper on the SQLAlchemy `join()` function that creates an automatically mapped class for the resulting selectable. To join between the

---

product and product_price tables, for example, we could use the following code, taking care to use the isouter=True to ensure we get a LEFT OUTER JOIN:

```
>>> join1 = db.join(db.product, db.product_price, isouter=True)
>>> join1.all()
[MappedJoin(sku='123',msrp=Decimal("12.34"),store_id=1,
... price=Decimal("0")),
... MappedJoin(sku='123',msrp=Decimal("12.34"),store_id=2,
... price=Decimal("0")),
... MappedJoin(sku='456',msrp=Decimal("22.12"),store_id=1,
... price=Decimal("0")),
... MappedJoin(sku='456',msrp=Decimal("22.12"),store_id=2,
... price=Decimal("0")),
... MappedJoin(sku='789',msrp=Decimal("41.44"),store_id=1,
... price=Decimal("0")),
... MappedJoin(sku='789',msrp=Decimal("41.44"),store_id=2,
... price=Decimal("0")),
... MappedJoin(sku='111',msrp=Decimal("22.44"),store_id=None,price=None)]
```

In order to chain the join object to other tables, just use the join() method again:

```
>>> join2 = db.join(join1, db.store, isouter=True)
>>> join2.all()
[MappedJoin(sku='123',msrp=Decimal("12.34"),store_id=1,
... price=Decimal("0"),id=1,name='Main Store'),
... MappedJoin(sku='123',msrp=Decimal("12.34"),store_id=2,
... price=Decimal("0"),id=2,name='Secondary Store'),
... MappedJoin(sku='456',msrp=Decimal("22.12"),store_id=1,
... price=Decimal("0"),id=1,name='Main Store'),
... MappedJoin(sku='456',msrp=Decimal("22.12"),store_id=2,
... price=Decimal("0"),id=2,name='Secondary Store'),
... MappedJoin(sku='789',msrp=Decimal("41.44"),store_id=1,
... price=Decimal("0"),id=1,name='Main Store'),
... MappedJoin(sku='789',msrp=Decimal("41.44"),store_id=2,
... price=Decimal("0"),id=2,name='Secondary Store'),
... MappedJoin(sku='111',msrp=Decimal("22.44"),store_id=None,price=None,
... id=None,name=None)]
```

In some cases, it's nice to label the columns according to their table of origin. To accomplish this, use the with_labels() SqlSoup method:

```
>>> join3 = db.with_labels(join1)
>>> join3.first()
MappedJoin(product_sku='123',product_msrp=Decimal("12.34"),
... product_price_sku='123',product_price_store_id=1,
... product_price_price=Decimal("0"))
>>> db.with_labels(join2).first()
MappedJoin(product_sku='123',product_msrp=Decimal("12.34"),
... product_price_sku='123',product_price_store_id=1,
... product_price_price=Decimal("0"),store_id=1,store_name='Main
... Store')
```

It is also possible to label a mapped table and then use the labeled table in joins:

```
>>> labelled_product = db.with_labels(db.product)
>>> join4 = db.join(labelled_product, db.product_price,
... isouter=True)
```

```
>>> join4.first()
MappedJoin(product_sku='123',product_msrp=Decimal("12.34"),sku='123',
... store_id=1,price=Decimal("0"))
```

Note that the columns from `db.product` are labeled, whereas the columns from `db.product_price` are not.

Mapping Arbitrary Selectables

Simple tables and joins are supported in SqlSoup, but what about mapping more complex selectables? The automatically mapping machinery of SqlSoup is actually exposed via the `SqlSoup map()` method. For instance, if we wished to add a column for the average price of a product over all the stores in which it is sold, we might write the following SQL-layer SQLAlchemy query:

```
>>> db.clear()
>>>
>>> from sqlalchemy import *
>>>
>>> join5 = db.join(db.product, db.product_price)
>>>
>>> s = select([db.product._table,
... func.avg(join5.c.price).label('avg_price')],
...             from_obj=[join5._table],
...             group_by=[join5.c.sku])
>>> s = s.alias('products_with_avg_price')
>>> products_with_avg_price = db.map(s, primary_key=[join5.c.sku])
>>> products_with_avg_price.all()
[MappedJoin(sku='123',msrp=Decimal("12.34"),avg_price=0.0),
... MappedJoin(sku='456',msrp=Decimal("22.12"),avg_price=0.0),
... MappedJoin(sku='789',msrp=Decimal("41.44"),avg_price=0.0)]
>>>
>>> db.product_price.first().price = 50.00
>>> db.flush()
>>> db.clear()
>>> products_with_avg_price.all()
[MappedJoin(sku='123',msrp=Decimal("12.34"),avg_price=25.0),
... MappedJoin(sku='456',msrp=Decimal("22.12"),avg_price=0.0),
... MappedJoin(sku='789',msrp=Decimal("41.44"),avg_price=0.0)]
```

A common usage pattern is to add such mapped selectables to the `SqlSoup` instance for access in other parts of the application:

```
>>> db.products_with_avg_price = products_with_avg_price
```

There's no magic here; this is just Python's ability to declare new, ad-hoc attributes on existing objects. Do note that if you happen to add an attribute with the same name as a table in your database, SqlSoup will not be able to access that table until you remove the new attribute.

Directly Accessing the Session

Although SqlSoup provides access to most session-oriented functionality through the `SqlSoup` object, it is possible to access the underlying SQLAlchemy contextual session through the global SqlSoup object `objectstore`:

```
>>> from sqlalchemy.ext.sqlsoup import objectstore
>>> session = objectstore.current
>>> print session
<sqlalchemy.orm.session.Session object at 0x2ae69954f210>
```

Using SqlSoup for SQL-Level Inserts, Updates, and Deletes

As mentioned in the list of automatically mapped class attributes and methods, mapped classes contain `insert()`, `update()`, and `delete()` methods. These are just thin wrappers around the corresponding methods on the underlying table. If we wanted to set the price for all products in all stores to their MSRP, for instance, we could do the following:

```
>>> msrp=select([db.product.c.msrp],
...            db.product.sku==db.product_price.sku)
>>> db.product_price.update(
...     values=dict(price=msrp))
>>> db.product_price.all()
[MappedProduct_price(sku='123',store_id=1,price=Decimal("12.34")),
... MappedProduct_price(sku='456',store_id=1,price=Decimal("22.12")),
... MappedProduct_price(sku='789',store_id=1,price=Decimal("41.44")),
... MappedProduct_price(sku='123',store_id=2,price=Decimal("12.34")),
... MappedProduct_price(sku='456',store_id=2,price=Decimal("22.12")),
... MappedProduct_price(sku='789',store_id=2,price=Decimal("41.44"))]
```

We can similarly use the `insert()` and `delete()` method to perform SQL-level inserts and deletes.

When to Use SqlSoup Versus Elixir Versus "Bare" SQLAlchemy

As we've discussed before, SqlSoup is useful when it's necessary to use an existing database, whereas Elixir is most useful when *Elixir* is the primary definition of the schema. This section compares SqlSoup and Elixir with "Bare" SQLAlchemy and gives the advantages and disadvantages of each.

SqlSoup Pros and Cons

Generally speaking, SqlSoup has the following pros and cons in comparison to "base" SQLAlchemy:

Succinct usage
> SqlSoup requires very little code to get started: just a database URI, and you're ready to go. Raw SQLAlchemy is much more verbose, requiring setup for tables,

mappers, and mapped classes. Even if you're using autoloading with SQLAlchemy, it still requires you to set up your mappers and mapped classes if you wish to use the ORM.

Ad-hoc queries and mappers
> Due to the ease of setting up SqlSoup, it is much more convenient to create queries and mappings from joins and other selectable objects.

Rich relation support
> Because SqlSoup's method of inference does not support SQLAlchemy `relation()`s, it is not well-suited to schemas where it is more convenient to use mapped properties to implement relations between tables.

Adding behavior to mapped objects
> Because SqlSoup creates its own automatically mapped classes, it is inconvenient to have domain logic from your application attached as methods. In this regard, SqlSoup mapped objects are little more than "smart rows" allowing convenient access to the database, with little ability to model domain objects.

Flexibility
> The convenience of SqlSoup generally comes at the cost of flexibility. Various SQLAlchemy ORM-level features, such as synonyms and relations, are either unsupported or not well supported.

Elixir Pros and Cons

Generally speaking, Elixir has the following pros and cons in comparison to "base" SQLAlchemy:

Succinct usage
> Although not as terse as SqlSoup, Elixir generally requires less code than raw SQLAlchemy to implement similar functionality. This is particularly true when using the *associable* and *versioned* extensions, for instance.

Rapid model development
> Because Elixir generally sees itself as the keeper of the schema, it can be more aggressive in what types of schema it supports. When using the *associable* extension, for instance, it is possible to create auxiliary tables with a single DSL line of code. This allows complex schema to be developed rapidly when your application is first being written.

Clear separation of concerns
> Due to the data mapper pattern used in SQLAlchemy (rather than the active record pattern used in Elixir), it is clear where the database schema resides (in the `Table()` classes), where the application logic resides (in the mapped classes), and where the mapping occurs (in the `mapper()` configuration). Elixir puts all this information into the `Entity` classes, making it a bit more difficult to separate these concerns.

Ability to use or migrate existing schemas

Elixir's aggressiveness in defining new tables and columns implicitly based on DSL statements in the `Entity` classes can make it challenging to use with an existing database. In such a situation, it's important to be aware of what schema changes are implied by each change to the `Entity` classes and/or to have access to a schema migration tool that can assist in migrating existing databases.

Flexibility

Raw SQLAlchemy's win over Elixir is much more limited than its win over SqlSoup, mainly because Elixir provides convenient ways to "drop into" the underlying SQLAlchemy tables, mappers, and classes. SQLAlchemy still wins on flexibility over Elixir, however, as it is, in fact, necessary to drop into regular SQLAlchemy to model some things when using Elixir.

## CHAPTER 11

Other SQLAlchemy Extensions

SQLAlchemy provides an extremely powerful method of defining schemas, performing queries, and manipulating data, both at the ORM level and at the SQL level. SQLAlchemy also provides several extensions to this core behavior. We have already seen one of these extensions, SqlSoup, discussed in Chapter 10. One of the nice things about the SQLAlchemy extensions package is that it provides a "proving ground" for functionality that may eventually make it into the core SQLAlchemy packages. When this occurs (the functionality of an extension is absorbed into the core feature set of SQLAlchemy), the extension is deprecated and eventually removed.

This chapter discusses the two remaining nondeprecated extensions available in SQLAlchemy 0.4, *sqlalchemy.ext.associationproxy* and *sqlalchemy.ext.orderinglist*. We will also describe the deprecated extensions, focusing on how to achieve the same functionality using "core" SQLAlchemy.

Association Proxy

The association proxy extension allows our mapped classes to have attributes that are proxied from related objects. One place where this is useful is when we have two tables related via an association table that contains extra information in addition to linking the two tables. For instance, suppose we have a database containing the following schema:

```
user_table = Table(
    'user', metadata,
    Column('id', Integer, primary_key=True),
    Column('user_name', String(255), unique=True),
    Column('password', String(255)))

brand_table = Table(
    'brand', metadata,
    Column('id', Integer, primary_key=True),
    Column('name', String(255)))

sales_rep_table = Table(
```

```
    'sales_rep', metadata,
  Column('brand_id', None, ForeignKey('brand.id'), primary_key=True),
  Column('user_id', None, ForeignKey('user.id'), primary_key=True),
    Column('commission_pct', Integer, default=0))
```

In this case, we might want to create User, Brand, and SalesRep classes to represent our domain objects. The basic mapper setup would then be the following:

```
class User(object): pass
class Brand(object): pass
class SalesRep(object): pass

mapper(User, user_table, properties=dict(
    sales_rep=relation(SalesRep, backref='user', uselist=False)))
mapper(Brand, brand_table, properties=dict(
    sales_reps=relation(SalesRep, backref='brand')))
mapper(SalesRep, sales_rep_table)
```

In such a case, we have completely mapped the data in our schema to the object model. But what if we want to have a property on the Brand object that lists all of the Users who are SalesReps for that Brand? One way we could do this in "base" SQLAlchemy is by using a property in the Brand class:

```
class Brand(object):
    @property
    def users(self):
        return [ sr.user for sr in self.sales_reps ]
```

This is not very convenient, however. It doesn't allow us to append to or remove from the list of users, for instance. The association proxy provides a convenient solution to this problem. Using the association_proxy() function, we can add the users property much more simply:

```
from sqlalchemy.ext.associationproxy import association_proxy

class Brand(object):
    users=association_proxy('sales_reps', 'user')
```

If we want to keep our domain object definition code ignorant of SQLAlchemy, we can even move the association_proxy() call outside our class into the mapper configuration:

```
mapper(Brand, brand_table, properties=dict(
    sales_reps=relation(SalesRep, backref='brand')))
Brand.users=association_proxy('sales_reps', 'user')
```

We can even append onto the users attribute to add new SalesReps. To enable this functionality, however, we need to create some sensible constructors for our mapped objects:

```
class User(object):
    def __init__(self, user_name=None, password=None):
        self.user_name=user_name
        self.password=password
```

```
class Brand(object):
    def __init__(self, name=None):
        self.name = name

class SalesRep(object):
    def __init__(self, user=None, brand=None, commission_pct=0):
        self.user = user
        self.brand = brand
        self.commission_pct=commission_pct
```

Now, we can populate the database and add a user as a sales rep to a brand:

```
>>> Session = sessionmaker(bind=engine)
>>> engine.echo = True
>>> session = Session()
>>>
>>> b = Brand('Cool Clothing')
>>> session.save(b)
>>>
>>> u = User('rick', 'foo')
>>> session.save(u)
>>>
>>> metadata.bind.echo = True
>>> session.flush()
2007-11-23 12:48:28,304 INFO sqlalchemy.engine.base.Engine.0x..90
... BEGIN
2007-11-23 12:48:28,305 INFO sqlalchemy.engine.base.Engine.0x..90
... INSERT INTO user (user_name, password) VALUES (?, ?)
2007-11-23 12:48:28,306 INFO sqlalchemy.engine.base.Engine.0x..90
... ['rick', 'foo']
2007-11-23 12:48:28,308 INFO sqlalchemy.engine.base.Engine.0x..90
... INSERT INTO brand (name) VALUES (?)
2007-11-23 12:48:28,308 INFO sqlalchemy.engine.base.Engine.0x..90
... ['Cool Clothing']
>>> b.users
2007-11-23 12:48:31,317 INFO sqlalchemy.engine.base.Engine.0x..90
... SELECT sales_rep.brand_id AS sales_rep_brand_id,
... sales_rep.user_id AS sales_rep_user_id, sales_rep.commission_pct
... AS sales_rep_commission_pct
FROM sales_rep
WHERE ? = sales_rep.brand_id ORDER BY sales_rep.oid
2007-11-23 12:48:31,318 INFO sqlalchemy.engine.base.Engine.0x..90
... [1]
[]
>>> b.users.append(u)
2007-11-23 12:48:33,668 INFO sqlalchemy.engine.base.Engine.0x..90
... SELECT sales_rep.brand_id AS sales_rep_brand_id,
... sales_rep.user_id AS sales_rep_user_id, sales_rep.commission_pct
... AS sales_rep_commission_pct
FROM sales_rep
WHERE ? = sales_rep.user_id ORDER BY sales_rep.oid
2007-11-23 12:48:33,669 INFO sqlalchemy.engine.base.Engine.0x..90
... [1]
>>> b.users
[<__main__.User object at 0xbdc710>]
>>> b.sales_reps
```

```
[<__main__.SalesRep object at 0xbe4610>]
>>> b.sales_reps[0].commission_pct
0
>>> session.flush()
2008-01-27 21:12:35,991 INFO sqlalchemy.engine.base.Engine.0x..50
... INSERT INTO sales_rep (brand_id, user_id, commission_pct) VALUES
... (?, ?, ?)
2008-01-27 21:12:35,994 INFO sqlalchemy.engine.base.Engine.0x..50
... [1, 1, 0]
```

This works because the association proxy extension will automatically create the intermediary SalesRep object by calling its constructor with a single positional argument, the User. To override this creation behavior, you can supply a creation function in the **creator** parameter. For instance, if we wanted to give sales reps added in this manner a commission percentage of 10%, we could define the proxy as follows:

```
Brand.users=association_proxy(
    'sales_reps', 'user',
    creator=lambda u:SalesRep(user=u, commission_pct=10))
```

Although accessing the underlying user attribute of the sales_reps property is useful, what if we prefer dictionary-style access? *associationproxy* supports this as well. For instance, suppose we want a property on Brand that is a dictionary keyed by User containing the commission_pct values. We can implement this as follows. (Note that dictionary-style association proxy creation functions take two positional parameters: the key and value being set.)

```
from sqlalchemy.orm.collections import attribute_mapped_collection

reps_by_user_class=attribute_mapped_collection('user')

mapper(Brand, brand_table, properties=dict(
    sales_reps_by_user=relation(
        SalesRep, backref='brand',
        collection_class=reps_by_user_class)))
Brand.commissions=association_proxy(
    'sales_reps_by_user', 'commission_pct',
    creator=lambda key,value: SalesRep(user=key, commission_pct=value))
```

Now, we can conveniently access the commission values by user:

```
>>> session.clear()
>>> session.bind.echo = False
>>>
>>> b = session.get(Brand, 1)
>>> u = session.get(User, 1)
>>> b.commissions[u] = 20
>>> session.flush()
>>> session.clear()
>>>
>>> b = session.get(Brand, 1)
>>> u = session.get(User, 1)
>>> print u.user_name
rick
```

```
>>> print b.commissions[u]
20
```

Note that the proxy and the original relation are automatically kept synchronized by SQLAlchemy:

```
>>> print b.sales_reps_by_user[u]
<__main__.SalesRep object at 0xbf2750>
>>> print b.sales_reps_by_user[u].commission_pct
20
```

Ordering List

A common pattern in many applications is the use of ordered collections. For instance, consider a simple to-do list application with multiple lists, each containing an (ordered) set of items. We might start with the following schema:

```
todo_list_table = Table(
    'todo_list', metadata,
    Column('name', Unicode(255), primary_key=True))

todo_item_table = Table(
    'todo_item', metadata,
    Column('id', Integer, primary_key=True),
    Column('list_name', None, ForeignKey('todo_list.name')),
    Column('list_position', Integer),
    Column('value', Unicode))
```

SQLAlchemy provides nice support for mapping the list items to a property and sorting them via the order_by parameter:

```
class TodoList(object):
    def __init__(self, name):
        self.name = name
    def __repr__(self):
        return '<TodoList %s>' % self.name


class TodoItem(object):
    def __init__(self, value, position=None):
        self.value = value
        self.list_position = position
    def __repr__(self):
        return '<%s: %s>' % (self.list_position, self.value)

mapper(TodoList, todo_list, properties=dict(
    items=relation(TodoItem,
                   backref='list',
                   order_by=[todo_item_table.c.list_position])))
mapper(TodoItem, todo_item)
```

We can now create a list with some items:

```
>>> lst = TodoList('list1')
>>> session.save(lst)
>>> lst.items = [ TodoItem('Buy groceries', 0),
```

```
...                    TodoItem('Do laundry', 1) ]
>>> session.flush()
>>> session.clear()
>>>
>>> lst = session.get(TodoList, 'list1')
>>> print lst.items
[<0: Buy groceries>, <1: Do laundry>]
```

This approach is certainly workable, but it requires you to manually keep track of the positions of all the list items. For instance, suppose we wanted to mow the lawn between buying groceries and doing laundry. To do this using base SQLAlchemy, we would need to do something like the following:

```
>>> lst.items.insert(1, TodoItem('Mow lawn'))
>>> for pos, it in enumerate(lst.items):
...     it.list_position = pos
```

Rather than "fixing up" the list after each insert or remove operation, we can instead use *orderinglist* to keep track of the list_position attribute automatically:

```
>>> from sqlalchemy.ext.orderinglist import ordering_list
>>>
>>> mapper(TodoList, todo_list_table, properties=dict(
...     items=relation(TodoItem,
...                    backref='list',
...                    order_by=[todo_item_table.c.list_position],
...                    collection_class
...                    =ordering_list('list_position'))))
<sqlalchemy.orm.mapper.Mapper object at 0xbcb850>
>>> mapper(TodoItem, todo_item_table)
<sqlalchemy.orm.mapper.Mapper object at 0xbcb710>
>>>
>>> session.clear()
>>> lst = session.get(TodoList, 'list1')
>>> print lst.items
[<0: Buy groceries>, <1: Mow lawn>, <2: Do laundry>]
>>> del lst.items[1]
>>> print lst.items
[<0: Buy groceries>, <1: Do laundry>]
>>> session.flush()
```

We can also customize the ordering_list() call either by providing a count_from argument (to use nonzero-based lists) or by providing an ordering_func argument that maps a position in a list to a value to store in the ordering attribute.

In some cases, you may also want to rearrange the entire list (rather than applying individual insertions and deletions). For such situations, ordering_list() provides the _reorder() method, which will generate new position values for every element in the list.

Deprecated Extensions

As mentioned previously, SQLAlchemy extensions function as a sort of "proving ground" for new functionality that may someday "graduate" into SQLAlchemy proper. There are several such extensions that have graduated in the transition from the SQLAlchemy 0.3.x release series to the 0.4.x release series. These extensions are briefly described here:

sqlalchemy.ext.selectresults

The *sqlalchemy.ext.selectresults* extension provided generative query support for ORM queries. Since version 0.3.6, this support has been built in to the native Query class. *sqlalchemy.ext.selectresults* also provides a MapperExtension that adds generative query behavior on a per-mapper basis.

sqlalchemy.ext.sessioncontext

The *sqlalchemy.ext.sessioncontext* extension provided contextual session support. This has been deprecated in favor of the scoped_session() support in core SQLAlchemy.

sqlalchemy.ext.assignmapper

The *sqlalchemy.ext.assignmapper* extension provided the ability to automatically save mapped objects and additional instrumentation on mapped classes above what the mapper() function normally does. This has been deprecated in favor of the Session.mapper() function available with contextual sessions created by scoped_session() in core SQLAlchemy.

sqlalchemy.ext.activemapper

The *sqlalchemy.ext.activemapper* extension provided a declarative layer implementing the active record pattern on SQLAlchemy. This has been deprecated in favor of the external package Elixir (Chapter 9), a more comprehensive declarative layer.

Index

Symbols

!= comparison operator, 76
& bitwise logical operator, 77
1:1 relationships, 107, 110
1:N relationships, 107
< comparison operator, 76
<= comparison operator, 76
== comparison operator, 76
> comparison operator, 76
>= comparison operator, 76
? (question mark) as a name value, 15
| bitwise logical operator, 77
~ bitwise logical operator, 77

A

active defaults, 48
"active record" patterns, 93
acts_as_versioned( ) statement, 186
adds( ) decorator, 119
add_column( ) method, 149, 150
add_entity( ) method, 149, 150
after_commit( ) (SessionExtension class), 138
after_delete( ) hook (MapperExtension), 120
after_flush( ) (SessionExtension class), 138
after_flush_postexec( ) (SessionExtension class), 139
after_insert( ) hook (MapperExtension), 120
@after_revert decorator, 188
after_update( ) hook (MapperExtension), 120
alias( ) method, 89
aliases, 88
all parameter, 114
all( ) method, 139, 150

allow_column_override parameter (mapper( ) function), 105
allow_null_pks parameter (mapper( ) function), 105
ALTER TABLE command, 46
always_refresh parameter (mapper( ) function), 105
AND boolean operator, 77
any( ) method, 140
append( ) function, 134
appender( ) decorator, 118
append_result( ) hook (MapperExtension), 121
application-specific custom types, 63
apply_avg( ) method, 150
apply_labels( ) method, 85
apply_max( ) method, 150
apply_min( ) method, 150
apply_sum( ) method, 150
arbitrary selectables, mapping, 105
architecture (SQLAlchemy), 10–19
*args argument
    Column constructor, 43
    Table constructor, 41
arithmetic operators, 76
asc( ) method, 140
AssertionPool pool type (sqlalchemy.pool), 38
associable( ) function, 184
association proxys, 199
as_scalar( ) method, 86
attribute Elixir keyword argument, 176
attribute-based syntax (Elixir), 178
attribute_mapped_collection( ) method, 119
autoflush argument (sessionmaker( ) method), 128

We'd like to hear your suggestions for improving our indexes. Send email to *index@oreilly.com*.

except_all( ) function, 88
except_all( ) method, 85
exclude_properties, 99
exclude_properties parameter (mapper( )
        function), 107
execute( ) method, 37, 68, 138
executemany( ) method, 69
expire( ) method, 137, 183
explicit execution, 40
explicit sequences, creating, 54
expression language (SQL), 14–16
expression-builders (Pythonic), 2
expunge parameter, 114
expunge( ) method, 137, 183
extending session, 138
extension argument (sessionmaker( ) method),
        129
extension parameter (mapper( ) function), 106,
        120
extension( ) method, 145
ex_setup.py file, 22

F

fetchall( ) method, 74
    ResultProxy), 37
fetchmany( ) method, 74
fetchone( ) method, 74
    ResultProxy, 37
Field( ) class, 175
filter( ) method, 29, 139, 150
    querying with joins, 142
filter_by( ) method, 18, 29, 139, 151, 183
    querying with joins, 142
Firebird database, 24
first( ) (Query object), 142
first( ) method, 151
flush( ) function, 28
    saving objects to sessions and, 129
flush( ) method, 136, 183, 191
for+update=False parameter (select( )), 73
foreign keys, 4
ForeignKey constructor, 45
ForeignKeyConstraint class, 46
foreign_keys parameter, 115
for_fields parameter, 186
for_update parameter (Sequence constructor),
        55
from_obj=[ ] parameter (select( )), 73, 89
from_statement( ) method, 147, 151

G

"generative" interface, 82
get( ) (Query object), 141
get( ) hook (MapperExtension), 121
get( ) method, 29, 137, 151, 184
    Elixir, querying using and, 183
__getattr__( ) method, 192
__get attr__( ) method (ResultProxy), 37
__getitem__( ) method, 153
get_as_of( ) method, 188
get_by( ) method, 183, 184
get_indent( ) function, 154
get_session( ) hook (MapperExtension), 121
GROUP BY clause, 80
group_by( ) method, 84, 151
group_by=Name parameter (select( )), 73

H

hand-generated SQL versus SQLAlchemy
        generation layers, 15
has( ) method, 141
has_and_belongs_to_many( ) statement, 180
has_field( ) method, 175
has_field( ) statement, 180
has_many( ) method, 180
has_one( ) statement, 180
HAVING clause, 80, 151
having( ) method, 84, 151
having=None parameter (select( )), 73
horizontal partitioning, 123

I

identity_map attribute, 138
idiomatically Python (Pythonic), 1
IF EXISTS clause, 56
IF NOT EXISTS clause, 56
"impedance mismatch" (object/relational), 4
implicit execution, 40
IN clause, 90
include_columns argument (Table), 42
include_properties parameter, 99
    mapper( ) function, 107
increment parameter (Sequence constructor),
        55
index argument (Column constructor), 44
Index object, 53
indexes, 52
Informix database, 24

plural_name argument (associable( ) function), 185

polymorphic
    class, 167
    identity of rows, 159
polymorphic_fetch parameter (mapper( ) function), 107
polymorphic_identity argument, 159
    mapper( ) function, 106
polymorphic_on argument, 159
polymorphic_on parameter (mapper( ) function), 106
polymorphic_union( ) function, 162
pool parameter (create_engine( ) function), 35
pool.manage( ) function, 38
pool.manage( ) method, 38
poolclass parameter (create_engine( ) function), 35
pools (connections), 11
    (see also connection pools)
pool_recycle parameter (create_engine( ) function), 35
pool_size parameter (create_engine( ) function), 35
pool_timeout parameter (create_engine( ) function), 35
POPOs (plain old Python objects), 1, 3
populate_existing( ) method, 152
populate_instance( ) hook (MapperExtension), 121
PostgreSQL, 1
    drivers, installing, 24
    passive defaults, support for, 52
post_update parameter, 116
prefixes=None parameter (select( )), 74
prefix_with( ) method, 85
PrimaryDeyConstraint object, 45
primaryjoin parameter, 116
primary_key argument (Column constructor), 43
primary_key parameter (mapper( ) function), 107
properties parameter (mapper( ) function), 107
property mapping, 99
PyPI (Python package index), 21
pysqlite binary module, 23
pysqlite driver, 24
Python Imaging Library (PIL), 14

Pythonic (idiomatically Python), 1

Q

queries, 26, 67
    constructing, 72–86
query( ) method, 137, 139
query_from_parent( ) method, 152
question mark (?), as a name value, 15
QueuePool pool type (sqlalchemy.pool), 39
quote argument
    Column constructor, 44
    Table constructor, 42
quote parameter
    Sequence constructor, 55
quote_schema argument (Table), 42

R

refcolumns parameter (ForeignKeyConstraint class), 47
reflect( ) method (MetaData), 43
reflection, defining tables, 42
refresh( ) method, 137, 183
refresh-expire parameter, 114
relation( ) function, 107, 114, 134, 143
    custom collections, using, 117
    Elixir attribute-based syntax and, 178
    parameters, 115
    self-referential mappers and, 113
relational model, 4, 167
relationships, 4
relationships (SQLAlchemy), 107
remote_side parameter (ManyToMany), 180
remote_site parameter, 116
remove( ) function, 134
remover( ) decorator, 118
removes( ) decorator, 119
removes_return( ) decorator, 119
_reorder( ) method, 204
replaces( ) decorator, 119
replace_selectable( ) method, 85
required Elixir keyword argument, 175
required parameter (ManyToOne), 179
reset_joinpoint( ) method, 153
ResultProxy class, 74
ResultProxy object, 36
revert( ) method, 187
revert_to( ) method, 188
rollback( ) method, 136

rowcount ( ) method, 75
rowcount( ) method
    ResultProxy, 37

S

save( ) method, 129, 136, 183
    Elixir, quering using and, 183
save-update parameter, 114
save_or_update( ) method, 184
scalar( ) method, 75
scalar( ) method (ResultProxy), 37
schema argument (MetaData.reflect( )
       method), 43
schema argument (Table), 41
schema definitions (database), 2, 12
schema( ) method, 191
scoped_session( ) function, 153
secondary parameter, 116
secondaryjoin parameter, 116
SELECT statements, 28, 72
    customizing in queries, 147
    WHERE clauses and, 75
select( ) function, 72–74
    "generative" interface, 84
select( ) method, 27, 72–74, 86
select_from( ) method, 84, 147
select_table parameter (mapper( ) function),
       107
self-referential mappers, 112
Sequence object, 54
Session object, 3, 18, 127–139
    creating, 127
    saving objects to, 129
session.commit( ) method, 30
Session.configure( ) method, 127
sessionmaker( ) function, 29, 127
set operations, 88
SetupTools package, 21
setup_all( ) method, 173
setup_entities( ) method, 173
"sharding" (horizontal partitioning), 123
single table inheritance, 157
SingletonThreadPool pool type
       (sqlalchemy.pool), 39
single_query( ) method, 165
SQL dialect management, 12
SQL expression language, 14
SQL Expression Language, 67
SQL injection attacks, 2

sqlalchemy package, 24
sqlalchemy.engine, 36
sqlalchemy.engine.Connection class, 36
sqlalchemy.engine.ResultProxy, 36
sqlalchemy.ext.activemapper extension, 205
sqlalchemy.ext.assignmapper extension, 205
sqlalchemy.ext.selectresults extension, 205
sqlalchemy.ext.sessioncontext extension, 205
sqlalchemy.orm, 36
sqlalchemy.orm.attributes, 36
sqlalchemy.orm.collections module, 119
sqlalchemy.orm.mapper, 36
sqlalchemy.orm.strategies, 36
sqlalchemy.orm.sync, 36
sqlalchemy.orm.unitofwork, 36
sqlalchemy.pool, 36
sqlalchemy.types package, 60
SQLite, 1
    drivers, installing, 24
sqlite3 driver, 24
SqlSoup, 189
start parameter (Sequence constructor), 55
startswith( ) method, 140
    ClauseElement, 78
_state attribute (mapped class), 9
statements (SQL), 67
StaticPool pool type (sqlalchemy.pool), 39
strategy parameter (create_engine( ) function),
       35
subqueries, 89
SUM( ) function, 150
sum( ) method, 153
synonym Elixir keyword argument, 176
synonym( ) function, 100

T

Table object, 13
table.c object, 15
Table.insert( ) method, 68
Table.select( ) method, 72
tablename parameter (ManyToMany), 180
Tables object, 40–43
table_iterator( ) method, 57
Text construct, 72
    WHERE clause and, 75
text parameter
    text( ) function, 80
text( ) function, 79
thread-local sessions, 153

threaded parameter (create_engine( ) function), 35

through Elixir keyword argument, 176

transactional argument (sessionmaker( ) method), 128

Transient state (Session), 130

translate_row( ) hook (MapperExtension), 121

tutorial.sqlite file, 25

twophase argument (sessionmaker( ) method), 128

TypeDecorator object, 63

TypeEngine object, 14, 16

TypeEngine objects, 59–65

typemap=None parameter (text( ) function), 80

type_ argument (Column constructor), 43

U

unbound metadata, 11

unbounded constructors, 39

undefer( ) function, 105

undefer( ) method, 146

undefer_group( ) method, 146

UNION clause, 88

union( ) function, 88

union( ) method, 85

union_all( ) function, 88

union_all( ) method, 85

unique argument (Column constructor), 44

UNIQUE clause, 80

UNIQUE constraints, 47, 52

unit of work pattern, 93

update defaults, 49

UPDATE statements, 69–71

update( ) function, 28
    SqlSoup, using, 191

update( ) method, 69, 137, 183

updates, 26

useexisting argument (Table), 42

uselist parameter, 116

use_alter parameter (ForeignKey constructor), 46

use_alter parameter (ManyToOne), 179

use_ansi parameter (create_engine( ) function), 35

use_labels=False parameter (select( )), 74

use_oids parameter (create_engine( ) function), 35

using_options( ) method, 173

V

values( ) method (ResultProxy), 37

version_id_col parameter (mapper( ) function), 107

vertical partitioning, 122

viewonly parameter, 116

W

weak_identity_map argument (sessionmaker( ) method), 129

WHERE clause, 72
    operators and functions, 75–78

where( ) method, 84

whereclause=None parameter (select( )), 73

with_labels( ) method, 192

with_lockmode( ) method, 153

with_options( ) statement, 181

with_parent( ) method, 153

with_secret parameter, 186

About the Author

Rick Copeland is a senior software engineer with retail analytics firm Predictix, LLC, where he uses SQLAlchemy extensively, primarily for web application development. He has been using Python full-time for development since 2005 in projects as diverse as demand forecasting, business web applications, compilers, and hardware synthesis.

Colophon

The animal on the cover of *Essential SQLAlchemy* is a largescale flying fish (*Cypselurus oligolepis*). Flying fish is the more common name for members of the *Exocoetidae* family, which comprises roughly 40 species that inhabit the warm tropical and subtropical waters of the Atlantic, Pacific, and Indian oceans. Flying fish range from 7 to 12 inches in length and are characterized by their unusually large, winglike pectoral fins. Some species also have enlarged pelvic fins and are thus known as four-winged flying fish.

As their name suggests, flying fish have the unique ability to leap from the water and glide through the air for distances of up to a quarter of a mile. Their torpedo-like bodies help them gather the speed necessary to propel themselves from the ocean (about 37 miles per hour), and their distinctive pectoral fins and forked tailfins keep them airborne. Biologists believe this remarkable trait may have evolved as a way for flying fish to escape their many predators, which include tuna, mackerel, swordfish, marlin, and other larger fish. However, flying fish sometimes have a more difficult time evading their human predators. Attracted by a luring light that fishermen attach to their canoes at night, the fish leap in and are unable to vault themselves back out.

Dried flying fish are a dietary staple for the Tao people of Orchid Island, located off the coast of Taiwan, and flying fish roe is common in Japanese cuisine. They are also a coveted delicacy in Barbados, known as "Land of the flying fish" before shipping pollution and overfishing depleted their numbers. The flying fish retains a prominent cultural status there, however; it's the main ingredient in the national dish (cou cou and flying fish) and it is featured on coins, artwork, and even in the Barbados Tourism Authority's logo.

The cover image is from *Dover's Animals*. The cover font is Adobe ITC Garamond. The text font is Linotype Birka, the heading font is Adobe Myriad Condensed, and the code font is LucasFont's TheSansMonoCondensed.

Related Titles from O'Reilly

Scripting Languages

Essential PHP Security

Exploring Expect

Jython Essentials

Learning Python, *3rd Edition*

Learning PHP and MySQL, *2nd Edition*

Learning Ruby

Learning PHP 5

Learning Python, *3rd Edition*

PHP Cookbook, *2nd Edition*

PHP Hacks

PHP in a Nutshell

PHP Pocket Reference, *2nd Edition*

PHPUnit Pocket Guide

Programming PHP, *2nd Edition*

Programming Python, *3rd Edition*

Python & XML

Python Cookbook, *2nd Edition*

Python in a Nutshell, *2nd Edition*

Python Pocket Reference, *3rd Edition*

Python Standard Library

Ruby on Rails: Up and Running

The Ruby Programming Language

Upgrading to PHP 5

Our books are available at most retail and online bookstores.
To order direct: 1-800-998-9938 • *order@oreilly.com* • *www.oreilly.com*
Online editions of most O'Reilly titles are available by subscription at *safari.oreilly.com*

The O'Reilly Advantage

Stay Current and Save Money

Order books online:
www.oreilly.com/store/order

Questions about our products or your order:
order@oreilly.com

Join our email lists: Sign up to get topic specific email announcements or new books, conferences, special offers and technology news
elists.oreilly.com

For book content technical questions:
booktech@oreilly.com

To submit new book proposals to our editors:
proposals@oreilly.com

Contact us:
O'Reilly Media, Inc.
1005 Gravenstein Highway N.
Sebastopol, CA U.S.A. 95472
707-827-7000 or
800-998-9938
www.oreilly.com

Did you know that if you register your O'Reilly books, you'll get automatic notification and upgrade discounts on new editions?

And that's not all! Once you've registered your books you can:

» Win free books, T-shirts and O'Reilly Gear

» Get special offers available only to registered O'Reilly customers

» Get free catalogs announcing all our new titles (US and UK Only)

**Registering is easy! Just go to
www.oreilly.com/go/register**

O'REILLY®

Try the online edition free for 45 days

Mapping Python to Databases

Essential
SQLAlchemy

O'REILLY®

Rick Copeland

Get the information you need when you need it, with Safari Books Online. Safari Books Online contains the complete version of the print book in your hands plus thousands of titles from the best technical publishers, with sample code ready to cut and paste into your applications.

Safari is designed for people in a hurry to get the answers they need so they can get the job done. You can find what you need in the morning, and put it to work in the afternoon. As simple as cut, paste, and program.

To try out Safari and the online edition of the above title FREE for 45 days, go to www.oreilly.com/go/safarienabled and enter the coupon code MITFZCB.

To see the complete Safari Library visit:
safari.oreilly.com

70502